The Secret Spiritual World *of* Children

The Secret Spiritual World *of* Children

Tobin Hart, Ph.D.

INNER
OCEAN

Inner Ocean Publishing, Inc.
P.O. Box 1239
Makawao, Maui, HI 96768-1239

Cover design: Bill Greaves
Cover photo: Taxi
Interior page design: Bill Greaves
Interior page typography: Madonna Gauding
Editor: John Nelson
Copy editor: Barbara Doern Drew

Publisher Cataloging-in-Publication Data

Hart, Tobin.
    The secret spiritual world of children / Tobin Hart. —1st ed.—Makawao, HI : Inner Ocean, 2003.

        p. ; cm.

    Includes bibliographical references.
    ISBN 1-930722-19-2
        1. Experience (Religion) in children. 2. Children—Religious life. 3. Spirituality. 4. Spiritual life—New Age movement. I. Title.

BV4571.3 .H37 2003
204/.2/083–dc21   0311 CIP

Printed in Canada by Transcontinental
Distributed by Publishers Group West

9 8 7 6 5 4 3 2 1

Contents

For Maia and Haley

Acknowledgments

*I*t feels like I have been collecting golden threads. I have had the grace to hear the intimate stories of childhood from so many individuals, too many to thank by name here. These accounts have been the heart and soul of this research, and I am extraordinarily grateful for them. Hopefully I have woven these threads into something that touches others, as I have been so deeply touched.

Special gratitude goes to my agent Stephanie von Hirschberg, whose expertise and vision have been instrumental in shaping this book; my graduate students, for their powerful and playful feedback, ongoing dialogue, research, and also hard work in helping to organize the First U.S. Conference on Children's Spirituality; John Nelson, for his thoughtful and sensitive editing, and Barbara Doern Drew, for her careful polishing; Peter Nelson and Kaisa Puhakka, for their guidance; Don Rice and my colleagues at that well-kept secret of innovation, the Department of Psychology at the State University of West Georgia, for their support; Scott Guffey, Carey Giles, Ted Smith, and Chris Johnson, for their expert assistance; and the team at the Child-Spirit Institute, for ongoing support with all phases of this project.

Love and appreciation beyond measure I give to Haley and Maia Hart, who have been the impetus and inspiration for this whole project.

My deepest thanks are reserved for Mary Mance Hart, for all she is and all she does. Her touch is on all of this work.

Foreword

One value of a book is its ability to disturb us, move us beyond our comfort zone, outside the boundaries of our platitudes and common assumptions, forcing us to look anew at issues we had explored and thought to be closed topics. Such has been my case with this extraordinary and magnificent book by Tobin Hart.

To be asked to write a foreword for such a work was both flattering and intimidating. Knowing something of the professional and spiritual stature of the book and author, I was flattered; after reading the work I was somewhat intimidated—for this book is an immense achievement and to introduce it is no casual task.

When I consider the brilliant observations and analyses made in the last century by the great pioneers in child development, I am astonished that the key element—given here, and summarily called *child-spirit*—was missed for so long. I had thought of "matters of the spirit" to be essentially adult fare, grist for the mill of mature minds. As father of five children, grandfather of twelve, and great-grandfather of one, I am chagrined that for so long a time I did not see what Tobin Hart has seen, even as I am delighted to be shown.

How, in fact, could the issue of "child-spirit" be other than that of our "species-spirit" as a whole, since the child and its wondrous world embrace the whole of life from the beginning? Surely the following examination of children's innate spirituality examines both our individual and specieswide spirit as well. And, as you will find here, the issue of spirit stretches us beyond religion, psychology, philosophy, or idle speculation.

Indeed, Tobin Hart courageously and clearly delineates between spirit and religion, an issue of serious import in this transitory age wherein we are, if unknowingly, shifting from the bonds and bondage of religion to the light and wings of spirit, that state toward which our great model pointed some two millennia ago. Hart's exploration of the spiritual world of children deals with the juice of life itself, that which pulses through our veins and lifts us beyond the beasts and perhaps a bit above the angels. And, just as with our species-spirit, a child's spirit is not some casual sentiment to be added to his or her curricula of life like a spice or bit of seasoning, but rather it is the essence of life itself. The subject of children's spirituality branches out until it embraces every aspect of the child's life, that of the eventual adult, and so all of us.

What is so striking here is in examining child-spirit as he does, Hart reveals, as few works have, the foundations and functions of adult spiritual life as well. Any adult or child can gain enormously from this book since self-revelation is the issue. And that is what we parents, teachers, or guardians will find when, through the wisdom shared and guidance given here, we move to protect, nurture, and mentor a child's budding spirit. Our own awaking, reawakening, or expansion occurs as well. In a neat twist we find that indeed a little child will lead us, to the extent we also lead that child. There are no one-way streets in life's dynamics.

A friend's five-year-old daughter asked him, "Daddy, do you know why children are sent into the world?" "No," my friend answered, "tell me." "To teach them to think in their hearts, so everything goes right," she replied. "Otherwise they think in their heads and life is hard."

Having read this book, I see more clearly than ever the reason for that enigmatic statement made some two millennia ago that if we can become again as a little child, a priceless inner realm may open to us. And who better than a child can demonstrate or model for us what that means? Even a brief survey of this book's table of contents spells out the major milestones of that royal road the child longs to travel: wonder, awe, exuberant excitement; seeing the invisible, the intuitive knowing beyond the senses; creative inner sight that, if allowed, turns every event into play—that play that is our divine right and the foundation on which intelligence and creativity grow. Providing for these in a child's unfolding can provide a bridge across the gap the years have wrought between our own hearts and minds. We, too, can discover divine play. Through mentoring and nurturing a child's spiritual life, we can find, revive, and/or enrich our own.

Years ago Gerald Jampolsky, a psychiatrist specializing in child dysfunctions, reported an influx of parents concerned that their children were having psychotic episodes. The children ranged in age from three or four to seven or so, the heart of that stage giving us what Jean Piaget called the "child of the dream" or Rudolph Steiner saw as the "ethereal child": one foot on earth, the other still in the imaginal world of the spirit, intuitively aware on levels later lost. I considered most of the events recorded by Jampolsky essentially "psychic" in nature—the children reporting sensory perceptions, events, and phenomena the parents themselves did not perceive. After reading Tobin Hart, I have revised my concept of psychic as well as spiritual.

Along about the time of Jampolsky's work, Blurton Jones, a British ethologist working with Nobelist Nikos Tinbergen, gave us, perhaps unknowingly, an invaluable clue to the inner world of the child. He reported that in cultures throughout the world, toddlers, on initially encountering an unknown object or event, will stop and *point* toward the novelty, looking back to check out the caretaker's or parent's response. Before following through with a tactile, direct sensory exploration of the new unknown, through which the brain builds its corresponding "structure of knowledge" of that event, a "parental check" is made, not just to see if the event is safe to explore but more to see if the parent cognizes and so gives *sanction* to that event. Most mammal infants go through the same safeguard maneuver.

Although most parents respond to the child's pointing by enthusiastically naming the "object-event," as nature prompts us to do, the "recognition signals" parents send can be very subtle, even unconsciously made. Either way, if the parent cognizes the event on any level, the child senses that cognition and, knowing the phenomenon to be part of his or her parent's world, moves to explore that object or event and build his or her own neural imprint of that now named and sanctioned novelty. In this way, his or her experience of the world grows as a fair copy, or duplicate, of ours—mirroring us, in effect. For, as Walt Whitman put it,

> There was a child went forth every day,
> And the first object he looked upon, that object he became,
> And that object became part of him for the day, or a certain part of the day,
> Or for many years or stretching cycles of years.

In every culture, however, Blurton Jones found that surprisingly often the parent *cannot discern* what the child gestures toward and so makes no response at all. "Whazzat Mamma, whazzat Daddy?" the pointing child then demands, over and over, generally to no avail. With no sign of a parental sanctioning response, and no corresponding word identification given, as a general rule the child will not follow through with those sensory explorations, though such are critical to a full-scale neural structure of knowledge. In all cultures Jones found this phenomenon occurring between parent and child so often that he coined the phrase "the quasi-hallucinatory fantasies of the early child," pondering why children should think they are seeing things that are not really there. That such "objects to be-come" are not really there is the case only in the parent-caretaker's eye, however, not the child's, and the distinction is critical.

Consider that the child, not exploring such unsanctioned object-events, will ignore such an event should it occur again, as well as other events of a similar nature. He or she will do this on behalf of those event-phenomena named and given sanction by, and so shared with, parents. On growing up and becoming parents themselves, such persons, in turn, will not themselves be able to discern events within that long-ago ignored category of "quasi-hallucinatory fantasies." Should their own child point toward something similar, demanding word-label sanction, that sanction will not be forthcoming. Thus it is we ensure that our cultural worldview becomes that of our child's, no matter the restricting nature, or paucity, of that shared world.

And so it is that a child's spiritual life can be "usurped," as En-glish poet Samuel Taylor Coleridge said, impoverished until finally made void, simply by being ignored or belittled by parents who have themselves been wrought spiritually void in the same manner. And so it is we parents may remain unchanged by our children, thinking in our heads instead of our hearts lifelong, wherein life is hard in-deed.

Back in the 1970s, James Peterson, a kindergarten teacher for many years, wrote a book, *The Secret Life of Kids*, concerning the con-tinual reporting of such "hallucinatory fantasies" by his young charges. Finding that he would listen to their experiences without negative censure, his young students would describe such events freely, and Peterson built up a rich library of anecdotes. Continual failure of parents—or teachers—to make that positive response that grants the child validity, will eventually compel that child's brain to select out such phenomena on behalf of those events shared by adults. Thus did we pattern our world after that of our parents on the one hand, while on the other losing our capacity to see in this intuitive way. Use it or lose it is nature's dictum, by which, all too often, new worlds may open to fade like morning mist. Hallucinatory fantasies indeed.

On reading Tobin Hart, I realized that these "psychic events" could be of overall developmental significance, expressions of the infinitely varied life of an expanding spirit. All too often, however, I realized that this expansion is crippled or curtailed by our "cultural imperative" of conformity: conformity to our standards for what is real and what is not, standards of behaviors acceptable or not, standards bringing inhibition and constraint instead of that boundless opening to imagination nature intends. And imagination is a prime language of the spirit.

The ancient Sufis considered imagination—that internal making of images not present to the outer senses—to be the very way in which we are made in the image of our Creator. Fostering a child's intuition, imagination, and capacity for play is a critical part of that spiritual growth that twines with intelligence like a double helix, giving birth to God in and as that child. Some two millennia ago our great model warned that "should we cause one of these little ones to stumble, it were better a mill-stone be tied about our neck and we be dumped into the sea." No subtlety in that stark statement—though we seldom stop to analyze what "stumbling" might entail.

Finally, here, recall that equally sobering question the Creator makes of We-the-Created, generation by generation: "And how do you account for those children I placed in your charge?" *The Secret Spiritual World of Children* can usher us into the joyful adventure such a "charge" can be, enabling us to stand *with* our children as the answer, equally accountable since equally enriched in spirit, mind, body, and heart.

Joseph Chilton Pearce
Faber, Virginia

Introduction

Children have a secret spiritual life. They have spiritual capacities and experiences—profound moments that shape their lives in enduring ways. These are sometimes stunning, often tender, and reveal a remarkable spiritual world that has been kept largely secret. From moments of wonder to finding inner wisdom, from asking the big questions about meaning and life to expressing compassion and even to seeing beneath the surface of the material world, these experiences serve as touchstones for our life as spiritual beings on Earth. In what follows I will show some of this secret world that lies within our own households, classrooms, and, perhaps, our own childhoods.

I have been interested in questions of spirituality and human potential for many years and have pursued this field as a university professor, researcher, and therapist. However, it was my role as a father that helped me to see more deeply into this secret spiritual world of children.

One evening I was sitting at my six-year-old daughter's bedside, saying good night and trying to help her settle down to sleep. I was gently rubbing her forehead when she said that she felt a little "weird," "light-headed," and "tingly." I asked her if this feeling was OK. She answered, "Yeah, it's OK; I've felt this way before." "When?" I asked. "One time when someone touched my forehead," she responded. "And one time when Madi's [a friend] grandmother was helping us get to sleep. I've felt like this at other times, too. When it happens, I feel very floaty, like I could fall asleep."

She hesitated for a moment and then added, "And then I see my angels." "Your angels?" I asked. "Yeah, I see them right now," she said in a gentle voice with her eyes closed. "You see them?" I repeated, more than a little surprised. "Yeah, I do *see* them and it's like I can *feel* them and know they're there. It's like they're having a tea party and they're talking about me." She paused for a moment and then said, "They let me know I'm loved." She fell silent and seemed to be drifting off to sleep.

I said good night and left her room. I wasn't sure what to make of this. As I wandered back downstairs, I decided that this would be a nice little story—a child's fantasy, I supposed—to write down in her baby book. I did write it down, but forgot about it until several months later when an angel paid her another visit. In fact, her angel became a regular visitor. On her own, Haley seemed to be able to shift her awareness and find the special state of consciousness almost at will. At those times she would feel a profound sense of peace and tap into insight and wisdom that were simply beyond anything I had previously noticed in a six-year-old, either as a parent or as a psychologist.

Perhaps you are wondering, as I did, Was she really meeting with an angel? Was there really an angelic tea party in the bedroom? I cannot verify the source of her insight by conventional empirical means—no one can. But I can listen deeply to the quality of the information she offers and watch the impact these experiences have had on her life. What I see and hear is that, on her own, she taps a source that serves as a remarkable wellspring of love and wisdom. I will return to Haley's angel in more detail later, but for now I want to say that bedside moments like these captured my fascination. They set me on a course of exploring this hidden world in a five-year-long research study. What I have found is that my daughter is not unusual:

children have remarkably rich spiritual lives that take all kinds of forms. But few adults are aware of this secret dimension.

Most people, in particular psychologists, educators, and religious leaders, assume that children are not able to be "spiritual." The belief is that children may conjure up a funny image of what God is or they may be able to repeat a prayer they have memorized, but that, for the most part, they have no conscious experience of a direct and intimate connection with the Divine. Their capacity for wonder and wisdom, for compassion and deep questioning, and for seeing beneath the surface of the physical world is largely unacknowledged. Children's spiritual experiences have been often misunderstood: dismissed as fantasy, labeled as pathology, or feared by a parent, teacher, or therapist who has no map for understanding them. Ultimately this attitude leads to repressing rather than refining the child's spiritual nature.

Alison's experience, at age eleven, captures the fear and confusion that adults often have when children know or see more than we think they should. Alison was enjoying the warm day at her home when suddenly, she recounted, "I knew that my mom's friend had just died. I was out in the yard and it hit me; I can't tell you how I knew; I was just absolutely sure. I came into the house and said to my mom, 'Ellen is dead.' My mom's face changed right in front of me, and she got very upset and said, 'Alison, that's not funny!' I tried to tell her that I wasn't joking, but she wouldn't listen.

"A few minutes later the phone rang and the message was that Ellen had just died. My mom got very angry and said, 'I don't know how you knew that, but I don't ever want you to tell anyone about this and I don't ever want you to do that again!' I began to wonder what was wrong with me, even if I had somehow caused her death. I worried that I was crazy. I was so confused about what I was supposed to believe." Until her conversation with me that day she had never told anyone else about this.

Some adults do offer religious education to children, most often teaching about the key figures, guidelines, and beliefs of a religious faith. Schools are increasingly asked to develop "character" in children. And parents often wonder what their role in their child's spiritual training should be. Both religious and character education have traditionally tended to mold from the outside in. However worthwhile this training may be, it does not assume that children have spiritual lives from the *inside out*. For example, if we look in nearly any textbook on child development or psychology, there is nothing on children's spirituality. *Nothing*. Most often when researchers have looked at children's spirituality, they have limited their consideration to "God talk," that is, how children think and talk about God. These researchers have generally concluded that children do not and cannot have a spiritual life prior to the development of formal reasoning, usually sometime in adolescence.

These conclusions are derived from defining spiritual life based on the rational thinking style of adults and on religious concepts such as that of a supreme deity. When we, as adults, use these assumptions to filter our understanding of children, we miss their innate spirituality. But spirituality lives beyond the rational and beyond thoughts about God. Without an image of ourselves as divine and of our children as spiritual, we may have trouble seeing the divinity in our children and, ultimately, in ourselves as adults.

Catalyzed by the glimpse first offered by my daughter, I set out to explore children's spiritual life as deeply as I could. In my role as a university professor I teach research to graduate and undergraduate students, consult with other professionals on their projects, and have conducted numerous studies of my own. Since 1998 I have conducted in-depth interviews with more than one hundred individuals and families, and have gathered written accounts from hundreds more children, parents, and also adults who recollect their childhood experiences. I have been trying to hear the delicate and often very private spiritual moments that can shape a life.

This is not the kind of research that takes place in a laboratory; instead, like the work of an anthropologist, it occurs *in the field*. The field includes a family's living room, a child's bedside, a parent's private journal, and the depth of our own memories. The data is the experiences themselves and the impact these events have on a life. With the gracious permission of these individuals, I will share some of these stories with you; in many cases I have changed names and identifying information in order to protect identities. Beyond this data I have teased apart other researchers' work in this area and searched the autobiographical accounts of scores of historic figures, from English poet and mystic William Blake to Indian nationalist leader Mahatma Gandhi, uncovering the surprising spiritual richness of their own childhoods. I have also dug into the literature of the wisdom traditions and across academic disciplines ranging from psychology to literature in order to help unravel and understand this mystery.

Even from casual conversations, I have discovered that these stories are often right under the surface. Whenever I have mentioned, say, in a conversation on an airplane, that I am exploring children's spiritual experiences, I often get curious looks in response. Once I explain my earnest interest a little further, I often hear, "Well, I've never told anyone about this but . . . " followed by a secret moment of childhood revelation that has shaped this person's life in a powerful way.

As part of this research, I have also helped to bring different families together in order to talk about their experiences with one another. As one mom reported after attending a camp for children and parents, "My daughter has been telling me things about what she sees and hears. I'm amazed especially because we've always been so close, yet she never mentioned these things before." Being in an environment where it is "normal" to talk about spiritual experiences simply made it safe for this ten-year-old to share more. And essentially this is the goal of this book: to help make it safe for children and adults to explore and share their spiritual worlds and to claim and develop their "spiritual intelligence" throughout their lives.

How many children actually have spiritual experiences and capacities? Are we speaking of a handful of unusual children or is the phenomena more common? I am not speaking of seeing angels particularly; as I will explain in a moment, spirituality is much more diverse and not always so dramatic. While children will often tell me that everyone has spiritual capacities, I wanted to see just how common this might be.

First, we can make some estimates based on previous research. For example, it appears that significant spiritual experiences are surprisingly common in the general population. Various polls have reported that between 20 and more than 60 percent of adults surveyed have had a significant religious or spiritual experience.[1] Results vary largely depending on the way questions are posed. But what about children? In a study in England in which those who had had a spiritual experience were asked to write about it, among the more than four thousand reports that were received, nearly 15 percent described an experience that occurred in childhood.[2] This was without being asked anything about childhood whatsoever.

To address the question more directly, a colleague and I conducted a sophisticated statistical survey of 450 young adults. The results suggest that childhood spiritual moments are very common. We questioned participants about a variety of different kinds of specific spiritual experiences rather than focusing on only one general question as has been more typical of surveys of this nature. For example, we asked about moments of wonder and awe, unitive experiences, and receiving spiritual guidance from a nonphysical source, to name a few. The affirmative responses to various questions in this anonymous survey ranged from about 10 percent to more than 80 percent. Of those who indicated an age at which experiences occurred, between 60 percent and 90 percent indicated that their first experiences of this nature occurred in childhood.[3] These data highlight how relevant children's spirituality may be for *all* families and *all* teachers.

From my research, a startlingly different picture of children's spiritual life emerges from the one we have been taught. The evidence overwhelmingly suggests that children have a rich and formative spiritual life. From the adults with whom I have spoken, we will see that childhood moments serve as touchstones for their entire lives. And sometimes they also serve as a source of confusion in a world that does not acknowledge these possibilities.

What Is Spiritual?

Before going further, we should consider what is meant by the word *spiritual*. But defining it is a bit like trying to hold water in our hands. We can hold some for a while and we may even bring some to our mouth and swallow, but a great deal just passes through unconfined, ungrasped. *Spiritual* naturally pertains to spirit, that unquantifiable force, the mystery that animates all things and of which all things are composed. There is really no separating us from it. Any aspect of this life contains an essence of the whole, just as any of our cells contain the code for our whole form. We might recognize that mystery as the power of creation or sense it as wholeness, homecoming, or perhaps a truth deeper than words.

Talking about spirituality can be like asking a fish to talk about water. By this I mean that spirituality is the sea within which we live, and water is even that which makes up most of who we are (the majority of our body is composed of water molecules). So rather than thinking of ourselves as human beings occasionally having spiritual experiences, I find it more helpful to think of ourselves as spiritual beings having human experiences. While this phrase is probably already a bumper sticker on someone's car, I think it captures well the notion that our life *is* a spiritual life. It is not that some of us are spiritual and some are not; our entire existence is a spiritual event. So how can we talk about it with useful distinctions?

First, it may be helpful to distinguish between spirituality and religion. Religion is a systematized approach to spiritual growth formed around doctrines and standards of behavior. Religions were generally inspired by spiritual insight and developed in order to spread that insight through various teachings, rituals, and rules of conduct. To be "religious" implies some adherence to those standards and practices. For many, religion serves as a kind of oasis and a community that provides comfort and guidance. But for others, religion has served as a source of oppression, especially when members of a particular religion assume that they alone know the truth and demand that others see it in the same way.

The original seed of religion—the "word in the heart from which all scriptures come," as Quaker William Penn wrote[4]—is the spiritual. *Spiritual* refers to an intimate and direct influence of the divine in our lives. Spiritual moments are direct, personal, and often have the effect, if only for a moment, of waking us up and expanding our understanding of who we are and what our place is in the universe. While the essence of the spiritual is mysterious, it also involves an invitation to dwell as near as possible to the channel in which our light, or spiritual essence, flows. Some come near that light through service or devotion; some find incomprehensible oneness in nature. But we also find the spiritual in small everyday moments: a small child hugs us tightly and our heart opens; we breathe in the softness of a spring day and our own hardness softens with appreciation; we assume a loving attitude instead of a defensive posture and in so doing heal a wounded relationship. But like the fish's water, whether it is recognized or not, the spiritual is always present.

Getting a little more technical, spirituality may be seen both as a *worldview* and as a *process* of development. A worldview addresses the big questions: Who am I? What is the nature of this life, this universe? Our answers to these questions affect the way we live in the world. Historically, the doctrine of materialism tells us that only what we can observe and measure is real. Materialism collapses the universe into a flatland that we call the physical plane.

On the other hand, a spiritual worldview locates the individual in a multidimensional, sacred universe. A spiritual view does not neglect the physical, but integrates it into a larger understanding of reality—matter and spirit coexist, and maybe are even different aspects of the same thing. In the Gospel of Thomas, Jesus says, "Split a piece of wood; I am there. Lift up a stone, and you will find me there."[5] The basic premise of a spiritual worldview is that all things, including us, are sacred and are infused with or part of spirit. The fish's water, that which is within him and surrounds him, becomes holy water. A child's openness and directness of perception allows for this intimate and intuitive awareness of the world; the child seems to dwell nearer the light. For a child, a worldview does not have to be carefully crafted in logic and language. It can be built from direct spiritual experience and housed in a feeling, an image, or a sense of belonging or truth.

In addition to a worldview, spirituality is also a process of development. The spiritual has been considered as the top of the developmental ladder or as a particular branch or line of development like, say, cognition. However, in this age of so much possibility and so much estrangement from self, society, and source, I think it is more important to focus on it as an ongoing growth process—a process of identity, of finding out more about who we really are. The crest of the wave of this process has been called liberation, transformation, enlightenment, and self-realization. It is also recognized as integration and wholeness; the more of ourself and the world we can integrate into our being, the greater our development. We claim our shadowy parts, learn to love our enemies, and experience ourself as an interconnected spiritual being, even as spirit itself. The world's sacred traditions tell us that the process ultimately unfolds in the direction of love and wisdom. Spirit simultaneously pushes toward creation and communion—toward increasing diversity and toward a sense of indivisible, indestructible unity.

Spiritual experiences serve as benchmarks and catalysts for spiritual growth. These are moments when our individual consciousness opens to the larger consciousness of which we are all a part. In other words, we wake up to some aspect of divinity in the here and now. It is increasingly apparent that children *do* have spiritual experiences, sometimes in remarkable and diverse forms. My daughter's encounters with her angel represent only one kind of experience that can be called "spiritual." This is not a book just about angels; the spiritual manifests itself in all sorts of ways. We will explore five general kinds of spiritual capacities: wisdom, wonder, wondering, the meeting between you and me, and seeing the invisible. These may even emerge as a kind of spiritual temperament—the style or styles through which the child's spirituality most naturally flows.

In spite of their inexperience in the world (or perhaps because of it), children have remarkable access to deep inner guidance and insight—they can often penetrate to the heart of an issue and open to an intuitive source of *wisdom* that provides comfort and counsel. For example, two-year-old Alissa insisted to her mother that she must "tell that lady something." The "lady" was a stranger who was giving a lecture at a workshop that her mother was attending. Her mother had no idea what Alissa was talking about, but she respected her daughter's insistence. After staring at this stranger and waiting patiently on her mother's lap for the lecture to finish, Alissa walked up to her and announced that she had to tell her something. She then announced to the stranger that she "must let her daddy into her heart."

The stranger was brought to tears and later shared that she had shut her estranged father out of her life and had been wrestling with what she should do. While children may not be able to explain logically what or how they know something, their wisdom can be crystal clear, just like Alissa's. Perhaps the most recognizable kind of spiritual experiences are those incredible moments of *wonder* and awe that the mystics describe. Childhood is a time of wonder and awe as the world grabs our attention through our fresh eyes and ears. It is not hard to find young children absorbed in a blissful moment on a swing or spinning just to feel the world move around them. Children are natural mystics. Sometimes that wonder opens all the way to ecstasy and unity.

At age eleven, Debbie was by herself lying back on her swing set. As she described, "I was looking at the sky, just watching. I don't know how it happened, but all of a sudden it all opened up to me. I don't know how to say it, but I felt everything was perfect and connected. I can't say I was thinking anything—it's like there was no room even to think. It felt like my chest could just burst open and fly into a million pieces. It felt like I could explode and be the sun and the clouds." Inevitably, powerful moments like these can shape the course of an entire lifetime. Children have a natural capacity for wonder and therefore feel the pulse of spirit directly and intimately.

At age six, Reed asked himself earnestly, Why am I here? What is life about? This pondering or *wondering* about life and meaning is what religion and philosophy attempt to address. Through big questions like these, we enter into a dialogue with mystery. We have assumed that children do not and cannot consider these "ultimate concerns," as theologian Paul Tillich named them.[6] However, the evidence I am presenting will demonstrate that many children seek spiritual nourishment through metaphysical reflection. And in the Sufi tradition, like so many others, deep reflection is said to make possible the deeper insights, the nourishment of the heart.[7]

Spirituality is often lived out at the intersection of our lives—at the *meeting between you and me.* The way we know and treat one another is the basis of a *relational* spirituality. Children have the capacity to connect or relate deeply with others. Through their connection they often sense pain, injustice, and hypocrisy very quickly. Sometimes they may be overwhelmed or confused by the feelings of another person; in other moments that deep connection leads to surprising expressions of compassion. Psychologists have described the capacity for empathy, for really feeling into another's world, as the basis for compassion and moral development. However, they have not often recognized that children, while sometimes tremendously selfish and self-centered, simultaneously have the capacity for deep empathy and compassion.

In addition to wisdom, wonder, pondering, and meeting, we will talk about another general type of spiritual experience, and this is the most controversial. When consciousness opens, we may notice things that we did not sense before—we may *see the invisible.* The revelation from the sages and mystics is that the world is not just physical form; rather, it is multidimensional—layers upon layers of existence— and children's natural openness often allows them to see into it. These insights may help reveal more of who we are and what the universe is. For example, at seven years old, Maia saw lights and color around people. "I see green and purple on you and colored strings coming off you," she told me. Many children with whom I have spoken, like many individuals from various cultures, also describe seeing colors, lights, or various shapes around people.

Children *see* in others ways as well. Gladys remembers when her sister awoke with a nightmare: "She was crying and saying that my grandpa's factory was burning; she was crying so loudly that she woke up everyone in the house. Several minutes later we received a phone call that the factory was on fire." Another mom reports: "When my youngest son was about two, we were visiting the home of relatives. He could see the garage window from the bedroom where he was supposed to be napping. Pointing out the window, he started to cry and said he couldn't sleep because he was afraid of the 'sad old man in the garage.' Nobody was in the garage at the time. What he had no way of knowing—although we discovered this later—was that an old man had killed himself in that garage several years before." The integration and refinement of this knowing may reflect a natural evolution of human consciousness that opens to a multidimensional universe. We will explore the natural range of these perceptions and along with it the roles and risks these present for a spiritual life.

Many of us recognize this range of capacities and events as spiritual; others might not be so sure about some of them. In order to provide a context for understanding these moments, throughout this book I have sprinkled the wisdom and insights of the great sages and mystics from a variety of sacred traditions to help guide and ground us both in terms of their understanding of the spiritual realm and through their spiritual experiences as children.

The great visions of Native American elder Black Elk began in a moment of awe as he walked through a "rainbow doorway" into a tepee. "I saw six old men sitting in a row," he related. "The oldest spoke, 'Your grandfathers all over the world are having a council and they have called you here to teach you.'" Each proceeded to give him a gift of power and understanding that would provide inner power and healing for his people during the difficult times ahead. He was unconscious for twelve days after the vision and nearly died.[8] These visions that guided his entire spiritual life began as a small boy of five and were crystallized at nine years old.

The influential Catholic nun Hildegard of Bingen, born in 1098, had visions throughout her life beginning at three years old. She described "so great a brightness that my soul trembled."[9] Saint Catherine of Siena had a vision of Jesus and various saints at six years old that would dramatically transform her life.[10] Ramakrishna, one of the great spiritual forces of nineteenth-century India, had his opening to the Divine at six.[11] William Blake described seeing "bright angelic wings bespangling every bough like stars" at nine years old.[12] Ramana Maharshi found incredible insight as a boy.[13] Gandhi had a hunger for truth even as a young child.[14] The Jesuit sage Teilhard de Chardin points to the beginning of his spiritual quest at five or six years old.[15] Clearly, our children are in good company.

To summarize, spiritual capacities may take the form of wisdom and moments of wonder. They may manifest themselves through wrestling with the big questions, through communion with and compassion toward others, and through seeing the invisible. While many of the children's stories in this book are somewhat dramatic, the simple spirituality of a compassionate act, an open heart, or a small moment of courage is just as much the stuff of a spiritual life. It is just a bit easier to see in the more dramatic stories; their greatest value may be to remind us to notice the more subtle impulses of spirit in our children.

Our encounter with divinity, our access to wisdom and wonder, does not wait until we have careers or cars. We live it as children, and it forms a center point for our lives. We could say that these experiences begin to reveal a "spiritual intelligence." And like intellectual capacity, spiritual capacity is diverse. It is something *all* of us possess to some degree. It can emerge at different times, and it may require cultivation in order to be brought to full bloom. Unfortunately, it has been neglected and even repressed in our consideration of children, and thus many of us are left developmentally delayed as adults. Having lost touch with inner wisdom and a sense of wonder, with compassion and deep meaning, our lives may be organized by fear or fashion rather than by the deep current of spirit.

But the mere presence of a child and the consideration of our own childhood can help us reconnect with the spiritual. Children can be our spiritual teachers if we pay attention. As one mother said,

"My eighteen-month-old came up and kissed me the other day; she was just so pure and tender that I started to cry. What immediately flashed in my mind was that this is the way I want to show my love to others—so purely, tenderly, with no holding back."

Few things can transform us as quickly as the presence of a child. The stories and insights that follow can serve as a pathway not only to understand the spiritual world of children but also to reconnect with our own divinity. Many of us can find the early tugs of spirit deep in our own memories. In reading this book, you may recall, reclaim, and renew your own early threads. It is meant to be an opening not only to our children's secret world, but also to our own. I will explore several main questions:

- How do children serve as spiritual teachers for adults?
- What are the varieties of children's spiritual experiences?
- How can parents, teachers, and other friends of children nurture spirituality?
- What problems and dangers do children face with respect to their spiritual capacities?
- What might a spiritual curriculum look like for children?
- How do early experiences serve as touchstones for a spiritual life?
- Are today's children different from those of previous eras? Do they represent a front edge of evolution?

Until now, it probably has not been safe to reveal this secret world in this very public way. Children would have been subject to persecution as heretics or prescriptions as they would have been diagnosed as mentally ill. They might have been ridiculed, dismissed, and left confused. Or perhaps just as painfully, a child might have been worshiped and turned into a showpiece, a spiritual novelty, and therefore laden with a huge burden to carry through his or her life.

But at this moment in history, as children's spirituality rises to the surface, as spirituality becomes of central importance to millions of adults, and as the state of the world demands the wisdom and compassion of a spiritual perspective, it is time to welcome and nourish our children's spiritual intelligence and reclaim our spirituality as adults. As we struggle to understand the contemporary world, to find a moral compass, to overcome selfishness, to develop character and compassion, and to uncover our calling, we may find a wellspring very close to home, in the authentic spiritual life of children. This spiritual world of children has been a *secret* world that deserves to remain *sacred*, but it is a world that can benefit from the light of thoughtful dialogue and fresh understanding. As part of that dialogue, this book is offered as a prayer to help us nourish the spirit within our children and within ourselves.

Part 1

A Secret World

Chapter 1

Listening *for* Wisdom

*I*n the information age, sacred texts, great ideas, and valuable information of all sorts is readily available. God is in the bookstore and on the Web. We no longer need permission, professor, or priest to gain access to the mysteries. But while we can buy an insightful book or find good advice about living, we cannot purchase wisdom. Wisdom is not an *object*, accumulated like possessions. Instead, it is an *activity*—a way of knowing and being that emerges through an opening of mind and heart. In wisdom we see into the heart of something or see it from a greater perspective.

We might assume that wisdom comes only with a great deal of experience, reserved for the elders or for a rare few. However, in spite of their naïveté in the ways of the world, children often show a remarkable capacity for cutting to the heart of a matter. While they may not have the language or thinking capacity of an adult, they have the capacity to open to the deep currents of consciousness. Through that opening may come a still, small voice, a pearl of insight, or maybe an angel.

Divine Homework

It had been several years since my introduction to Haley's angel. This whole relationship was unexpected enough for her mother and me, but one afternoon we were further surprised when her angel offered some unusual help with a fourth-grade homework assignment.

My wife and I had been very careful not to make too much of Haley's angel in front of her or to lead the conversation about it in any way. Generally, we had simply listened and asked questions whenever she mentioned it. Deep into one Sunday afternoon, Haley, nine at the time, had a report to write for her class on a significant black figure in history. She had chosen Mahalia Jackson, the great gospel singer who had been a powerful voice for civil rights during her lifetime. Over the previous two weeks, Haley had found a book and downloaded a couple of brief one-page articles from the Internet on the singer's life. She was now finishing typing this report. However, she was not much of a typist, and so this was a slow and sometimes painful process.

As I walked into the room where she was working, it was easy to feel the tension and imagine her teeth grinding away. She had worked pretty hard on the paper and done a respectable job so far. Most importantly, she seemed to have learned a few things about Mahalia's life and about writing a paper. But as time and patience were running out, it had reached the point that the goal was simply to finish the thing, which was due the next morning. Frustration was setting in, and she was still in need of a conclusion and desperately in need of a shift in mood.

While she was walking out of the room to take a short break, I spontaneously asked if she wanted to try an experiment. As she began to climb the stairs to her bedroom, I suggested that she lie down on her bed and ask her angel if she knew anything about Mahalia Jackson. I had never suggested anything even remotely like this before, and I am not quite sure where my suggestion came from. Haley, more than ready for any distraction from her typing, agreed.

Fifteen or twenty minutes later, she hopped downstairs. "How ya' doing?" I asked. She said, "Good—I just saw Mahalia." "You did?" I said, not being sure what to expect. "I was kinda' surprised that I actually saw her and how easy it was to find her," she announced. She then started to tell me about what Mahalia had said to her. I stopped her in midsentence and quickly grabbed pen and paper so I could take dictation. She then proceeded to tell me a wide range of very subtle and personal information about Mahalia Jackson that I could not find in the materials she had read—I checked.

After nearly ten minutes of relaying this rich material, Haley said that Mahalia wanted to tell her a "main thing" about her life. "Mahalia said that her life was filled with three things: joy, happiness, and fear. She felt joy that black people *and* white people were giving her a lot of attention. She felt happy that she was able to do just what she wanted to do: sing her [gospel] music and sing about love and God. She also said that she was afraid—afraid because she was getting so popular and helping black people and white people to come together that some people would not like it and might try to hurt her." These specific ideas were not at all explicit in the materials she had read. But they seemed to capture Mahalia Jackson's life with riveting clarity and directness.

After I finished taking dictation, Haley added some of this information as a conclusion to her report. She suddenly had a new sense of intimacy and excitement for this woman and for her research paper. Because of her very personal "chat," she now felt like she really knew Mahalia firsthand. This was a very different sensation than she had had just thirty minutes earlier. A project that had been sliding toward drudgery now became one of inspiration, especially fitting for the nature of Mahalia Jackson's life, whose voice and presence inspired so many.

I asked Haley how she'd gotten in touch with Mahalia. She said, "It was easy; I just got relaxed on my bed and asked my angel for help. Then, in my mind, I went to www.mahaliajackson.com, and there she was standing right in front of me. We talked and she told me about her life."

Did Haley meet with the consciousness of Mahalia Jackson? Does she really see an angel? Great sages and mystics have recognized the possibility for hearing deep guidance, just like Haley does. Abraham, Moses, Mohammed, and Mary all claimed to tap a deep source of wisdom. So, too, did Martin Luther King, Mahatma Gandhi, George Washington Carver, and Winston Churchill. Socrates called his inner voice Daimon, which means divine.[1] In first-century China, individuals called the *wu* received guidance from inner voices.[2] Medieval Jewish rabbis conversed with disincarnate teachers known as the Maggidim.[3] Christian mystics attributed their inner guidance to the Holy Ghost, deceased saints, and angels. The ancients used the word *genius*, which meant a guardian spirit and is the origin for the word *genie*. In the Middle Ages, the genius came to be known as a guardian angel.[4]

In addition to thinking of wisdom as connecting with a source outside us, like an angel, the mystics and sages also talk about the source as emanating from deep within. Rumi, the thirteenth-century Sufi mystical poet, offers an image:

> *There is another kind of tablet, one*
> *already completed and preserved inside you.*
> *A spring overflowing its springbox. A freshness*
> *in the center of the chest. This other intelligence*
> *does not turn yellow or stagnate. It's fluid,*
> *and it doesn't move from the outside to inside*
> *through the conduits of plumbing-learning.*
> *The second knowing is a fountainhead*
> *from within you, moving out.*[5]

Would it be more accurate to think of Haley's angel as part of herself, "a fountainhead from within"? The source of guidance and knowledge, like Haley's, may indeed be thought of as on the inside— an inner fountainhead—or on the outside—the muses of the ancient Greeks or maybe a guardian angel. What is most significant is not the concept we use to describe this knowing, but the fact that, by whatever name, it is available. Its value is measured by the quality of what is heard and how it impacts a life. Haley is able to tap a source of insight, loving comfort, and guidance. Children open to these depths of consciousness naturally and regularly. But most contemporary maps of child (and adult) psychology underestimate the complexity of the human being's spiritual self. We need to rehabilitate the idea of our larger nature. The point is that it may be hard to recognize the inner wisdom, and especially to appreciate it, in children if we do not acknowledge its existence.

A Flowing Stream

Many traditions describe two main aspects of the human: what we might call the "Big Self" and the "small self." The small self is understood as the ego in Western psychology; in Buddhism this is called the "lesser self." We all have this self and it develops over time. But in the sacred traditions, the lesser self is not mistaken for our whole being. Rather than being directed by its fluctuations, worry, and grasping, we are told that we must learn to use this small self instead of being used by it.

As a source of wise guidance and insight, Sri Aurobindo, the Indian sage, called the Big Self the "inner teacher."[6] Meister Eckhart, the thirteenth-century Dominican priest, referred to the "inner man."[7] Ralph Waldo Emerson spoke of the "oversoul."[8] Italian psychiatrist Roberto Assagioli wrote about various dimensions of this Big Self as the "higher self," "transpersonal self," and the "universal self."[9]

Around the end of the nineteenth century, American psychologist and philosopher William James likened consciousness to a flowing stream.[10] Through the Big Self, in some moments children are able to tap the deeper currents in the stream. A simple map of this stream may be useful before we go further.

The surface of our being is the small self, or ego. The small self helps us operate in the world—it assesses danger, worries about the past, and thinks about the future. The small self generates the internal dialogue that occupies so much of our daily existence: Do I like this? Why did I just say that? It also sees itself as separate from others and therefore often seeks fulfillment at the expense of others.

Beneath this surface lies the subconscious mind. Actions, thoughts, and feelings of the ego both influence and are influenced by the subconscious. If part of us makes a directive, the subconscious can follow. For example, we can drive a car without thinking of every arm motion necessary to turn the wheel; we brush our teeth without having to think through every step. The subconscious not only responds to the ego, it also affects it. We may have personal traits that are "hardwired" from birth or we may have internalized the voices of a parent or the media, and these may shape our actions, feelings, and thoughts. Maybe these are the expectations of our family or the media about who we should be, what we should look like, and so forth.

Dipping deeper into the subconscious, we could also think of perinatal experiences, for example a difficult birth, or karma, as Hindu tradition maintains, as expressing its influence through the subconscious. We are generally not fully aware of these, but they form a kind of programming that automatically influences our responses, for better or worse. A challenging situation may activate the programmed response in a child, such as "I can do this; I'm competent." Or, on the other hand, "I'm no good; I can't handle this." Most approaches to psychotherapy are attempts at overcoming or recognizing this programming.

The realm of the subconscious is not only individual—mine or yours—but it is also *ours*. The stream meets other streams. Individual subconscious currents intermingle and form a shared region of the subconscious. Haley can find Mahalia Jackson because her consciousness exists in this collective mind. You and I may have a feeling about a relative or close friend at a distance and then have our intuition confirmed. Insight from this level is often personal and personalized. For example, Mahalia spoke about her life specifically.

Descending slightly further in the stream, the collective region also contains universal patterns or archetypes, as Carl Jung described.[11] These "first patterns" may be thought of as deep structures of human consciousness that form the internal architecture of the mind. Hints of this come in common images or concepts that emerge across cultures and time, such as the image of a circle representing wholeness or universal notions of roles like warrior or healer, which form a kind of template of human personality. Subconscious currents intermingle to form a shared subconscious. Streams flow, mingle, and merge.

There is still more to who we are. Deeper into the stream is what we will call the superconscious. When our awareness opens to this level we may experience inspiration and universal insight, or feel wholeness and unity. This is deep into the Big Self, which is not neatly contained within an individual. The particularities of the subconscious often serve as a filter between the self and the superconscious, personalizing or coconstructing the forms or patterns that are recognized as safe friends. As you will see later in the chapter, two-year-old Alissa says a dolphin tells her things, Diana feels the presence of her deceased father.

We might recognize and describe the deepest currents and our most expanded awareness as Christ Consciousness, Buddha nature, Tao, oneness, God, void, cosmic consciousness, and so forth. John Steinbeck described this recognition of unity in his work *The Grapes of Wrath*: "Maybe a fella ain't got a soul of his own, but on'y a piece of a big soul—the one big soul that belongs to ever'body."[12] And physicist Erwin Schrodinger concluded, "Mind by its very nature is a *singularte tantum*. I should say: the overall number of minds is just one."[13]

The task of spiritual development is regularly described as expanding our awareness in order to meet more of who we really are. The Christian Gnostic Gospels refer to this as revealing what truly exists.[14] The Russian mystic G. I. Gurdjeiff called this "waking up."[15] We might say that "wisdom is the process by which we come to know that the limited thing we thought was our whole being is not."[16] This implies that we grow in wisdom as we recognize, accept, and live from more of ourselves—recognizing our whole being and even the unity of all life—not just a limited ego. I should note that this is not just about accepting our higher angels, but also about facing and integrating our shadows, all those aspects that we have not owned; we grow as we face our fears and limitations as well as our inspirations.

This simple map gives an image of the depths of our inner nature and how we are simultaneously both separate and interconnected, as the sacred traditions often point out. While there may be different currents in a stream, ultimately the currents are all stream, all made of the same stuff, an undivided unity of consciousness.

Life Is about Love

"Life is about love," my five-year-old pronounced one day on a bookmark-shaped slip of paper. There had been no religious training, no prior discussion, just this private note that she wrote when she was playing by herself. We have kept it on the refrigerator for years because it serves as such a pure and wise reminder about what is important. Wisdom is distinguished from bare intellect especially by the integration of the heart.

Leslie described an opening to insight that took place when she was eight years old. "I was in church thinking about praying," she related. "Suddenly, in a flash, I understood that I should be praying for love and wisdom. I suddenly 'got' that this was the way to use prayer. This was never suggested to me or even really talked about, but this insight came to be my regular way of praying. Whenever I prayed, I prayed for love and wisdom. This sounds simple, but it provided an incredible focus for me. This was my special secret. Even up until this moment, I have never told anyone about it. Up until my late twenties, I continued this style of prayer. Around the time of my marriage, it changed somewhat. I started to pray to have my heart opened. . . . This seems like a different version of the same theme.

"I think that at some point I was expecting transcendence or something from my prayers, and it wasn't until later that I realized that what I was getting were small glimpses, a direction, an insight, or an attitude about handling situations. I didn't have the maturity to realize until later that wisdom involves acting on what we know— walking it out in the world. I had to take those glimpses and live them in order to learn from them."

Wisdom is not just about what we know, but especially about how we live, how we embody knowledge and compassion in our lives and, as the great essayist and poet Emerson said, blend a sense of what is true with what is right.[17] While this is often the daily challenge played out over the course of our lives, some children seem to have it all together remarkably well.

An eleven-year-old boy named Mattie Stepanek seems to have a remarkable embodied wisdom. He is wise like an old guru, but with the funniness and liveliness of a child. The clarity and simplicity of his being and his single-minded mission to "spread peace in the world" are amazing. Mattie has multiple sclerosis and for many years has been precariously poised between life and death. His three older siblings have already died of the disease. Mattie had three wishes for his life: (1) to get his book of poetry published; (2) to meet his hero, former president Jimmy Carter; and (3) to be on Oprah Winfrey's talk show so he could "spread peace."

By 2003 all three wishes had already been accomplished. In an interview, talk show host Larry King asked Mattie about his meeting with Carter. Mattie described it in a lively and funny way, and said they had a wonderful one-on-one conversation. Jimmy is his hero because he is a "humble peacemaker." He said they are still in touch and are on a first-name basis, and he likes to "make sure that Jimmy stays on track" with his peace work.

In response to the 9/11 tragedy, Mattie wrote three poems. The first he wrote when the World Trade Center Towers were falling, and he was "very, very sad and scared." The poem expresses this sadness, almost despair, about what is happening to people and their suffering, without in any way getting stuck in the "good" here and the "evil" there. In the third poem, he called on all people to "STOP" and stay still—just to "BE" before making any move in reaction to what just happened. It is a very profound and impassioned poem in which a Buddhist might recognize that he took the "stopping" all the way to the emptiness of the Buddhist notion of *sunyata* (although Mattie is a Catholic). During the interview Mattie said he was "sometimes a little sad" about his own illness, but said with conviction that he thought it somehow was meant to be—that God meant it to be this way.

Sometimes knowing opens us to all sorts of unexpected places. Levi, a very verbal two-year-old at the time, and his grandmother were playing in the backyard while Krista, Levi's mother, was cleaning up inside the house. When they came back inside, Krista noticed that her mother had a very peaceful look on her face, quite different from what she had had before she had gone out. Krista asked what had happened outside. Levi's grandmother answered, "Levi just told me about *my* mom." (She had died more than twenty years earlier.) "He taught me to play a game that he said he learned when he was in heaven. It was a game I used to play with my mom when I was little, a word game—a riddle game. Levi said he learned it from 'Great-Grandma Brown.'" (Neither Krista nor her mother had ever mentioned her as "great-grandma.") "I asked how he knew Grandma Brown, and he corrected me. 'It is my *Great*-Grandma Brown, your mom. And, Grandma, she is so pretty and you look just like her.'" "And she does," Krista confirmed. "He went on to tell her specific things about Great-Grandma Brown—like she was very funny, hard to keep up with, and full of energy—he described her personality to a T." Once in awhile Levi, now several years older, still tells his grandmother about Great-Grandma Brown.

Comfort and Counsel

The gateways to wisdom are diverse. Some children just seem to know; for others, inner comfort and counsel seem to come in the form of a helper. Spirit guides in the form of angels, saints, and ancestors have been part of every major sacred tradition. For example, there are 294 references to angels in the Bible. Animals, too, have been a common representation of spiritual energies and are featured in many religions. The animal is seen as a power, or "medicine," as Native Americans call it, which serves as a link, symbol, or totem between the invisible world and the physical one. When a shaman, for example, adopts the guise of an animal in a ceremony, he or she attempts to call forth those energies for the purpose of healing and guidance. The idea is that somehow the image, idea, or form of this animal embodies and represents certain qualities; they may be thought of as archetypes—primary forms or patterns deep in our shared consciousness. In most explanations of animal guides, you do not choose

the animal, it chooses you—it pays you a visit. Native American elder Black Elk described a horse and an eagle that came in visions to
him as a young boy and provided guidance.[18] Contemporary author
Ted Andrews told of a wolf from the spirit world that spoke to him
when he was four years old.[19]

Adam, the family dog, had just died and Laura, seven, was having a very difficult time getting over the loss. She had really loved
Adam and she didn't know how to deal with losing him. According
to her mother, "Laura was crying a lot about him and I just didn't
seem able to comfort her very well. We were driving in the car and
Laura was talking a lot. I was tired and I asked her to please just lie
down and rest for a few minutes. Thankfully she did, and after about
twenty minutes she sat up and said, 'Mom, something wonderful happened! I left my body and went to talk with Adam. He told me that
my being so upset about him dying was making it harder for him and
if I really wanted to help him, I should send him love and light. So I
did and it feels better.' Laura paused and then added, 'Adam said the
reason he came to see me is that when somebody else close to me
dies, I'll know what to do.'"

A few weeks later, Laura's aunt gave birth to a baby with a ter-
minal illness. It was a very difficult situation for everyone. Laura
insisted on visiting the baby in the hospital. Her mother said, "I wasn't
sure about this. Normally, given Laura's emotionally charged personality, I would have expected her to fall apart, to be really hysterical,
and I didn't think this was what the family needed. But we went to
the hospital, and in the middle of all this grief, Laura insisted on
holding the dying baby. She was unbelievably calm and clear; she
was not upset or crying, but was working hard to help this dying
baby by sending him love and light. She helped all of us."

Two-year-old Alissa said that a dolphin would take her for rides
on his back when he wanted to tell her something. Alissa's mother
described her introduction to her daughter's special friend: "We were

in our family room watching a dolphin video one evening. There were lots of dolphins in the scene, and suddenly Alissa ran up to me and said, 'Mom, that looks just like Kiwa.' I had no idea what she was talking about. I said, 'Who's Kiwa?' 'Kiwa is my dolphin,' Alissa replied. 'Well, how did you meet her?' I asked. 'Way back in Cincinnati. [They had moved recently from Cincinnati; however, Alissa had never physically been with a dolphin in Cincinnati.] I swim with him in the dolphin area. But I can't stay in very long,' Alissa explained. 'When he needs to tell me something, he sees me on the beach and then he takes me. He lets me ride on his back.'"

At first, Alissa's mom assumed this was a cute fantasy. It was not long before she saw that her daughter's visits with Kiwa offered something more. "Kiwa tells me how to fix things. He told me how to fix Jane's head," Alissa announced one day. Jane was a friend of her mother's who suffered from migraine headaches. Her mom said, "I had never told Alissa about Jane's headaches, and we had never talked about them at our house. I had no idea that Alissa had any idea of Jane's problem until one day when Jane was over. Alissa was telling me that Kiwa had something to tell Jane. She wouldn't tell me what Kiwa was telling her because, she said, 'It isn't for you; it's for Jane.' Finally Alissa walked up to Jane, touched her and whispered very gently in her ear, 'Relax.'

"This sounds pretty simple, but Jane experienced it as a profound event. She has great trouble relaxing, is really high strung, and doesn't take the time to calm herself, to relax. It seemed that it was not just the words that moved her because somehow Jane felt a healing in that moment." This little two-year-old knew nothing about Jane's migraines, yet she was able to offer a direct and healing prescription.

While intelligence is usually associated with an ability to identify or articulate complex patterns of thought, wisdom often emerges as an elegantly simple proposition. This is not simplicity born of ignorance, but a simplicity that is tuned into what is essential in life. It cuts through the cloud of complexity. Children often go right to the heart of an issue. They often recognize pain, injustice, and phoniness very quickly. Wisdom cuts to what is of importance, not through calculations or shrewdness; the deepest insights, the authentic revelation, the healing vision come more directly, as an intuition.

Several months after the incident with Jane, Alissa's mom witnessed another encounter that dispelled any remaining doubts about the importance of Kiwa in her daughter's life. Alissa was with her mother at a lecture, more than a thousand miles from home, given by Katherine, whom they had never met. As she was sitting in the audience with her mother, Alissa became very insistent about needing to talk to Katherine. "I was holding Alissa on my lap and she was clinging to me and staring at Katherine through the whole presentation. She kept whispering in my ear, 'I need to talk to her. I need to talk to her. Kiwa wants to talk to her.' Katherine was addressing the audience, and Alissa just kept waiting and staring.

Finally, when Katherine was done talking, we went over to her. I just walked up and said, 'My daughter, Alissa, said that Kiwa needs to talk to you. She says Kiwa is her dolphin.'" Initially, Alissa wouldn't talk to Katherine directly; instead she used her mother as a conduit. She looked right at Katherine and quietly told her mother what her message was. Her mom said, "I simply relayed it to Katherine. I guess I was a safe way for her to say what she needed to. Alissa said, 'Tell her that she needs to play with her daddy. He is swimming in the ocean and they are playing. Tell her that her mommy and daddy love her and tell her they are playing with bees.'

"I told this to Katherine and then asked Alissa why they were playing with bees. She then said directly to Katherine, 'Because they need the honey; the honey, it's sweet—the honey—and they love you a lot. You need to let your daddy into your heart.' She said one more thing about the daddy and Katherine playing, but I don't remember what it was. When she was finished I had this sense of the energy going back into Alissa, and then she jumped up and was ready to play.

"Katherine and I looked at each other for a moment. Then Katherine seemed to gather herself and said to me, 'I know that didn't make any sense to you, but she just cleared up an issue that has been going on for five years between my father and me. It has to do with a daughter not being able to see how a dad loves her. The bees and the honey have to do with making something sweet and innocent and healing.'"

I was able to speak with Katherine soon after her encounter with Alissa. Katherine reported that the child had given her deep insight into and healing in her relationship with her father. The information from this little two-year-old had helped her to understand and resolve a deep-seated and very private problem in her life. Although Alissa had had no previous contact with this woman, she was somehow able to provide a picture that Katherine understood.

How often do we dismiss as frivolous such insight from children? Whether the insight comes through a dolphin, an angel, or "just knowing," this wisdom represents children's openness to an expanded consciousness that can help and heal. While they may not be able to explain eloquently and logically what or how they know, their messages, just like Alissa's, can still be crystal clear.

Diana's comfort and counsel came from a source that had been very close to her. She said, "When I was twelve, my father passed away very unexpectedly. Following his death, I was convinced, much to the consternation of my family, that he was still there. I distinctly felt his presence in my room with me, and we would be having a conversation about how his body could be gone, but that *he* was still there. I was talking to him and I was almost in a panic, wanting to see him so badly, but what I got instead was a sense of his presence and the understanding that I could talk to him and that it would be OK.

I was just talking with him about how we were going to continue our relationship when someone came in and found me having a conversation with him and made me go to my mother's room to spend the night because they thought I was hysterical.

"My mom was very ill for years after my father's death, and he helped me through all of that," Diana continued. "I journaled constantly through those years, and I often felt, as a child, that he was journaling with me. I could sit down and put a pen to paper, and he would teach me. It was as if he would give me the words that I was looking for. I just felt that he was right there with me as I sat and wrote in my journal, like a cat who would sit on my shoulder.

"I felt like there was a point where we were so unified that I didn't even have to ask a question—I would just know the right thing to say or do or write," she explained. "I felt this confidence through his presence. I felt like I had all of his experience rolled into my nonexperience. When I was twelve or thirteen and would experiment with writing, I often felt that this writing was better than I could do and that it was coming out of the power of his ability as well as mine. I felt that I had the great gift of his store of knowledge. His abilities had somehow merged with mine, and I was carrying something forward that was starting with him.

"When I do have direct communication with him, the answers come back to me so quickly. His sentence starts before my question completely ends. It's like when you and your closest friend finish each other's sentences. It has that quality. It travels so quickly and with such precision."

After high school, Diana went into extremely demanding writing programs at Duke and Radcliff and was a senior editor of a major magazine by the time she was twenty-four years old, a rare feat in the industry. "I remember in my midtwenties I realized that my dad wasn't as close to me as when I was a kid," she revealed. "When I asked about it, he answered, 'I need to do some other things. I'm going to be moving away a little bit and you need to do some things on your own.' He would be around, but he would be farther away. This was so clear that it was really unsettling. His message was, 'You can do this on your own. You don't need to run to Daddy every five minutes.' I understood later that he never moved away from me, but he gave me more space. There were things I needed to work out on my own. He was still whispering in my ear, but in a different way. He didn't want me to go through life not knowing my own strength. But he says that he often holds me.

One day I felt this so deeply, and when I saw this white cocoon that was so beautiful I just cried harder than I had cried in twenty years. Just to experience the beauty of it was excruciating. I can't explain it. I was just in the place of divine love that was so profound that it felt like it would be a disservice if I were not changed forever. When I feel the divine love of where my father is, I see how unnecessary any anger is—mine or my husband's or my mother's—how thin the wall is between here and there, how vast our souls are, how silly any day-to-day squabbles are, how unnecessary it is to react to the small irritations in life. I feel divine forgiveness of all human frailties. I want to hold onto this feeling, but I won't be able to articulate it."

Like Diana, many great writers (among many others) tell us that their work sometimes feels as though it originates from a source that is beyond them. The English poet John Keats said that his poetry seemed like the production of another person.[20] Hildegard of Bingen, whose first encounters with the Divine occurred when she was three, said her writings were dictated to her by the Holy Ghost: "I hear these things not with the bodily ears or the thoughts of my mind, but entirely with my soul."[21] William Blake, who saw angels as a child, said of his poem *Jerusalem*, "I have written this poem from immediate dictation, twelve and sometimes twenty or thirty lines at a time. . . . I may praise it, since I dare not pretend to be any other than the secretary—the authors are in eternity."[22]

Comfort and counsel, especially when things get difficult, are often what spirituality provides. Haley says that her time with her angel provides both guidance and also comfort: "It lets me know I'm loved." Just as for Haley, the comfort is often direct, personal, and "profoundly real," as Martin Luther King Jr. described it. During the Montgomery bus boycott, King faced tremendous opposition and even death threats. But in the midst of it all, he reported that an inner voice sustained him: "God has been profoundly real to me in recent years. In the midst of outer dangers, I have felt an inner calm. In the midst of lonely days and dreary nights, I have heard an inner voice saying, 'Lo, I will be with you.'"[23]

As it did for King, this deep wellspring may serve as the biggest lifeline for a child. One day I was having a telephone conversation with an old friend, a professional in her midforties. Meg asked me what I was working on these days, and I told her about some of the research I was doing on the inner spiritual life of children. I offered an example or two of the kinds of experiences that children were telling me about.

The next moment on the phone was silent. Then I heard her voice; it sounded both matter-of-fact and a little dreamy, as if she had closed her eyes and was describing a scene in her memory. With no prompting from me she then said: "Beginning around age five, I had a friend named Gigi. She would sit on the end of my bedpost in my bedroom. I remember her quite distinctly. She was like a spirit who watched over me much in the way that I watched over my dolls. I had no confusion that she was quite real; our interactions were very distinct from the kind of imaginary play that I had with toys and dolls. As a child I wondered where her name came from; it was so different from the names that I heard in my family and neighborhood. In sixth grade, I started taking French in school and it just clicked for me; I realized that my Gigi must have some French heritage." (Meg happens to have a gift for languages, especially French.

Native speakers often remark that she speaks their particular dialect, whether from Montreal or Paris or some more remote region of France, with no trace of an accent.)

"I didn't see her the way I saw my dolls, but I did see her in some inward way; I knew very clearly when she was there," Meg explained. "We had this very special connection. A couple of years later, my life changed. I went through extremely difficult times—some abuse in my home—and I starting feeling just horrible about myself. During these dark days, Gigi would speak to me and comfort me. I never talked to my dolls for help or protection, but I knew I could talk and listen to Gigi and I'd feel better. She helped me to survive. Later in [Catholic] grammar school, we learned about patron saints, and I felt that my Gigi was kind of like this.

"I just knew that in order to stay safe I needed to keep Gigi a secret. She started fading when I was ten years old, when there was much more imposition of morality. I picked up what was OK to believe and what was not. It became unsafe to have this relationship, and so I started burying this and burying everything. Gigi went so far inside even though this was the being that kept me feeling safe." I asked Meg if she had ever shared this with anyone. She said, "I haven't thought about this until recently, and until now, I've never told anyone about Gigi."

I was moved by her story and amazed that she had never shared this before, although I would learn that keeping secrets of this sort is pretty common. In fact, most of the adults with whom I have spoken had never shared their childhood visions with anyone before, often out of fear that they would be dismissed or derided.

Patron saints, French names, and inner guidance bring to mind the life of another young girl who found her own inner source. Beginning at thirteen, Jeanne saw a brilliant light and said that she touched, smelled, and heard various saints. Her first encounter occurred in her father's garden when, she described, "God sent a voice to guide me. At first I was frightened."[24] But in time she came to trust and rely on this guidance. At seventeen, the voice, steady throughout her teens, instructed her to leave home and join the army. Remarkably, in time she was put in charge of the army that led the liberation of France from the invading British. Jeanne is better known as Joan of Arc, who lived in the fifteenth century. Jeanne was also persecuted and ultimately executed because of charges related to her inner knowing.

Sometimes the voice of inner wisdom is called Gigi or has the face of an angel; sometimes it appears as an animal, like Kiwa or Adam. Sometimes there is no apparent messenger; there is just direct knowing—intuition and inspiration. While wise guidance seems remarkably available, I have been so intrigued to see how individualized it comes to children (and adults), like a fingerprint. It becomes uniquely crafted or coconstructed in a way that we can perceive it.

Once again, the important goal may not be to name the ultimate source of insight and inspiration—the spiritual world is simply too vast and mysterious for us to pin it down in this way. Instead, the more important considerations are the quality of the insight, how it affects our life, and also how we can tap into it.

The Contemplative Eye

Parents, teachers, and society as a whole are concerned with what our children know. However, *how* we know, not just *what* we know, is fundamental to the pursuit of wisdom. In the twelfth century, Saint Bonaventure wrote about three different "eyes of knowing": the eye of the senses, the eye of reason, and the eye of contemplation.[25]

The contemplative mind offers a direct nonrational mode that complements the analytic. There is a long history of contemplative knowing. In the East, practices such as meditation, which were designed to open the contemplative, have endured for thousands of years. In the West, ancient philosophers such as Plotinus (third century A.D.) understood that the highest truths were revealed only through a contemplative state of mind.[26] Nineteenth-century German philosopher Fredrich Nietzsche suggested that this nonrational mode is so important because it "opens the way to the Mothers of all Being, to the innermost heart of things."[27]

In the West, however, the dominance of a largely Aristotelian emphasis in logic, the natural sciences, and theology beginning at least by the twelfth and thirteenth centuries pushed the contemplative out of favor. Today we often discount the direct knowing that emerges as an inner sense or voice in favor of the measurable observation or logical deduction that science and reason value. Essentially, adult society has grown a cataract on the eye of contemplation—we have made it cloudy with mistrust. But the direct sight of contemplation is alive and well in most children; they are natural contemplatives.

The opening for children and adults often occurs spontaneously, seemingly out of the blue. Two-year-old Alissa said that when Kiwa, her dolphin friend, needs to tell her something, he meets her on the beach in the "dolphin area" and takes her for a ride. The process remains completely mysterious. And whether catalyzed by a strong need like Diana's loss of her father or Haley's curiosity about Mahalia, the opening of wisdom is considered "grace." In the Sufi tradition, for example, liberating knowledge does not originate from the seeker, but is received as a gift from the Divine. While a gift, the contemplative traditions also indicate that certain practices and techniques such as prayer and meditation help enhance the process by shifting consciousness and opening up awareness, inviting the "present"—meaning both *gift* and the *now*—this moment. Being in the present moment is the gift, and it is also the place where gifts of spirit are received.

Sometimes the busyness of daily life makes it more difficult to open to and dip into the deep currents. I asked Haley when she was ten years old if she had heard from or spoken to her angel recently. She said, "Not in a couple weeks. I've been too busy." The velocity and stimulation of the information age and the lack of contemplative space in the day often keep us on the surface, absorbing information from our senses and racing right along with our chattering minds. For children, there can be a rush to go from school to after-school activities like sports and music, to homework, to a bit of TV or computer if there is time, or to some reading, and then it is off to sleep. In the lives of children and adults, there is often little time and encouragement to be still and feel the deeper currents within and without. Our lives are shallower as a result.

But Maia, our youngest daughter, reminded us that even the very first moments of a day offer a kind of natural contemplative space in which we dangle between worlds. Maia, six at the time, had a class field trip to a very small local airport. The children examined several airplanes, and they watched their teachers take a quick flight given by a local pilot. On the way home, they chatted about the planes, and especially a little Ultralight that almost promised the sensation of flying without any plane. My wife asked, "What would it feel like if you could fly all by yourself, without a plane?" Without hesitating, Maia said, "I do fly. It's like before I wake up in the morning when I'm still flying. It's hard for me to get up sometimes. When I wake up for school, sometimes I'm not all back yet." If we can simply allow children to relax for a few minutes in that soft, listening space before the chatter of the mind and the force of the day's schedule kicks in, they may be able to carry into the day a bit of the awareness that comes from beyond logic and beyond the senses.

Children do not need to practice meditation for ten years to open intuition; it is working all the time. For example, when a child meets a new person, he or she may immediately pick up "vibes" from that person. But in the midst of all the external stimulation of today's world, we can help children tune in their intuitive receiver by inviting them first to be still and quiet. Maybe they have a special place where they can be alone and safe, like in their bed. Slowing down enough to pay attention to the inner flow helps to welcome it. Taking just a few moments before rising or before sleep to relax and see what comes to mind, or turning the car radio off and sitting quietly on a car ride, or taking a few deep breaths and pausing in any situation may provide enough space to hear and feel the whispers of inner knowing.

As a young teenager, George left home to try to find a person who would inspire and serve as his spiritual guide. He came away from each visit with a different preacher more disappointed and discouraged. Finally, sitting in silence one day, he began to hear a deep inner source, what he called the "inner light." This was George Fox, who founded the Society of Friends, better known as the Quakers, in the seventeenth century.[28] In recognition of the inner light, Quaker worship services are dominated by silence, so that worshipers may listen for their own inner voice. In the heart of silence, we find that "still, small voice," that "word in the heart" that is beyond shrewdness and calculation.

Children sometimes find their own unique ways to open the contemplative mind. Haley knew that to meet her angel, she must relax and quiet down. She discovered that taking slow deep breaths, closing her eyes, and straightening her spine seemed to help. She had never had any instruction or example of this, yet somehow she just knew.

Meg found a way to open to her friend Gigi. She said, "We had a small tile floor in a bathroom. It had those inch-square tiles with a pattern of black and white, but with other colors too, almost like a mosaic. I would be in the bathroom at times and I would just fall into the pattern. I don't know exactly how to describe this, but I would begin to see 3-D layers of things superimposed on one another. I would be sitting there and she would be on my shoulder. As I focused on the floor, it was like going into a trance. During that time and in those superimposed layers, I would understand things—things about the world and my life; I just 'got it' intuitively. It felt like it came from some deep place within me."

Ellen said that staring does it for her: "There is a deep focus that comes from staring. Then I seem to move into this other, deeper level where I see and know things. We're taught not to stare, but little kids do, and staring moves you into another dimension. I am able to see and understand things in those moments. It's like these images have a wave of intuition that goes along with them. You see them and know their meaning."

There are two general ways the mind operates. One is a kind of self-contained chatter in which we mentally process events, recycle the past, and anticipate the future. The other is a present-moment awareness in which we feel in the flow. When children (and adults) find a way to be quiet in their own special way, there is a subtle shift away from the chattering mind toward the larger stream of consciousness.

In addition to being still, the chatter also quiets when we break the mind's routine by things such as witnessing great beauty, encountering the unexpected, being in nature, taking a vacation, experiencing exhaustion, and just being playful. Even a little shift in perception or activity can help the mind move out of its little loops. For example, we could ask a child to notice something new about a family member, to doodle, hop, move around, change his or her body posture, walk in a silly way, think out loud, hum, sing, take a different route home, take a bath, or switch the color of pen he or she is using. All these things can break automatic thought processes; that is, they free us from the usual routine of thinking in order to help us open into the present moment, where wisdom lives.

Intention can also help open the contemplative eye. So many spiritual traditions advise some form of "Ask and ye shall receive." Focusing through asking inwardly is akin to tuning the radio receiver to whatever station you want to hear. We can attune to intuition by writing down a clear question before going to bed or formulating and asking a question out loud or silently, such as, How can I be of help to this person? or What is Mahalia Jackson like? We can also focus by inwardly asking a wise person, our higher self, or perhaps our angel for advice. This intention, in the form of an earnest question or prayer, can focus us toward the depths of consciousness.

Children have a natural sensitivity and openness that allows them to hear the inner wisdom. Listening to intuition means noticing those subtle cues that we often tell children not to pay attention to—a gut feeling, a vague discomfort, a fleeting idea. Sometimes what is heard is remarkably beautiful.

Marshall is a child who cannot speak or walk and writes by pointing at an alphabet board. He needs someone to support his elbow, providing a fulcrum, so that he may point to the letter and have a helper write the letter down. While Marshall's parents suspected delays in development when he was nine months old, by the time he was three, they realized that he understood the world at a very deep level. He began writing his own unique wisdom at age five. To everyone's amazement, he used words that he had not been exposed to in writing, yet he knew how to spell correctly. While his process takes more time and effort than simply sitting with pen and paper or a computer keyboard, his mother reports that he writes effortlessly. At six years old he captured the importance of inspired listening in a poem entitled "My Harmony Prevails to Free," later published in his book *Kiss of God*:

> *Even though my individuality finds*
> *sweet knowing perfection, I listen*
> *for the answers to wishes from above.*
> *I listen to good thoughts like something cloudy over mountain tops.* [29]

And these next lines capture the importance of finding "our right place"—that shift in consciousness that allows the contemplative eye to open.

> *Answers come when we are in our right place*
> *Perfect love will kindly give each thought special direction.* [30]

The listening of which we are speaking does not come by way of the ears particularly; it is listening with the heart. The contemplative mind and heart know through direct, intuitive feelings, not through abstractions and logic. As Marshall wrote at age seven, "Poetry is the magnificent kindness of the heart."[31] These are not the more superficial feelings of our moment-to-moment reactions, but the deep intuitive feeling from our core.

Through his gracious parents, I asked if Marshall had any insight to offer the readers of this book. In his response, he gives us clues into the world of the intuitive heart—what he calls "real feelings":

> *Tell the children feelings need to come about a perfect God and His children.*
> *Real feelings will take us to God.*
> *Can you feel God?*

When asked whether he makes some particular shift in order to listen, he writes:

> *Marshall is constantly hearing Good God. We all are. Will you listen?*
> *Feelings come when we listen.*

These "real feelings" were familiar to other spiritually oriented writers. They were experienced as "love" by Dante, a "golden chain linking heaven and earth" by Homer, "a spring overflowing its springbox" by the poet Rumi.

We can get information from all sorts of levels and currents in the stream of consciousness. With practice, children can learn the difference between feeling the ego's desire and that of their deeper self, between the inflation of their lesser self and a sense of the greatness and perfection of creation, or between some fear of their subconscious and a warning from the universe. Adults can help children develop discrimination by comparing notes and framing some simple questions: Which is a better choice? Is this person trustworthy? Which choice seems to have more light or flows better? With practice we can help children distinguish between "real feelings," as Marshall calls them, and the ego's tug.

Mostly we honor the contemplative mind when we use it. Test it out. Try it. Ask your inner voice, and follow it into the outside world as an experiment to see what the results are. We help our children listen to their intuition by trusting their inner sense and exploring our own.

Wisdom is a way of knowing and being that takes us beyond the limits of the small self, beyond the repository of our experience, and into the deep stream of consciousness. Children live immersed in and are a part of this stream. Before we develop the limits of our sense of self and the notions of what we can and cannot know, all possibility remains open and available to our minds. In some moments children find remarkable insight as they open their minds and hearts to what is right and what is true. As they inevitably grow in experience, in ego strength, and intellectual capacity, they need not give up the way of wisdom. Through honoring their contemplative knowing and exploring our own, we help children balance their ways of knowing and keep the inner light in view.

Can we begin to recognize children in all their depth and complexity? Can we see the spirit and the capacity for wisdom in them? Can we even help them to stay open to the deep currents of consciousness and remind ourselves to listen along the way? In his poem "Free the World," Marshall Ball poses one more question that serves as a simple prayer of hope for this book:

> *Will we free the world to think perfectly*
> *about the listening*
> *and marvelous children?*[32]

Chapter 2

Wonder

Mark and his eight-year-old daughter, Miranda, were at a quiet beach one warm, sunny day. Miranda soon wandered into the soft and steady waves pulsing against the beach. She stood in the water up to her waist, just moving back and forth with the waves. Ten or fifteen minutes passed, and Mark thought that her eyes were closed. Thirty minutes went by, and she was still swaying in the gentle surf in the same spot. After an hour, he found himself swaying with her as he sat and watched from the beach. It was as if she were in a trance. He wanted to make sure she was all right. *Is this some kind of seizure? Does she have enough sun screen on?* he wondered, but he managed not to intrude.

It was nearly an hour and a half before she came out of the water, absolutely glowing and peaceful. She sat down next to him without a word. After a few minutes, he managed to gently ask what she had been doing. "I was the water," she said softly. "The water?" he repeated. "Yeah, it was amazing. I was the water. I love it and it loves me. I don't know how else to say it." They sat quietly until she hopped up to dig in the sand a few minutes later. "Somehow I felt completely overwhelmed, like I had witnessed grace," Mark said.

Childhood is a time of wonder and awe. The world is sensed through fresh eyes and ears. We hear wonder in the squeal of joy during a first game of peekaboo, in the dropped jaw and wide eyes in seeing an elephant up close, or in the curl of a smile in discovering a new favorite food. As adults, we taste wonder in moments when we are stopped by the color of a perfect sky or maybe as we behold a child speaking, walking, or reading for the first time.

By wonder I mean a constellation of experiences that can involve feelings of awe, connection, joy, insight, and a deep sense of reverence and love. For children (and adults) sometimes these moments open so far and so deep that we find unity and ecstasy. Moments of wonder can be difficult to describe or fully comprehend, although they are recounted in poetry, stories, and spiritual texts throughout all cultures and ages. The poet and mystic Walt Whitman described a moment of wonder in this way:

> *As in a swoon, one instant,*
> *Another sun, ineffable full-dazzles me*
> *And all the orbs I knew, and brighter, unknown orbs;*
> *One instant of the future's land, heaven's land.*[1]

Physician Richard Maurice Bucke described his own experience of "cosmic consciousness." One evening he found himself enveloped in what first appeared to him as a flame-colored cloud. "I knew that the fire was within myself," he said. "Directly afterward there came upon me a sense of exultation, immense joyousness accompanied or immediately followed by an intellectual illumination impossible to describe."[2]

These are moments in which we feel divinity firsthand and perhaps recognize how it touches us, and *is* us. These experiences serve as a cornerstone for a spiritual life. Many people assume that such ecstatic incidents are the province of the rare "mystic." But the mystic is more common and more familiar than we might think. I have heard mystical stories from hundreds of "ordinary" folks over the last twenty-five years. These reports from both children and adults are indistinguishable from those of the great mystics of the world. Children especially have an inherent openness to mystery, wonder, and delight. They are natural mystics.

What wonder does is help us see the sacred in the world. Mechanism, materialism, and modernism tend to "desacralize" the world, leaving it as inert matter for our manipulation. Wonder keeps the sacred in view and recognizes it alive in our midst. As Richard Bucke, like so many others, has said, he did not merely come to believe but *saw* that the universe is not composed of dead matter but is, on the contrary, a living presence.[3]

Wonder comes in all shapes and sizes, ranging from awesome spiritual epiphanies to a small moment of appreciating the warmth of the sun on our face, perhaps that seems to warm our soul. But these special moments typically also have some things in common that serve to define them. As William James recognized more than one hundred years ago, they are *ineffable*—words fail to convey their depth and meaning.[4] Miranda said of her oceanic experience, "I don't know how else to say it." Like so many others, Black Elk said he was just speechless in trying to convey his own childhood spiritual visions: "As I lay there thinking of my vision, I could see it all and feel the meaning with a part of me like a strange power glowing in my body; but when the part of me that talks would try to make words for the meaning, it would be like a fog and get away from me."[5]

These special moments are also *timeless*. A few hours in the surf may feel like a few seconds when we are absorbed in the "eternal now," as theologian Paul Tillich called it.[6] The capacity for being lost in the moment—absorption—is a capacity that is natural for children and necessary for experiencing the mystical moment.[7]

During such a moment, *boundaries blur* between me and "notme." Miranda didn't say she was *in* the water, she said, "I *was* the water." While the spiritual has often been portrayed as separate from us—beyond our reach or not of this world—what children tell us is that the other world is right here and right now. This profound sense of unity often comes with a sense of perfection, understanding, appreciation, and love—"I love it and it loves me." For many, a "reverence" or "compassion" toward life arises naturally out of wonder and forms a moral backdrop. The influential humanitarian Albert Schweitzer called this reverence the most profound attitude that we can have as human beings.[8]

However novel these moments seem, there is often a sense of their being both *absolutely true* and *strangely familiar*. Plato called this depth of knowing "anamnesis," the soul's remembrance of truth.[9] A moment of such communion announces our spiritual homecoming and serves as a reminder of our spiritual address. Fifteen-year-old Jane said, "I'm having the hardest time finding the right words. Sometimes I feel like what I experience isn't really another reality at all, it's just a bigger view of this one. A few months back I had this experience while taking a walk where I felt so connected to everyone and everything—I could see, feel, and hear the web between us. It dissolves all fear. It felt so totally fresh and like coming home at the same time."

Wonder is also nonrational; it involves a *direct knowing*. Saint John of the Cross described this mystical knowing that is beyond our intellect's ability to pin down as "infinite incomprehension."[10]

Moments of deep wonder are available to children (and adults) here and now. They serve as nourishment for our soul and as touchstones for our spiritual identity. Dana described her first memory of wonder: "It was early one morning, and I was sitting outside our house on a cinder block wall that was to be a foundation for a garage. I was facing and gazing at a chain-link fence that had honeysuckle all grown into it. The morning light was so soft, and the dew was sparkling on everything. It was almost like sensory overload. I was totally absorbed by the smells, the way the light was. And then the world just seemed to stop and I was completely transfixed. I had a sense of perfection, and I don't know how I grasped this at three years old, but I clearly did. It was a very distinct sense that everything is perfect—this is absolutely perfect."

Dana had other experiences of bliss and unity throughout childhood, usually in the outdoors. Then, at seven years old, something different occurred. "I was dangled out into the void," she explained. "It was not a peak experience like some others that I had had. It was so divorced from my everyday life and was bigger than all of it. It provided a whole new backdrop; I felt like I was out in nothing and yet it was everything. It was the strangest sensation. Emotionally, it was like at any moment I could feel every emotion in the universe by focusing on it. I just had to change my awareness—like a dial or something. I could enter it and yet I felt them all at the same time. It felt like this is everything and nothing, and I remember being blown away by it as a child. This must sound confusing, but I don't know how else to say it. It overtook me, and I had to just sit back and experience it. It was a little scary, but it was also so amazing. Those visions were deeply convincing, matter-of-fact, like 'this is how it is.'"

Profound wonder sometimes involves insight and understanding, and sometimes a sense of a void as Dana describes. Buddhism refers to this as "nothingness," Taoism as "absolute emptiness," and Hindu tradition might recognize this as the pure, undifferentiated consciousness that exists beyond individual thought.

We have an innate capacity and even a need for wonder, but our society, for a variety of reasons orbiting around fear and a desire for control, tends to misunderstand and therefore to repress wonder, even in children. In schools, for example, we are not interested in tremendous mystery but in tremendous certainty, and so activities direct children away from wonder and toward things like multiple-choice examinations. The daydreamer is made to pay attention; giggles have little place in a typical classroom. In the child's day-to-day life, emphasis on material possessions overwhelms mystery; a demand for control closes off openness; fast-food-style stimulation (TV, video games, etc.) overwhelms stillness.

Children in the midst of wonder are often a source of concern to well-meaning adults. *Are they on drugs?* one might speculate. *Do they have some attention problem?* They may also be disruptive to a tight schedule and a preset worldview. As a result, the vision may be denied and misunderstood, becoming a source of pain and shame for a child: *Nobody else is saying anything like this—I must be weird.*

Dana learned to keep her visions to herself and tried to shut them out. She learned to shut down in order to fit in and win the acceptance of her family. In time she came to doubt her own knowing, and buried herself in a rigid scientific worldview throughout much of early adulthood. In our culture, wonder and especially its kin ecstasy are generally met with suspicion, disbelief, and hostility rather than welcomed as gifts, as the ancients understood them to be. They do not fit neatly into busy schedules or predetermined answers.

Wonder is one way we connect with the pulse of spirit. Mythologist Joseph Campbell advised individuals to "follow their bliss."[11] He did not mean hedonistic indulgence—the "pleasure principle," in Freudian language—but instead what we can call the "wholeness principle," that drive for union and the sustenance of joy. *Joy* means literally "an exultation of spirit." Following our bliss means to follow those feelings of wholeness that arrive through the heart of wonder. Hedonism increases selfishness, whereas wonder increases a sense of connection that leads to increased responsibility to spirit, society, and self. The mystics regularly report that their experiences of wonder are not the end point but serve as a reminder of the *center point* out of which our life flows.

Dana sums up her many childhood experiences: "What these have in common is that they all seem to point to what I really feel is the core of what I am, because when I'm in touch with that, it clears everything else away. These moments seem to stop my going in circles with questions and always trying to figure everything out. These moments clear everything out; it's like coming home. It leads me to a calmness, like a still pond that feels more real than all this other stuff. It's like, 'This is who I am.' It's a feeling like remembering your name. It brings me back in alignment with what feels like my center, and it's here [points to her heart]. It's not up here [touches her head]."

Childhood moments of wonder are not merely passing reveries. They shape the way a child sees and understands the world, and they often form a core of his or her spiritual identity, morality, and mission in life. And while we may have a dramatic awareness—a wondrous vision at eight years old, for example—it is worked out, integrated, and lived over the course of a lifetime. Those visions or words remain *living words*. Like the holy texts of all the wisdom traditions, the meanings are brought to life as we walk them out day by day, directed by a deepening sense of wholeness and participation.

Black Elk describes how he, too, was changed by his vision and explains that visions have to be explored throughout our lives in order to reveal their meaning:

> It was the pictures that I remembered and the words that went with them; for nothing I have ever seen with my eyes was so clear and bright as what my vision showed me; and no words I have ever heard with my ears were like the words I heard. I did not have to remember these things; they have remembered themselves all these years. It was as I grew older that the meanings came clearer and clearer out of the pictures and the words; and even now I have known that more was shown to me than I can tell. . . . I remember that for twelve days after that I wanted to be alone, and it seemed I did not belong to my people.[12]

Childhood visions may serve as a measuring rod and a moral barometer. One woman described her vision as "the fundamental measure against which all else was measured in my life. I tested everything else. I saw people and things in terms of quality and quantity of light: the presence of light or its lack was my only yardstick of right and wrong. . . . When I tried to speak to adults of the light, or tried to live by its implicit truth, this was often met with blank astonishment or, as I grew older, active annoyance."[13]

Once we see the world and ourselves as interconnected or dangle into the void of nonbeing or feel bliss, we cannot help but be changed. In her study of children's near-death experiences, researcher P. M. H. Atwater finds evidence for significant mind and brain shifts, including an enhancement and alteration in intellectual capacities and an improvement in creative and inventive thinking, following a near-death episode.[14] Many experiencers also develop acute sensitivity and sometimes a desire for solitude. A child may be uncertain how to integrate or make sense of an experience, especially within a culture or a household that does not understand or welcome such visions. But however it weaves itself into a lifetime, the wonder remains within us as a touchstone. "It remembers itself," as Black Elk said.

As parents, teachers, and friends, the challenge is to honor and work with what the child knows rather than assume we are starting from scratch, writing on a blank slate. Many children already have a firsthand knowledge of unity, perfection, and unconditional love— profound mysteries that they are trying to understand and live out. What they may need help with is integrating that vision into daily life. And we may be able to help by making space for wonder in our own lives as adults.

Home for Peggy at age five was a farm in rural Louisiana about thirty miles from the nearest town. One Sunday, she and her mother had just returned from church. She quickly ran out to the fields in her pretty sleeveless dress. Her older brother, whom she loved dearly, was burning off the weeds to get the fields ready for plowing. She plopped down on the ground near the burning field still in her church dress with petticoats all fanned out around her. A few moments later she noticed an ember was burning a hole through the petticoat. She was kind of excited, but not really scared by it, and stood up and shouted to her brother, "Look Jimmy, I'm on fire!"

Suddenly a gust of wind came up and the dress burst into flames. Peggy screamed and started to run, only fanning the fire. Jimmy chased after her to knock her down. From the house, her mother heard the screams, saw this horrible scene, and rushed to her. She finally got her on the ground and patted the flames out, burning her own hands severely. When the fire was out, all that was left of the dress was three inches of cloth circling around each shoulder and armpit. Peggy had third-degree burns over two-thirds of her body, second degree over most of the rest. Only her face and feet were spared. Jimmy put his arms, folded over his forehead, against an oak tree and wept, assuming she was dead.

It took an hour to get Peggy to the nearest hospital. She said, "I could see everyone panicked around me. But I was totally calm; I didn't feel any pain. When we got to the hospital, I was asking questions about the equipment around me: 'What does that do?' 'What's that for?'" The staff was making plans for her to be airlifted to a better-equipped hospital in Galveston, but her doctor said not to bother. "She won't make it until daylight," he pronounced.

"I remember them putting on orange gauze, and the next thing I remember I was repeating that the 'light was too bright.' I was squinting and the light was so brilliant that it hurt my eyes. I looked up and saw these silhouettes over me, but it wasn't the nurses or doctors. They were larger and their voices were different. They were reassuring me, 'You're going to be OK.' And they started telling me about animals in the winter who hibernate, like taking a long sleep. And they said to think of this as sleep, as hibernation. 'We'll take care of you while you're sleeping,' the voices said.

"The longer I was there, the softer the light got," Peggy

reported. "It became like a pinkish glow, like you see at sunset some-times. There is no way my words can capture what it was like. It was wonderful; I felt so engulfed with love, in complete acceptance. I knew that nothing is separate about you and me. Nothing about you is judged. You're completely known and you know everything; words aren't spoken—every thought is known instantly. There's no right or wrong, it's just part of your existence. There's a reason why you're experiencing this and everything."

Peggy went into cardiac arrest, and after several minutes the hospital staff told her father that she was gone. With nothing left to lose, the doctor tried a procedure that he had only recently read about. To everyone's shock, it worked: her heart started again.

Peggy came out of a month-long coma on April 19, her sixth birthday. She would have thirty-eight surgeries and would spend the next four years, except for an occasional weekend furlough, in the hospital. She had to grow her own skin, as there was no alternative at the time. Every time she made a wish during those years it was al-ways the same: "God, please just let me grow skin."

"I got to the point where I could leave at will," she told me. 'The bright light would return, then soften to that pinkish glow. On the other side, colors were deeper, smells more intense, and people would always be there to greet me. Before the fire, I loved to climb a mi-mosa tree near our house. Many times when I crossed to the other side, I would find myself at the base of a huge mimosa tree that was full of children. They would ask me to climb with them and call me to go higher. The higher up I went, the brighter the light became. I would sit on branches and talk with them. I still know them inti-mately; it feels like they're part of me.

"At other times I would be surrounded, like a circle of friends holding hands around me. It felt like complete love. I still see them," she said sheepishly. "I know they're always with me. I always have a special one with me. He was the first one I saw. Sometimes he would be there with his arms open and just envelop me with love. Sometimes it would be hours and he wouldn't say a word. He would just love me. I would come away much stronger. The charge he would give me might last three days, and people would say I looked different or had a glow. My family would notice and say things like 'Your face looks different,' or 'You're glowing.'"

I asked Peggy if there was something she felt she was supposed to do with this experience now as an adult, many years later. "To tell my story," she said without hesitation. "People need to know they're not being judged: this is just a school yard, and we're in a semester. No one is upstairs keeping a scorecard. We're all connected. We're eternal. I can feel great compassion for others now. I know things about them that I have no way of knowing, but I'll find myself offering a word or a touch to a stranger and they burst into tears of release and appreciation. I know my purpose is to help, to heal, and to tell without letting my ego take center stage. I'm still trying to do that, everyday. . . . I'd gladly go through it all again to learn what I know."

Peggy has tried to live her life aligned with the childhood vision of love, acceptance, and healing that she experienced. Wondrous moments provided a touchstone and a beacon for her spiritual development, just as it did for a remarkable number of historic figures, such as Saint Catherine of Siena, William Blake, Joan of Arc, Teilhard de Chardin, Black Elk, Hildegard von Bingen, and Ramakrishna, among many others.

As just one historic example of how childhood revelation set the course for a spiritual life, we can consider a six-year-old boy who was walking in a large open meadow when a huge dark rain cloud filled the sky above him. Looking up, he saw the flight of white cranes passing across the dark cloud. In this moment he was completely overwhelmed, "seeing light, feeling joy, and experiencing the upsurge of a great current in one's chest, like the bursting of a rocket," he revealed. "Since that day, I have been a different [person]. I began to see another person within me." Within his body were two persons: one the devotee and the other his Lord. This young boy began to experience the Divine as immanent, that is, in form, right here and right now, in him and in all things.

One day he was taking food as an offering to the Divine Mother. The custom was to place it on an altar as he said prayers. This day he stopped as he was approaching the altar and noticed a cat nearby. He said, "I clearly perceived that the Divine Mother Herself had become everything, even the cat." Instead of leaving the food on the altar, he gave it to the cat.

He described another incident a few years later, during his adolescence: "I felt as if someone had hold of my heart and mind, and was wringing them like a towel. . . . In my heart of hearts there was flowing, a current of intense bliss. . . . It was as if houses, doors, temples and everything else vanished from my sight, leaving no trace whatsoever. However far and in whatever direction I looked, I saw a continuous succession of effulgent waves madly rushing at me from all sides, with great speed." He collapsed into unconsciousness.

This boy was Ramakrishna, born in 1836. He became one of the great spiritual leaders of India. The heart of his vision, as it is for many children who experience ecstasy, was that divinity is immanent—it is here and now in all things, including you, me, and even the cat.[15] Our children are in good company.

A Bliss Station

Do you remember a special spot you had as a child, a secret place where you went in person or in your imagination? Children sometimes find a special place of spiritual sustenance in their own backyard—a "bliss station," as Joseph Campbell called it. Karla found the steps outside her house to be a place where she could escape the conflicts of her parents and watch the seasons pass. Sam never fights going to bed at night; he says he loves to travel in his dreams. Margaret's special place has become a stable and the horse she loves so tenderly.

Karen remembers a powerful moment in her own secret place. "I was fifteen, sitting in silence in my 'special spot' outside a short walk from my family's house. I was just sort of tuning in to nature—the little birds and insects here and there. Then suddenly I had this experience of everything being connected. Both in the sense of just part of the same, but then, what was most amazing to me was that there was also a sense of everything being equal—the majestic mountain, the blade of grass, and me."

As it was for Karen, the most common "trigger" for ecstasy is nature, for example, noticing a beautiful sky or looking at honeysuckle.[16] Sometimes the outside helps us to go deeply inside. Emerson, Thoreau, and Saint Francis of Assisi along with many others understood this nature mysticism. One day I noticed that my daughters had been visiting their tree house quite often. They insisted on lighting candles, even in the middle of the day, and I would often find one of them alone there, singing softly. I didn't dare interrupt or even ask, but I could remember my own ecstasies, little and large, in nature, and I imagined my daughters' own depth and delight. Nature seems to resonate deeply within us. While the lure of electronic entertainment is large these days, few gifts we can provide as parents are probably more enduring than unstructured time in nature.

The bliss station is not simply a favorite tree or spot beside a stream, but a place within us—a gateway in our consciousness that opens into the depths of mystery, perhaps like Peggy's mimosa tree. The shift of awareness usually occurs unexpectedly, without any plan. Ramakrishna was watching white cranes pass under a dark cloud; Dana was just being still on a quiet, misty morning. As she said, "It's not like I made any of these experiences happen; they just come, maybe as I'm absorbed in some sight—the steam rising off the driveway after a summer rain, the smell of the flowers." Wonder occurs beyond our control; we seem to be grabbed or graced, but there is something that children have that seems to welcome it.

Beginner's Mind

When we hear the peals of delight of a child seeing a hummingbird up close or witness a child's sheer awe at a huge thunderstorm, we have a sense of the wonder of the world when seen through a child's eyes. And like children, mystics and sages often discover that everyday events—a bird's song, a cup of tea, a loving hug—become extraordinary when we fall deeply into them and simultaneously into that place from which our life flows. This moves us from living in front of things to living *with* them.

The spiritual is revealed not by traveling to some distant place in the clouds, but by opening to it wherever we find ourselves. In ancient Aramaic, the words *heaven* and *leaven* were sometimes used interchangeably. For example, "The kingdom of heaven is like unto leaven."[17]

Leaven is what makes bread rise. The implication is that heaven is not a location distant in time and place, but a rising (or opening) of our consciousness in the here and now. Heaven, a name for the spiritual, is eternal—beyond time—and infinite—beyond space. Especially for children, divinity is near, neither distinct nor distinct from them; it is immediate and alive. William Blake understood something about this closeness of spirit:

> *To see a world in a grain of sand*
> *And a heaven in a wildflower*
> *Hold infinity in the palm of your hand*
> *And eternity in an hour.*[18]

Religionist Abraham Heschel says it is awe and wonder that open us to the divine: "Awe enables us to perceive in the world intimations of the divine, to sense in small things the beginning of infinite significance . . . to feel the rush of the passing of the stillness of the eternal. . . . The beginning of awe is wonder, and the beginning of wisdom is awe."[19]

One of the greatest lessons that children have to teach adults is the power of awe. Wonder and awe do not only describe a spiritual experience but also a spiritual *attitude*. In Zen Buddhism, this attitude or way of seeing is called "beginner's mind." It means being open to the world, appreciating and meeting it with fresh eyes—just watching it (and ourselves) without preset expectations or categories. In precisely the same vein, the Bible tells us that one enters the kingdom of heaven by becoming like a child: "And calling to him a child, he put him in the midst of them and said, 'Truly, I say to you, unless you turn and become like children, you will never enter the kingdom of heaven.'"[20] This means to have an openness and purity of heart.

The same principle is captured in Taoism, whose founder's name, Lao-tzu, means "old child."[21] This does not mean "childish," but "childlike"—full of wonder and openness, allowing one to see as if for the first time. The goal is to maintain that openness and freshness of wonder throughout our daily life. Sometimes this means slowing down and taking a time out to just appreciate the moment at hand. There is no way to force wonder; it just does not work that way. But we may be able to welcome it.

Appreciating and Judging

Wonder begins as appreciation. Appreciation is a way of looking at the world that complements judgment. A quick evaluation about something—*Is this dangerous? Do I know other things like this?*—puts the world in categories: *These are my friends*, or *I don't like things like that*. Appreciation tends to just let things be and see what we can learn and understand about them. While children learn early on to judge, manipulate, possess, or protect themselves from the world, we may also be able to help them to remember that natural sense of open appreciation, of beholding the moment.

One way to introduce this is to give a raisin or perhaps a piece of fruit to a child and take one for yourself. Say to the child, "Take as long as you can to eat it. It isn't a race to see how long it takes, but instead an opportunity to notice as much as you can about the experience. Soak in the texture, the taste, and your body's and mind's reactions to it. Just savor the moment patiently, slowly." This mindfulness slows us down so that we can actually be in the middle of our life rather than racing through it.

In a similar vein, we could take our young friend (and ourselves) on an adventure. We could suggest, "Pretend that you're new to this world—you have been living underground and arrived on the surface just a short while ago [maybe we help the imagination by hiding in the dark under a blanket for a few minutes]—then go outside in nature and just take in the sights, smells, sounds. Give yourself enough time to do nothing but appreciate what is before you. In time, come back and let's share what we found." Small acts like these slow down the judging mind so that we might live more fully in the appreciation of this moment.

Being and Doing

Most of us, including children, are busy these days. This is not necessarily good or bad; it is just the way it is. But when we consider moments of wonder, we are told they most often arrive when we let our mind drift, "hang out," and just be. Do we make time just to be and not always to do? In such a production-oriented culture, it can sound like heresy or a sign of moral bankruptcy to not do anything. But we may all benefit from moments of being—under the tree in the backyard, on the swings, in our favorite chair—especially when we are alone. Following is a simple exercise in *not doing* that is easy to explore at home or in a classroom. These few moments can help children to put the brakes on in order to arrive in the here and now, the place where wonder lives.

First, invite the children to find a comfortable place to sit. If available, we might ring a bell three times to signal the beginning of the exercise; this can add to the power of ceremony that helps mark this as a special time. We might then say, "Take a few deep, slow, clearing breaths. Let your body release and relax; let any parts of you that need to wiggle or stretch do so. Feel the gentle pull of gravity, and allow the chair you're sitting on and the floor beneath you to support you without any effort on your part. Just let go and allow yourself to be silent and *not do* for a few minutes [anywhere from two or three to ten or fifteen]. Focus only on your breathing, allowing it to flow in and out without effort. If you find yourself thinking, distracted, working on a problem, don't fight it, but don't get stuck in it either. Just allow it and you to be, and bring your attention back your breath and to *not doing*. Perhaps you can imagine those thoughts or concerns floating up like bubbles from under water. When they reach the surface they simply burst and disappear."

When you feel that enough time has elapsed, ring the bell one more time to indicate that the exercise is ending. You may then say, "As you gently come back to the room you may notice sensations such as feeling more peaceful, or maybe your mind is clearer. As you move through your day, even and maybe especially when things get difficult, you can take a deep breath and find that freshness again." *Not doing* in this way is a simple and powerful balance to the rushing minds and rushing bodies that characterize so much of contemporary society.

Surrender and Control

Our lives are a dance between will and surrender, yang and yin, masculine and feminine. Will involves the power of intention that throws (or holds back) our weight, our heart, and our effort in one direction or another. However, the power of will alone is insufficient to enter the mystery. It is through willingness *and* surrender that we are able to drop into the current of creation. The act of surrender has been described with such paradoxical phrases as "choiceless willing" or in the prayer of "Thy will be done." This is an act of faith and a statement of hope. It can occur out of both deep trust and, sometimes, great desperation, when we are brought to our knees to ask for help or when we can no longer hang on. While children can surely be willful in moments, they also have the capacity for surrender, for letting go, for trust. Sometimes children even develop their own strategies of surrender, such as when they spin and spin just to get dizzy and be out of control, or in their simple willingness to be held in an adult's arms.

Ceremonies of holding on and letting go can help make the point as well. At New Year's or a birthday or maybe just at the end of the day, we can ask a child to name or write down privately what they want to hold on to—a memory, a bit of insight, even a possession—and what they want to let go of—a frustrating event, anger or hurt, a toy or clothes that they really do not need any longer. Perhaps we put this note of what we want to let go of in an envelope, seal it, decorate it, and, with the appropriate weight and fanfare of ceremony, shred and burn it. We might tell a story of nature cleaning itself out each year with the change of seasons—how trees have to let go of their leaves in order to grow new ones and how what is left behind becomes compost for creation. It is amazing how we hold on to resentments, fears, and unhappy memories that clot our consciousness. Instead, we can help children get into that natural rhythm of constructive surrender that frees them for new delights.

Like many of the great sages and mystics, our children naturally have moments of awe, both tiny and tremendous. They sometimes find themselves in rapport with the greater mystery that surrounds us, which leaves them with a deep reverence for life and perhaps also a demand to live out and make sense of what they have seen. Children help remind us that we live in a vast sea of wonder and mystery. As poet and potter M. C. Richards tells us, "Mystery sucks at our breath like a wind tunnel. Invites us into it. Let us pray and enter."[22]

Chapter 3

Between You *and* Me

*E*arly in their new preschool program a three-year-old boy, who was having trouble fitting in, bit Chessie, also three, on the arm. She was naturally upset and was then very vigilant about this boy's whereabouts for the rest of the day. The next day, when he was sneaking up behind her and was just about to pounce, she spun around, pointed her finger at him, and shouted, "No!" like a parent. He stopped dead in his tracks and then moved away, leaving her alone for the remainder of the day.

The next day, he again tried to sneak up on her. Once again, Chessie spun around just as he was about to strike. He stood up straight and froze. She then stepped up and gave him a big hug. From that day on he never sneaked up on her. She made sure he wasn't left out during games or other activities and made certain that he had someone to sit next to during a video or story. As her teacher said, "She seemed to know exactly what this boy needed and took care of him while still setting limits."

"Spirit is not in the I but between the I and you. It is not like the blood that circulates in you, but like the air in which you breathe,"[1] wrote theologian Martin Buber. This is a *relational* understanding of spirituality in which the spiritual life is lived out at the intersection of our lives—in the "between," as Buber named it. This is about how we treat the other and how we know one another. Do we know the other as an object to possess or manipulate, or as a friend to understand, serve, and appreciate? When we know with an open heart, we see something or someone in a deeper way, and love and compassion arise naturally. Relational spirituality is about communion, connection, community, and compassion. It is about the way we know and meet the world. The spirit is brought to life in a genuine and open meeting, and Buber tells us that, ultimately, "all real living *is* meeting."[2]

What we meet—a tree, our neighbor, a holy book, the day in front of us—may not be so important as *how* we meet it. While modern conceptions generally locate "knowing" in the head, sacred traditions identify the most essential knowing with the heart. For example, the Chinese word *hsin* is often translated as "mind" but includes both mind and heart.[3] Heart knowing is recognized as the eye of the Tao in Chinese philosophy. Plato called it the eye of the soul.[4] And the power of the heart is identified as "south" on the Native American medicine wheel.[5] In this chapter, we will explore how children experience and express this heart-full meeting, or knowing, that is itself the heart of love and compassion.

Natural Compassion

When a child hugs us out of the blue, or when we hear the cry from a skinned knee, or when we really understand another or feel understood by him or her, something arises from within us that builds a bridge between us. Our heart opens and we can feel the impulse to comfort that child and soothe the pain of a knee, or maybe we just feel love for the one with whom we have an understanding. This natural compassion lies within all of us, especially children, and it comes to life in the space between us just as it did for Chessie.

Compassion is sympathy for the suffering of others and often involves the desire to help. Even small children can feel that concern and care for a dead squirrel along the roadway, a dying tree, or nature as a whole. On the way to school just yesterday my daughter asked, "Dad, will you go back and make sure that turtle [that was in the middle of the road] gets across OK?"

Sometimes children may even feel compassion for their teacher. "I had been having a difficult day and I must have shown it," Kathy, a kindergarten teacher related. "I was frustrated and snapping at my kindergarten class in that way that felt justified at the time, but seems so utterly embarrassing, even cruel, when you look back on it. Basically I had 'lost it' and was taking it out on them. I had insisted that the students be quiet, stay in their seats, and put their heads on their desks.

"I was sitting at my desk writing something when the tip snapped off my pencil—no doubt I was pressing pretty hard in my frustration. As I continued to fume, Jamie, risking more of my wrath, raised his head off his desk, got up from his seat, and walked over to my desk. 'Here,' he said, holding out his hand, 'you can take my pencil. We know you're having a hard day.' He put the pencil down in front of me, then turned around and walked back to his seat; he put his head back down. My frustration melted, and I felt pretty ashamed of my anger toward these 'selfish' kids and grateful for his kindness and his courage. Kids can be so provoking, but here was Jamie offering me this perfect gift."

Developmental theorists typically tell us that children are self-centered and incapable of real empathy or compassion; they have not developed sufficiently to really put themselves in someone else's shoes. Indeed, children can be enormously selfish and self-centered, but they can also be deeply empathic and compassionate. They do not have to wait until adulthood to act unselfishly, feel into another's pain, or share their heart. Their openness allows them to experience deep interconnection with the world, and their compassion can arise very naturally. The capacities for separateness and connection, selfishness and compassion exist simultaneously.

Stacey had been visiting her parents' home for the Thanksgiving holiday. She had had a very difficult marriage, and it finally had come to a point where she knew the relationship was ending. She left the large group of family and friends (husband included) who had gathered that day for the holiday meal. She went into a room alone and found herself letting go, and she started to weep with the deep grief and exhaustion of a dissolving marriage. She didn't think anyone would hear her until her one-year-old nephew walked up to where she was sitting. He simply stood there and touched her arm. In that moment it was like a current went through her. "It simply blew me away," she said. "I have never forgotten it, and it has always stood for me as a supreme example of the healing capacity of a silent, loving presence."

Compassion arises because we come to know the other in a very special way—with an open heart. Chris says, "My father and his wife adopted five foster kids. Jack [Chris's son], five, was asking about it: 'Are they really your brothers and sisters?' We were just chatting and I certainly didn't bring up any emotional stuff, and, *boom*, he says very gently, 'Mom, didn't that make you feel kind of left out?' It was exactly what I felt. I was happy for those kids, but I hardly saw my father from the time I was a freshman in high school to the time I was a senior, and I remember thinking, *He's adopting all these kids, but what about me?* My five-year-old understood perfectly."

Jeff remembers a moment of deep recognition as he was turning ten. "More than anything I wanted a wristwatch for my birthday, and I kept letting my mother know. I had never had one before, and I thought this would be the greatest thing I could get. But we were poor. My birthday came and my mother gave me an unwrapped box. I opened it and saw my new watch. But in the next moment, I looked into my mother's eyes and I saw this incredibly deep pain. In that instant I saw that she was someone's child, she was someone's mother, and she would become an old woman. I knew that my mother was feeling pain and a sense of desperation. I had no way to talk about it then, but I knew who she was and what she felt, although I'm sure she had no idea of what I saw. I knew that somehow I was different after that moment. I went out to play and lost the watch before I returned for dinner.

"At the age of twenty-two, more than a dozen years later, I had been reading Martin Buber on the 'I-thou' experience. It was then that I had an image for understanding what I had felt with my mother on my tenth birthday. I decided that I should telephone her. I asked her if she remembered that day and that gift. She did. I told her about the pain that I knew she was in. She was amazed because it seemed exactly right to her. She wondered how I could have known and understood it so clearly."

Compassion in Action

One way that children express their natural compassion is through giving. As much as children love to receive presents, they also can find the joy that comes along with giving. Children can be selfish and stingy, but they can also be naturally expansive and generous: I watch out the window as my very young neighbor picks our daffodils to take them to her mother; a two-year-old whom I do not know very well insists on giving me a kiss; Jamie offers his pencil to his frustrated and snapping teacher. A true gift—one with no strings attached and given for no gain—has power and medicine for everyone involved.

Pay It Forward is a family movie expressing the natural compassion and power of giving.[6] The theme is that instead of paying back a gift or favor to the person who gave it, you pay it forward to three people who look like they could use your help. The world is changed in such acts. The feeling and expression of compassion is the secret that takes us beyond separateness and selfishness into a new aeon—a new age, as the apostle Paul (then Saul) recognized on the road to

Damascus. Paul suddenly understood that this divine radiance resides secretly in all hearts, waiting to be realized and lived out in our daily lives.

The strongest medicine comes when the giving is personal. Children can invest themselves in making that special card, or picking out the present that they think the person would like, or pursuing their own idea about what a gift might be for someone. Maia, five, picked out some silky and silly boxer shorts with big hearts on them for her ailing and gruff grandfather, who has always been impossible to buy for and pretty impossible to live with. This got a big and playful chuckle out of him, and it was clear that she felt enormous pleasure in giving a gift that brought a smile to this stern old man.

Albert Einstein understood the importance of these exchanges between one another. He observed, "Without deeper reflection one knows from daily life that one exists for other people—first of all for those upon whose smiles and well-being our own happiness is wholly dependent, and then for the many, unknown to us, to whose destinies we are bound by the ties of sympathy."[7]

Being of service is one powerful way of giving. We can think of all sorts of ways to be of genuine service, from an older student helping a younger student with his or her reading to caring for the classroom bunny over a long weekend. Mother Teresa understood the heart of service: "To me, God and compassion are one and the same. Compassion is the joy of sharing. It's doing the small things for the love of each other—just a smile, or carrying a bucket of water, or showing some simple kindness. . . . The fruit of love is service, which is compassion in action."[8]

When service is seen in instrumental ways, as something one does to "be good" or earn a place in heaven, then its intrinsic power as a way of knowing and connecting with others is diluted. No longer is there the pure joy that Mother Theresa names. Rather than seen as a moral issue or a way of doing good, service may be best understood as a way of *knowing* the world directly; it is a chance to come in close and assume responsibility for something or someone, if only for a moment. And the result can be monumental.

When a dove got out of its cage in class, Megan, an elementary school teacher, gave seven-year-old Kendrick—an extremely disruptive and uninterested student—the responsibility to capture, hold, and care for the dove before placing it back in the cage. Megan said, "When another student came up to my desk and tried to help, he politely told him it was his job and he could finish it on his own. He had rarely spoken politely to adults before that moment, much less to his classmates. For the first time, I saw a loving and caring side of him. Before that incident, when I had tried to hug him, he would freeze up, as if he didn't know what to do. Now we can't get him to stop giving us hugs. At the end of the following day, he approached me and said that he wanted to come back to school the next day. Before that he would often and only say, 'I hate school.'"

Kendrick's school performance suddenly made dramatic improvement. One day, when asked to describe his favorite teacher, he wrote, "Mrs. Partain I like." Describes Megan, "I was amazed to have gotten that much structure, since most days I just received a conglomeration of letters copied at random. Often I could not even read them. Now, he had not only written words that were not displayed on the word list, but had organized them into a phrase to answer the question. A few weeks later, he read his first book. I was so proud of him that I started crying as he was reading to me."

We know the world differently when we serve it. A teacher serves a child, a child serves a dove, and this becomes power and medicine that serves the heart of the world. This is a power that has no end—a cup overflowing.

The Golden Root

One of the things we usually associate with "spiritual people" is the quality of their moral and ethical choices. This usually means choices guided by care for others (relationships) and for what is right and just (universal principles). Especially in these days when we fear a growing hole in the moral ozone, what is the living source of this ethical center?

Sometimes we make rules; The Golden Rule is a pretty good and universal one. Rules are simple reminders of what is good or acceptable and serve as a safety net for a civil society. But we do not necessarily uncover and activate natural compassion simply from rules. A child can follow a rule because he or she wants to avoid punishment or wants approval—from parents, teachers, God. Yet sometimes breaking a rule and putting oneself in peril is the right thing to do— think of Martin Luther King, Gandhi, or Jamie, who left his seat and delivered the pencil to his frustrated teacher. Choices at the high end of moral development are made not to avoid something or to get something, but because they serve the best of humanity and divinity. These kinds of choices invoke our highest nature and highest hope as human beings; they call for and draw out our best.

The real root of the Golden Rule, the place within us where loving, kind, and just action toward others comes from, is what we often find in children. Typically, theorists say this kind of moral maturity comes only in adulthood, if at all. But children have tremendous capacity to recognize injustice, hypocrisy, and suffering, and to speak a true word, to empathize, and to offer spontaneous expressions of compassion, mercy, and forgiveness. How can we nourish this natural capacity within children, especially when we know the tug toward selfishness and self-interest can be so strong in our world? Because the messages from the world can be very confusing, we want to make sure children get the message that they can anchor their lives in the power of their compassionate hearts.

One way to assist is through the models we provide. It is no big surprise that children take a test-drive of values by modeling what they see. First and foremost, we help children listen with their hearts through our own expressions of love—toward our children, ourselves, and the world around us. How we treat our spouse, what we say about our difficult neighbor, and what we express toward the person who cuts us off in traffic give our children a map for their own actions. Mostly, we teach by who we are and how we live. Our own development and that of our children are intertwined—we grow up together. And so the first question is, When and how do we live from our hearts? We support a child's natural compassion when we live from our own.

The stories of great beings like Buddha and Jesus, King and Gandhi, or maybe someone closer to home, provide images that can serve as touchstones when a choice of how to listen and act arises. They help draw out the best within us. Stories about people who express radical courage and love provide an alternative to the gratuitous violence of Rambos and professional wrestlers, and create questions and paradoxes that are seeds of self-creation.

Alongside sharing stories and biographies of compassionate heroes, we can ask children about difficult situations with difficult people—bullies, for example—and explore the natural tensions for revenge, fear, and anger on the one hand, and love and understanding on the other. For example, when do you turn the other cheek and when do you defend yourself, and is there some way to do both? How can we be strategic and strong, facing situations with courage, and not back down from what we know to be right? How can vulnerability be an expression of strength, courage, and faith? Why does the word *courage*—an expression of inner strength—mean to "have heart"?

Beyond role models and rules, the way we know, see, and look upon the world affects how we treat others. Most of us notice that when we really pay attention and are simply open to the person in front of us, we come closer to understanding his or her experience. This is simple enough, although it can be easily forgotten when we are caught up in agendas and the hurry of daily activity. But when we really meet another, we begin to *feel into* his or her world, which means we *empathize*. When this occurs, there is often a feeling of really having met the other person: "Oh, this is who you are. I didn't really see you before." The person in front of us begins to take on new dimensions, like a cardboard cutout coming to three-dimensional life. They have depth and substance, meaning and complexity, value and beauty beyond what we have seen previously. And often, our own fantasies of who we thought the other person was or who we wanted him or her to be are revealed as the individual steps into existence outside the gravity of our projections.

This is a spiritual experience especially because it awakens our interconnection, compassion, and our love. Because of the profound importance of this kind of meeting, empathy has been described as the basis of moral development and even the trait that makes us most human. We realize our humanity and our divinity through the depth of our meetings. And when we really meet others, feel into their world and understand them, it becomes much more difficult to perpetrate violence against them. This is the root of a living morality.

Two Ways of Seeing

There are two ways of seeing. One puts things in categories, decides what is useful and what is not, assesses danger and opportunity, and serves our self-interest. It may be thought of as objective, which means to "stand apart or against" the object at which we are looking. The other way of seeing leans into others, feels into and makes contact; it allows them to be who they are. It understands, which means "to stand under or among." Instead of objectifying the world into objects to be measured, controlled, and manipulated, this way of seeing meets the other firsthand, whether a person or a peach. Antoine de Saint-Exupéry's Little Prince understood this way of seeing. He said, "And now here is my secret, a very simple secret: it is only with the heart that one can see rightly; what is essential is invisible to the eye."[9]

In the midst of a conflict or frustration, in the middle of a hurried day, or as a regular "tune-in," you and I, and our children, too, can get a look from the heart by simply sitting quietly for a few moments, taking a deep breath, and gently bringing awareness to the area of the chest. There is often a *felt shift* involving a sense of tenderness, spaciousness, slowing down, and settling in. This process can change the scene that is in front of us or the one that is spinning in our mind. Few activities are so simple and powerfully beneficial, but so infrequently practiced.

Research on heart-rate variability has confirmed the bodily changes that occur when we shift awareness to the heart.[10] When the heart is beating at, say, sixty beats per minute, we think that each beat is one second apart and that the heart muscle is pushing the same amount of blood through in each beat. But during normal waking consciousness, each beat is actually quite variable in terms of its timing and power. One beat may be 1.2 seconds, the next .7, the next .9, and so on. However, when we are relaxed and "in our hearts," the beats become very consistent in both time—about one second, one second, one second—and in pressure or power. Because the heart is the biggest electrical generator in the body, the brain may follow or entrain with the heart (or maybe they are just entirely interwoven in function), and we see an increase in alpha brain waves, associated with deep relaxation. These outer technologies have begun to confirm the physiological changes that occur when we *see through our hearts*.

Children often find their own ways to tune in through their

hearts. Julian, six, was singing and seemed to be concentrating very hard as he was sitting near his little brother. His mother asked him what he was doing. He said, "I'm just singing so I can feel his [brother's] brain." In a very real sense, he was adjusting his own frequency in order to match his brother's. He may be synchronizing the heart-brain system or the two brain hemispheres, which has been associated with high performance in everything from golf to creative writing. While it may take time to confirm the mechanisms at work, Julian describes the function perfectly; his singing helps him tune in to his brother.

This way of knowing is not limited to human relationships. The entire world is revealed to the degree that we open to it. Nobel laureate in genetics Barbara McClintock described a less detached empiricism, one in which she gained "a feeling for the organism." The organisms with which she worked were simple corn plants. The key to her astounding and extremely advanced understanding of genetics was, as she described, "the openness to let it come to you."[11] With this feeling and openness, the other is no longer separate, but becomes part of us in a profoundly intimate way. The Indian sage Krishnamurti said this feeling is critical for the spiritual life: "To help him to be alive, it is imperative for a student to have this extraordinary feeling for life, not for his life or somebody else's life, but for life, for the village, for the tree."[12]

The children's book *The Animal* demonstrates this way of seeing.[13] A strange visitor to the animal kingdom takes in everything that he looks upon with deep appreciation. He sees so deeply because "he loves it," we are told. We might ask ourselves or our child, "Do you ever see like the animal? Can you just stare and feel into that person, flower, and tree? How does it feel when you look from your heart?" We can honor and come to understand children's natural ability to see through their heart by asking questions like these, perhaps following a reading of this sweet book.

The boundary of what is me and what is not-me shifts when we see through the heart. Buddhist monk Thich Nhat Hanh calls this awareness "interbeing," which refers to the fundamental connectedness of all things.[14] Listening deeply to a particular piece of music, beholding a bird, thinking about a loved one, reading inspiring words or a story, and imagining a joyful or beautiful scene open and join us with the world. Walt Whitman recognized this special way of seeing and connecting that children can be so good at:

There was a child went forth every day,
And the first object he look'd upon, that object he became.
And that object became part of him for the day or a certain part of the day,
Or for many years or stretching cycles of years.[15]

Silver Strings

When two violins are placed in a room and a string on one is plucked, the other violin will also sound the note. This is called acoustical resonance. The sound waves from one vibrate the string tuned to the same frequency on the other. The violins become connected along this frequency. Empathic resonance works in much the same way. One's thoughts, feelings, moods, and all sorts of things are vibration, energy, and information transmitted from body-mind to body-mind.

Children often experience interconnection as they resonate with the feelings or thoughts of other persons. A child may be naturally tuned in to certain frequencies, such as those of a loved one. As Julian's mom said, "Julian reads my mind all the time. Even before he could talk he would grab things that I was thinking about and just give them to me. It was pretty weird, but it kept happening. I would mention this to my husband, but he dismissed it until one day they were riding in the pickup truck together. They arrived home and my husband came in the house and said, 'OK, I believe you! We were in the truck just driving along, and out of the blue he said, 'Well, why don't you just stop the truck and go pee if you have to!!!' I was definitely thinking about this, but I'm sure I wasn't giving any outward signals.'"

Jean said, "My daughter [eight] will have a headache and I'll have it too. Or she might say, 'Mommy does your stomach hurt?' or 'Are you feeling sick?' We seem to naturally be tuned to each other. By checking it out, she's learning how to figure out when it's her and when it's me. Sometimes she'll get mad at me because she thinks I'm the one whose causing it, like the stomachache. And I might have to tell her, 'No, I'm not hurting right now.'"

Sometimes children are tuned to feelings in general. Now a midlife professional, Ellen says, "I was always aware that I knew what other people felt. When someone would be talking about what they thought or what they felt, I could tell whether they were honest or not. I felt a lot of people were not really talking about what they really felt and I could tell. It was a just a very deep knowing that was confirmed later."

The connection may be with a very old friend. "Lissy [three] had a strange experience at gymnastics yesterday," her mom said. "A little boy, I'd say about 1 1/2, walked by her and they were nodding their heads at each other and laughing. He said, 'Hi!' to her and she nodded her head again and laughed. Then she watched him walk away. She turned to me and said, 'He remembers me from when I was his brother.' I said, 'You were a brother?' She said, 'Yes. His. But then someone dropped me and I became your Lissy.'"

Deep empathy, as I call this, can develop over time, and one of the big challenges is to help children sort out what is theirs and what is not, as Jean and her eight-year-old daughter were exploring.[16] The easiest way to do this is just to compare notes, to talk about it in order to refine rather than repress the capacity. Children do not develop ego and then have empathic resonance; it works the other way around. They are naturally open and in time develop perspectives that help to differentiate "mine" (feelings, thoughts, etc.) from "yours," along with developing interpretations of the information. But if they discount and deny the natural resonance, deep empathy is never refined and may even become a pathological boundary problem.

As I have said, the word *empathy* literally means "feeling into." We feel into, not merely with the physical brain but with the body-mind, this amazing system of flesh, chemicals, and neurons mixed with the magic of consciousness. Several studies have given scientific verification for communication between bodies. Researcher and former professor of psychology Dean Radin conducted a study in which two men who did not know each other were placed in different rooms isolated from one another. The man in one room was asked to think a loving thought about the man in the other room. At the moment that he did, the man who received that thought registered an immediate decrease in blood pressure. When the first man was asked to think an angry thought about the other man, the second man's blood pressure immediately shot up. The men had never met, neither was aware of the nature of the experiment, and neither had any direct physical or verbal contact with the other. While the second man had no conscious awareness of angry or loving thoughts, his body registered it.[17]

We are often trained not to pay attention to the body as we grow. There is a tendency to live in our heads and discount the subtle cues of our body's wisdom. But because children start out knowing through their bodies more than their heads, they may have even more sensitivity to those bodily signals. However, they do not always know what to make of that feeling, and this sometimes becomes a very real problem for the empathic child—as Ellen said, it can be overwhelming sometimes.

As an extreme form of this body resonance, there are well-documented cases of even physical markings, like stigmata, that occur on the body of sensitive souls. Ramakrishna of Bengal, who as a child realized the unity of all things, provides one dramatic example. Ramakrishna was observing from the temple garden two boatmen exchanging blows out in the River Ganges; witnesses swore that marks from these blows appeared immediately on his own body.[18]

On occasion I have asked a group of parents and children to pair up with someone whom they do not know very well in the group; we try to have one adult paired with one child. This could also be done in a group of children or just with you and a child. First I walk folks through a brief relaxation exercise in order to help them shift consciousness into a deeper state of receiving. (Adults usually feel like they need the time to shift; children are often able to tune in more quickly and easily.) Then, as they are sitting quietly across from one another, I will ask them to "empty themselves out" and then to take turns respectfully and with permission "tuning in" to or receiving each other as they gaze very softly at one another (or many like to close their eyes).

After just a few minutes they take turns reporting what they felt or saw or heard. The results are often surprising, especially for adults when they hear a child describe their personality, pinpoint their state of mind, or offer a bit of wisdom. This is an extremely simple exercise and one we can practice again and again. I ask them to just describe what they sensed and ask for their partner's feedback. We then get back together as a group and compare the different ways that impressions arrived and how accurate they felt, noticing both the similarities and the different ways each person resonates with others.

Because these impressions are subtle and often discounted or ignored by adults, it is important to recognize the many ways and forms in which they emerge. Impressions may be experienced as a physical sensation (for example, a tightness in the chest, a pain in a hip), a feeling (sadness, love, fear), a geometric shape or a sense of movement, a life script (I must work hard) or core belief (I'm unlovable), a symbol (a leaf that is frozen but will shatter if it is touched), an image (a hole in the abdomen) or a scene (a small child running through a field), or an urge to ask a question (What happened when you were eleven?). Sometimes information comes as a message for the other person. We might say that the higher self of the child attunes to the higher self of the other in order to offer a word of insight. Empathic information comes in all sorts of forms; the challenge is to listen and check it out.

"What's it like when you meet someone in this way?" I asked twelve-year-old Steve in the middle of our conversation. He said, "It feels like I connect to their energy, they connect to mine, and something is passed back and forth. If I met with somebody for the first time, a lot of times I could get a feeling in a split second, like 'This person is feeling pain or they're acting this way, but they don't mean what they say,' or whatever. Sometimes it's a feeling that I should do something like offer help or a feeling like this person needs to be held or something."

Jacques Lusseyran, who was blinded as a seven-year-old, describes how it felt for him to "see" objects and others deeply: "It is more than seeing them, [it's] allowing the current they hold to connect with one's own, like electricity. . . . This means an end to living in front of things and a beginning of living with them. . . . for this is love."[19]

Sometimes we float along the same frequencies in sleep. Debbie's tale is typical of many I have heard from parents. "The other night I was having a horrible nightmare in which I was riding in a car with my mother that plunged off a cliff. At the moment that the car in my dream went off the cliff, I heard my daughter, who is three, start screaming in her sleep in the other room. I immediately woke up and went in to see what was the matter. She was already back to sleep." My daughter Haley, at six, had some unprompted insight into the reality of meeting one another during sleep: "I think there is another part of me that's inside, but it's lighter and it travels around when I'm sleeping."

Gladys confirmed that our sleep can contain vital information: "My mother always had such vivid dreams about things that would come to pass, and I always thought as a kid that she was exaggerating. But when my sister awoke with a nightmare, crying that my grandpa's factory was burning, and minutes later we received a phone call confirming it, I began to have more respect for the messages in dreams. When the same grandpa died sometime later, I already had learned of it in a dream the night before."

Sometimes a child does not just tune in to information about one person, but into messages regarding whole groups of people. As one mom described it, "Last year my seven-year-old daughter had a terrible nightmare. She said there was a huge monster coming and he was going to kill us all. We gave her a little milk and calmed her down. Well, an hour later we had a terrible earthquake (we live in Istanbul) and hundreds of people were killed."

Physician Larry Dossey has helped to explain the idea that communication of this sort can take place at a distance—it's nonlocal.[20] This term is taken from quantum physics and in physics refers to the distant interactions of subatomic particles. While we pick up signals from others, we can also intentionally send signals to others.

Lynn had dropped Michael, eight, off at his father's, but neglected to remind either of them that Michael had baseball practice that night. Later, when his mom realized that they probably did not know, she simply kept imagining Michael calling and kept saying to herself, "Michael, call me." Within a few minutes the phone rang and it was Michael. His first words were "Mom, what do you want?"

After the powerful effects of several near-death episodes in her own life, researcher P. M. H. Atwater sought to explore the effect of near-death experiences in adults and, more recently, in children. Several children who were pronounced clinically dead and then were resuscitated *saw* prayers being said for them. They describe how prayers could be seen as beams of radiant, golden, or rainbow light that arched from the one saying the prayer, no matter how many miles away, to where they themselves were. Once the prayer beam reached them, the feeling was like a "splash" of incredible warmth and love.[21] Dossey's work highlights the evidence of the effect of prayer on healing. He suggests that there is a quality that correlates with the effectiveness of the prayer, and as he says, it is something that sounds very old fashioned. It is love.

Not only can the resonance of love transcend space, it also seems able to look around the corner of time. Stephanie, six, her older brother, and her parents had gone to visit her grandmother for several days. The neighbors had some children who were about the same age, and they had a rope swing out in back of their house. Some of the children were swinging, then landing in a huge pile of leaves, several feet below. Stephanie was a tomboy and would always attempt everything that her brother would do. But for some reason she wouldn't touch this rope swing. She just sat off to the side. Her brother asked, "What's going on?" Stephanie answered, " Something's wrong, something's not right here." He didn't pay any attention and they went off to swing.

They swung a couple more times and Stephanie was getting more and more agitated. She called out this time, "Brian, something's wrong! Something's going to happen on the swing!" She was shaking. Brian was next on the swing. He took a big leap and swung way out, missed the pile of leaves, fell off the rope, and started to tumble down a very steep hill. He came to a stop when his chin and chest crashed into large tree; he lacerated his chin badly and broke several ribs. Brian has listened to Stephanie's "feelings" more carefully ever since.

Listen with Your Heart

How can we help nourish and even deepen children's natural capacity to listen with their hearts, especially when there are so many messages to do the opposite, to live from selfishness or self-protection? We have talked about role models, service, empathic exercises, sensitivity to messages of the body-mind, and just taking a breath and feeling from the center of our chest. Following are some other ways we can help children (and adults) honor their natural empathy and compassion.

Giving Thanks

With children, often all that is required for the heart of love and caring to rise to the surface are simple questions, perhaps about thankfulness. We can ask, "What's one thing that you're thankful for?" or "How does a special person or creature in your life make you feel? How would your life feel without them?" Feeling a sense of appreciation vibrates the heart; expressing it makes it sing. When the child has identified someone or something we might ask, "Can you send that person [pet, object, etc.] your feelings of thanks? Maybe through a prayer, a hug tonight that lasts a little longer than usual, a note, a word, or just a warm thought."

One evening Christina's parents decided to encourage her to say a little prayer of thanks at bedtime: "I'm thankful for . . ." They expected a short, dutiful moment of thanks. But Christina was so taken by the opportunity to express her thanks that she said thanks for every friend, relative, favorite food, toys, feelings, birds, the sky, and everything else she could think of. It was as if a dam of gratitude had just burst open by this simple invitation. It was so completely genuine and spontaneous, and the more she let it flow, the more things and people she could find for which to give thanks. This went on night after night and her parents didn't want to interrupt, although they wondered whether they would need to adjust her bedtime in order to make time for all these nightly prayers!

Forgiveness

"Imagine that our enemies can do more harm than the hate we hold against them," Saint Augustine wrote.[22] Bitterness and resentment become poisons that eat away at our life. Forgiveness can come as quickly as just letting go, or it may take years to fully unwind. But we can help children move toward genuine forgiveness in the way we help them navigate conflicts. Sometimes children find their own magnificent solution to conflict, as Chessie did as mentioned at the beginning of this chapter. But sometimes children get stuck or get interrupted before things get worked out. In this case parents and teachers may need to become referee, police, judge, therapist, and peacemaker all rolled into one.

While all of these roles are sometimes necessary, the peacemaker has the most power. The truly great peacemakers, whether in international or more local conflicts, first and foremost make sure that all parties are heard and understood. It is especially important that their sense of hurt is understood. "*Why* did you hit her?" usually just cycles the blame around: "Because she pushed me first." And on it goes in endless recriminations. Instead, questions such as "What were you feeling when you did this?" have a better chance to move past the anger to the hurt, violation, and injustice that usually lies underneath. And adding a simple turn to that question, "What do you think *they* were feeling?" allows the child to move past the surface of blame and justification toward understanding and empathy—listening with the heart—and even toward a chance at genuine forgiveness.

Delight

Play, joy, laughter, ecstasy, beauty, dance, and celebrations of all sorts tease open the heart. The architecture of a spiritual life includes the structure of delight, and children often show us delight so effortlessly. Like eating our vitamins does for our body, delight nourishes our spirit. We can monitor ourselves: Have we had our draft of delight today? Our dose of beauty? A playful laugh? Did we sing or hum? Delight is an affirmation of spirit.

Music may be one of the most universal and direct ways to shift consciousness and move into the vibrations of delight. We know the power of music—both listening and making it—to evoke feelings of all sorts. Former Beatle George Harrison, paraphrasing the Indian poet Rabindranath Tagore, put it this way: "God likes us when we work, but loves us when we sing."[23] On occasion in our house my youngest daughter gets us to sing our conversations with each other in a kind of domestic opera: "What would you like to drink?" "Milk please, milk please . . ." and on we go. It is hard not to smile.

What are the songs that open your heart? They may not be the same for your children, but they may help open the dialogue to discover all the timbres and tones that resonate in our chest. When I have worked with difficult teenagers, I have sometimes asked them to bring me a couple of songs that are important to them so that we can listen to them together. In the few minutes of listening and then chatting about what the music feels like to each other, we enter into a private world so intimately and so quickly that we are usually both surprised at the vulnerability and understanding that we share. We can do this in our own families or schools and be surprised at how hearts move toward one another on the waves of this music.

Try a Little Tenderness

Love can be tough sometimes, like when we no longer enable irresponsibility, or when we set firm and fair limits and stick to them, or when we speak as directly and honestly as we can. But on a day-to-day basis, the heart is also welcomed through gentleness, kindness, and tenderness. We rub each other's shoulders with tender care; we make a lap when one is needed; we offer an appreciative word. Can we leave ourselves enough time in the morning to approach a sleepy child with softness, maybe crawling in bed to snuggle for a few minutes and then finding a spot that is ready for the wake-up call of a gentle tickle? And we can help children find ways to be gentle with themselves, to self-soothe. My daughter, for example, took a (very) long and (very) deep bath with candles the other night.

Can we play soft as well as play rough? The language we speak, the mood of our home, a gentle meal, a sane pace, an unconditional tone in our voice, the right music, or a candle or flower at the dinner table all can balance toughness and excitement with tenderness. Tenderness makes it safe for the heart to rise to the surface. We can also ask our children to think about who in their day could use a little kindness or tenderness and explore ways to give it, such as paying a visit to someone who would appreciate it, sharing a cookie at the school cafeteria, or saying "hi" or "thank you" to someone who gets overlooked.

Simplicity and Priorities

In the midst of all we have to do today, what is really important? The heart is at home in simplicity—a cup of warm cocoa on a cold day, a kiss on the cheek, a walk in the woods. The complexity of these modern times is shuffled and sifted by keeping the heart in view. Is there time before bed for a moment of holding one another? As we are rushing them off to catch the ride to school, can we still hold each other in our hearts or leave them with a genuinely felt prayer, such as "I wish you love today [a little kindness, delight, etc.]"? And priorities come into focus with big questions such as "If this were your last day on Earth, what would you do, who would you be with, what would you tell those you were leaving behind?"

These invitations do not make children spiritual. They are already spiritual. They simply make it safe and normal for them to feel and express their spiritual nature; they are invitations to be who they truly are.

Chapter 4

Wondering

"Why am I here?" seven-year-old John asked his father at the grocery store. "We're getting food for dinner. You said you wanted to come," his father reminded him. "No! No! Why are we *here*; you know, alive?" John said. "Huh? You mean why are we on Earth?" his dad asked, a little stunned. "Yeah!" John said with some exasperation in his voice, as if it was the most obvious question he could ask. His father quickly gathered himself together and began to wind up an answer in his mind. But before he offered it, he had the good sense to ask John instead, "Why do *you* think we're here?" "I don't know yet; I'm working on it," John replied. Fair enough.

Children are natural philosophers. Much to our amazement, they often wonder about the big questions. They ask about life and meaning, knowing and knowledge, truth and justice, reality and death. These big questions are precisely what philosophy and religion have attempted to address. For many people the spiritual quest is focused and explored through pondering, puzzling over, and playing with such questions. As we marvel at a starry night or consider some injustice, a yearning to know more may start to germinate inside us, growing into profound questions and a life of thoughtful seeking. For individuals like Gandhi, who was famished for truth even as a child, entertaining the big questions is a way to enter a dialogue with mystery, with the spiritual.

Swiss psychologist Jean Piaget mapped the development of

children's thinking capacity. He concluded that cognition develops through certain stages as a person matures—from the very body-based knowing of an infant to increasing abstraction. He concluded that early on a child lacks the ability to reason and reflect with any degree of sophistication.[1] His work has been hugely influential in shaping how psychologists and educators view children. However, there is increasing evidence that he was both right and also quite wrong or, at least, incomplete. It does appear that children do go through cognitive development in stages. But these stages are general and broad, and represent merely a rough sketch. When we look a little closer, we can find grand exceptions to Piaget's model. Even young children have shown a capacity for thoughtful consideration of the big questions (metaphysics), inquiring about proof and the source of knowledge (epistemology), reasoning through problems (logic), questioning values (ethics), and reflecting on their own identity in the world.

In addition to analytic processing, which Piaget was attempting to describe, children (like adults) also have an intuitive capacity. They may grasp a key insight or a broad understanding that captures the heart of an issue. They may not be able to explain in adult logic and language, but they comprehend at a very deep level. As children grow, both the developing ego and societal expectations of how we should think become more pronounced; the intuitive function sometimes gets drowned out by ego-generated analysis and repressed by social norms. However, this is not a developmental necessity as some have suggested. So many of the children I have seen have kept their intuitive function alive and well while at the same time developing sound analytic capacity and healthy ego structure. I believe fostering this balance is a critical challenge for parents and teachers interested in nourishing children's full potential.

Children's openness, vulnerability, and tolerance for mystery enable them to entertain perplexing and paradoxical questions. Philosopher Gareth Matthews said that children may be especially good at philosophy because they have "fresh eyes and ears for perplexity and incongruity . . . and a [high] degree of candor and spontaneity."[2] Especially important to the consideration of spirituality, they can ponder what theologian Paul Tillich called "ultimate concerns": "Why are we here? What is life about?" Or as my youngest daughter asked the other day, "Where did the first people come from?"[3]

The Great Thing

Questioning, whether for little children or accomplished scientists, is not just about finding an answer. As physicist David Bohm explains, "Questioning is . . . not an end in itself, nor is its main purpose to give rise to answers. Rather, what is essential here is the whole flowing movement of life, which can be harmonious only when there is ceaseless questioning."[4] If you are around young children, you may be familiar with ceaseless questioning—Why? Why? Why?—or maybe those difficult questions that defy easy answers. At six, Julian asked, "What are heaven and hell?" and "What about the devil—is it real?" He not only ponders how to get his little brother to leave him alone, but also earnestly puzzles over infinity, zero, God, and death. Radical questioning or pondering like this focuses priorities and serves as spiritual nourishment and direction.

The poet Rainer Maria Rilke instructs us regarding the questioning process:

> Be patient toward all that is unresolved in your heart. . . .
> Try to love the questions themselves. . . .
> Do not now seek the answers, which can not be given because you would not
> be able to live them—and the point is to live everything.[5]

Rilke's advice treats questions not as something to beat or to conquer, but as something to dialogue about and live with. Such an attitude toward questions does not necessarily seek intellectual certainty, but may actually seek new questions, like looking for the best fruit on the tree. The invitation is then to bite into the question, living it, allowing it to fulfill its purpose as nourishment. Whereas adult intelligence will typically cut, dismantle, and reconstruct the question in order to work toward certainty, the openness of children often allows them to ride the question to see where it goes and what it turns into. While answers may be satisfying, questions are *motivating*: they push us to go beyond where we are and what we know—to live everything.

But we have come to expect convenient answers at the cost of entertaining rich questions. In schools, one right answer, often on a multiple-choice test, determines value, worth, and truth. Schools do not lack answers, they lack depth. Depth is associated more with asking good questions than with having all the answers. Researcher Patricia Arlin had said wisdom is the capacity not so much for problem solving as for *problem finding*.[6] Children have a remarkable capacity for identifying problems that we may have overlooked or taken for granted as adults. Dan, aged four, wondered, "How did everything begin? Just tell me—is there a God?" Julian, five, asked, "Why are there more black people in jail?"

Jim, fourteen, looked back on his earlier school career: "I couldn't get my teachers to take my questions and ideas seriously. I thought this was what school was going to be about. There was such a big deal about going off to first grade, but I kept waiting for us to talk about life—you know, why we're all here, what this world's about. The nature of the universe. Things like that. When I'd ask or say my ideas just to sort of get things going, there would be dead silence, and then the teacher would move on to spelling or something. I thought, *OK, I guess we're getting the basic stuff this year, and then we'll get into the good stuff in second grade. I can wait that long if I have to.* Well, second grade came and went and it wasn't any better—maybe worse—since we didn't even get to play as much. By fourth grade I remember thinking, *I must be an alien. These people don't understand. I'm not a social zero; I have friends. But no one, especially not the teachers, are talking about this. School seems not to be very interested in my questions or any questions really; it is all about the answers. We're only supposed to give them the right answer.*

As a parent, friend, or teacher, what do we do when a child asks genuine questions? Christina said, "Adults would give me 'kiddie' answers. I would ask, 'Why are we here? What's the purpose?' I just felt like I wanted to know, but they wouldn't answer or take the questions seriously."

When a child asks a question, I find myself sometimes defaulting to a thin, quick answer; it is just easiest sometimes. But when I can catch myself and catch the heart of the question, I remember how much I wanted the truth as a child, like Jim or Christina. If my questions were dismissed or the answers lacked substance or vitality, it was like pouring water on a fire —on *my* fire. I rarely found playful answers lacking substance or vitality, though. Sometimes the goofy way of looking at something led to some breakthrough.

And I don't mean that I expected the ultimate truth, although I'm sure I wanted that, but the truth of an honest answer that was thoughtful and genuine. Without deep responses, I remember feeling like I was being taught to lie or at least to live on the surface. But answers that had substance kept the questions alive. Even when I left more perplexed, with more questions, it felt like really living. The tidy answers flattened the world. Honest answers, including and especially "I'm not sure; what do you think?" are nourishing.

So when a child asks a genuine question, I try to remember to be honest and rich in my response and to think of the question more as an invitation to dialogue and less as an opportunity to be the smart adult. The question always holds a whole world of ideas within it.

The idea at the heart of the question is, as Rilke named it, the "great thing."[7] The child's question, the half-baked hypothesis, the guess (and also the challenge and the acting out) read as an invitation that says, "Come sit with me at the table of this *great thing* right now, in this moment, and maybe at another time, too; and mull it over, turn it over, poke it, and chew on it with me, please. RSVP as soon as you can." And what is our response?

Living Words

In the wisdom traditions, pondering is sometimes developed into a spiritual discipline in itself. A Hindu might contemplate the nature of the self—Who am I?—as part of his or her daily practice. A Buddhist might structure his or her meditation around considering a concept such as "dependent origination"—the law of causality that implies everything comes from prior circumstance—and watch what arises into awareness as he or she does so.[8] A Jew might reflect on a biblical passage as it applies to a current difficulty in his or her daily life. This insight-oriented contemplation uses the question or idea to concentrate one's gaze, just as children's questions absorb and focus their attention.

All sorts of ideas, images, and feelings may arise during pondering. But the sages tell us that we never can quite solve the big questions in some purely intellectual fashion. Contemplative practice is sometimes even designed to frustrate our rational thinking, as with a Zen koan such as "What is the sound of one hand clapping?" Holding paradoxical or opposing views simultaneously absorbs and then frustrates the normal chain of analytic thought, opening up the possibility not for logical problem solving, but for intuitive insight. In the Sufi tradition, for example, metaphysical reflection and reason are the starting point said to make possible the deeper insights of intuition and *the heart*. The powerful energy of intention in the form of a question both focuses and opens our mind and serves as a magnet that brings us what we need.

Christina's deep questions, blended with the lull of a long drive and a beautiful landscape, opened to profound intuitive insight at five years old. "The six of us in my family were driving through northern New Mexico to Colorado for a vacation. I was in the back seat with my brother and sister, looking out the window at the beautiful scenery. At that age, I was always thinking about things like God and asked lots of questions, although I don't know why because my family didn't talk about religious or spiritual things. I was just really trying to understand how this world worked and what God was about. At that moment in the car, I was wondering what things were like before we were born and before there was a world, a universe.

"Suddenly, I could see everything gradually disappearing. The cars and the road and the poles, even the trees and land, were disappearing. At first it was sort of sad as I considered losing all these things. But it wasn't really empty; there was an incredible fullness in the emptiness. There was such a strong sense that everything was OK because I knew in that moment that everything was connected and that there is something bigger. It was a moment of truth and pure peace. It's hard to find the words. Everything seemed so clear and obvious. I've thought about it a lot, but I've never talked or written about it until now."

I cannot help wonder if the same kind of experience would have been available if there had been a steady stream of movies buzzing through a video player in the back of the family minivan? Would Christina have had the space and time for wondering that bore such nourishing fruit? Electronic entertainment is such a powerful attention magnet and so easily available that while something can certainly be gained by it, something may also be lost, and what is lost may be monumental. Contemplative insight can be framed by rich questions, but it emerges out of the spaciousness of silence.

The great texts of the wisdom traditions are often taken as inspired words. But most agree that these are "living words" requiring exploration and personal engagement. It is as if the words are encrypted and compressed, showing us only their outer surface. They need to be considered again and again so that we begin to decompress the words according to the quality of our awareness. Christina concluded from her epiphany, "The vision and connection that I had were always available. I just had to be open for them. The answers are always there. You just have to feel them."

In order to break the code, we must enter into relationship with the symbols and signs of the universe and allow ourselves to both open to them and be further opened by them. This is like a two-headed key opening a series of locks that lead simultaneously into ourselves and into the data. For the Sufis, uncoiling the mystical data comes from "knowledge by presence," which involves critical introspection—looking closely into our selves.[9] As the prophet Mohammed said, "Who knows himself knows his lord."[10] The code is broken, the words come alive, and the world is opened only through a corresponding opening within us.

The twentieth-century Indian sage Ramana Maharshi had momentous epiphanies as a teenager that opened him to his own spiritual identity. The center of his own quest and the heart of his spiritual teaching was a very direct question: Who am I? He understood that if this question is asked honestly and fully, it leads deeper and deeper, through layers of identity, roles, and attachments, to the eternal radiance at our core.[11] In some moments, children like Lynn and Ellen find this question naturally and spontaneously.

Lynn describes such an opening at seven years old. "I remember standing in my dad's apartment," she said. "My mom, dad, sister, and I were all very happy. My divorced parents were getting back together; it was a dream come true. Suddenly, the phone rang. I found out later that another woman was on the phone looking for my dad. My mother answered and then slammed it back down. My mother shouted that my father was a two-timer. I didn't know what this meant, but I knew it was very bad. She grabbed her pocketbook and took my sister and me outside to her car. It was dark and the sky was filled with stars. My heart felt like it was flying apart. I didn't want this to happen, and all I could do was watch.

"The color red filled the car as my mother backed out of the parking lot (my father's knuckles were still tapping on the window trying to get my mother to stop). It was a silent ride home. No one spoke; no one cried. I looked out the back window and made a wish on a star. I was wishing so hard to become part of this star, wondering what it would be like to be the star. I felt a strange tingling of butterflies in my stomach, then it rose up through my body and out of the top of my head. It suddenly stopped. I felt very light, like I was floating. I saw my mother and sister in the front of the car; I could see their laps like I was looking through the windshield, but I had been sitting in the back seat—just a second before I had been looking at them, and all I had seen was the back of their heads.

Then I looked back and saw myself, like I was hovering above the car looking down. A thought came to my mind: *Who am I? Is Lynn the person who is asking the question or the body I'm looking at?* I was worried about how I would return to my body. But as soon as I imagined myself back in my body, I was back in. I spent the rest of the ride home wondering, *Who am I?* I didn't say anything to anyone. A few months later my parents remarried." For Lynn, an emotionally powerful event, some moments of silence, and her strong wish (to become part of the star) led to the most fundamental question of identity: Who am I?

Ten-year-old Ellen also had an experience that forced her to question who she was. "We were biking all day and running around," she described. She became "really tired" and decided to go upstairs to her attic bedroom and take a little rest in the middle of the afternoon. She said, "I just lay down and the whole room started to spin, and in a few moments I felt like I was on the ceiling and my body was asleep on the bed. I could see myself lying there and wasn't sure what was happening. Where was I? Who was I? Was I on the ceiling or was I on the bed? This changed how I began to think about me. I wasn't just a body. I was something more."

I Am Air

The depth of children's concerns and questions can surprise us. Jesse was about to turn nine years old. It was the night before his birthday and his father was saying good night and giving him a kiss on the head. Jesse started to cry. "What's wrong?" his dad asked. Jesse couldn't control himself; he was sobbing heavily as his father looked on helplessly with no idea what was happening. Was it about a present that he was afraid he might not get? Did he get in trouble at school? His dad had no idea. Finally, Jesse was able to calm down enough to explain: "My birthday means I'm another year closer to death, and it means you are, too. I know that there's such a thing as reincarnation, but I don't want things to change." His dad didn't have an answer. They held each other while they both cried. Children certainly do think about toys and getting in trouble at school, but they also ponder deeply the mysteries of being human—like death and love—and therefore their questions and concerns deserve our deepest respect and reverence.

As humans, we are meaning makers—we hunger for and create meaning all the time. We inevitably try on various answers to our questions and see how well and for how long they fit. Denise pondered big questions and tried out some remarkable answers. I will call her a quantum philosopher because her reflections on the nature of matter and reality sound like both an explanation of quantum physics and the revelation of interconnection and indestructibility of the mystics. These were mainly spontaneous offerings, the kind that happen over morning cereal or a ride in the car, and occasionally answers to questions posed by her father, as I have indicated. Her father had the presence of mind to listen well and write down these pearls. He said, "As a parent I never gave her any direct answers to her big questions. Instead I always suggested first that she think about it and work it through herself." Here is a sampling of her musings between four and six years old:

> I am air. I think everything is air like me: plants, rocks, and animals, buildings and everything. You can feel it when the wind blows. People have different flavored airs. Mine is grape and cherry. God did not make us because he is air like we are. Everything is air—the hamster, the picture, and everything. We are all the same thing.

> I am not my brain, I'm nothing. [She then pointed outside herself.] I am like all this—air. I was never anything before; I came from nothing. I came from air.

> We are not made out of any real stuff. Nothing in this room is made of real stuff. Real stuff cannot be changed or hurt. See this bedspread, it is not real stuff—it can be torn. We are made of something, but not real stuff. The only real stuff is the air.

> We are air. There are all colors of air. I don't think air even sleeps because it is always moving. We sleep, but if we are air, then why do we have to sleep? Are we air?

You know how I know I'm air? I know because that is what I was before I was born. That's what I came from.

[What happens when an animal dies?] He is still air. The air is inside us, around us, everywhere. This air moves even when there is not any wind.

[Why are we alive?] I don't know now." [Do you mean you will know when you get older?] No! I might know sometime later today.

Contemporary teacher Gary Zukov offers a thought very similar to Denise's: "If there is any ultimate stuff of the universe, it is pure energy. . . . the world is fundamentally dancing energy; energy that is everywhere and incessantly assuming first this form and then that."[12]

How do we invite pondering? Sometimes we need basic information garnered most efficiently by "closed-ended" questions, for example, "What time do I need to pick you up from the party?" or "Do you have homework tonight?" But questions with tidy or prepacked answers constrict and categorize consciousness; they do not invite epiphany. Open-ended invitations open the world more deeply. "What stood out about school today?" "What do you see in those clouds?" and "Please tell me about that picture you drew" are more engaging than "What's that supposed to be?"

Teachers and others can balance the more answer-oriented approach with one that invites deeper exploration: "OK class, you've just read this story [chapter, article, or whatever]. Instead of giving me answers about it, I want you to give me as many questions as you can think of." Such a simple turn begins to shift the focus from closing things down to opening them up by balancing the need for closed facts with the hunger for expansive questions. When I have done this in a classroom or our living room, I am always surprised by questions I had never thought of; they move us past the information given.

As a parent, teacher, or friend, we also keep the space open for deep pondering in our children by pondering ourselves. I recall the feeling of mystery and intrigue each time I entered Mr. Simpson's sixth-grade science classroom. He was an environmentalist and naturalist well ahead of his time, at least in my little rural town. I would see this tall, respectable man walk home from school and pick up all the trash between his house and the school; he spoke of pesticide-laden poison apples and the particularities of the coloring on birds. He developed a nature trail behind the school. His classroom always seemed to have layers of fascinating stuff, from a wasp's nest and a human skeleton to rocks and minerals.

While I had some interest in these things, it was his fascination with the world around him and slightly eccentric personality that drew in many of my classmates and me. There was mystery here, and the most remarkable, the most important thing was that he was still fascinated and did not hide it. He might get "off track" for a few minutes speculating on the development of some rock or just "thinking out loud," wondering. Most significantly, this meant that we could be fascinated and wonder, too. Amid our growing concern with social stigmatization and how to be "cool," we did not have to be afraid to show our fascination. The teacher or parent who wonders right along with his or her charges, who enters the mystery rather than mystifying, opens the clearing. His wondering gave us permission to do the same, and it took us all deeper.

So much of our society races at such breakneck speed these days. The demands on our time and energy splinter us and eventually make a populous looking for ready-made answers; there is no time for anything else. And education tends too often to glaze the surface of learning by training children to repeat prepackaged answers at the expense of looking for deeper questions. This skimming along the surface can close off the clearing of education and of thoughtful pondering in our society at large. The promise of education is often unfulfilled and thus betrays students, teachers, and society. And what is worse, in order for teachers and students to fit in and adapt, they must betray themselves by remaining on the surface, and thus they miss the sustenance that comes from opening more deeply. We may not be able to make dramatic changes in the runaway pace of society or the flood of information, entertainment, and marketing vying for our attention, but we can begin to change this from the inside out by nurturing the natural openness in children, encouraging their big questions, and making time for pondering.

Our lives are full of moments when we have a choice between going a little deeper or moving on to the next item, person, or task. When we eat a morsel of food, how much do we allow the taste and texture to wrap around our tongue before bringing in the next mouthful? When an idea comes before us, in which moments do we open to it and in which do we ignore it or simply catalog it in our minds? In the times when we do go a little deeper, experience is not measured by quantity but is perceived as quality or intensity. Both experiences have value, but our lives are most significantly shaped by the intensities, the moments of greater depth and meaning.

In a previous book, *From Information to Transformation: Education for the Evolution of Consciousness*, I have described six interrelated layers that can deepen the practice of education.[13] As the surface layer, *information* is given its rightful place as currency for the educational exchange. Going deeper, information can then open up into *knowledge*, where direct experience often brings together the bits of information into the whole of mastery and skill. Knowledge opens the possibility of intentionally cultivating *intelligence*, which can cut, shape, and create information and knowledge through the dialectic of the intuitive and the analytic. Further down lies *understanding*, which takes us beyond the power of intelligence to look through the eye of the heart, a way of knowing that serves character and community. Experience then has the possibility for cultivating *wisdom*, which blends insight into what is true with an ethic of what is right. Ultimately, the depths lead to the possibility of *transformation*. This process of going deeper can happen in an instant or over the course of an assignment or exercise. Opening to the moment and into these depths does not take away from the information exchange but makes it richer, gives it context, and brings it alive. This keeps the big and intimate questions at the center of learning.

A Dark Knowing

Children's questions and comments reveal that they do not take for granted the same things that adults do. One mom described a moment when she and her daughter were sitting on their couch in front of the television: "I was laughing at something on TV, and my eight-year-old was scared by it and she said, 'You know, Mommy, I don't know yet what's real and what's not real.'" This both reflects a powerful self-awareness and poses a bedrock philosophical question about proof and evidence: How does one know what is real? What are the requirements to determine truth?

After pondering the idea that Jesus was the only perfect person, as had been explained to her in church, nine-year-old Kathy offered a flurry of questions. "This is so weird," she said. "I can't understand how he could be the only one. What about all the other people around the world who don't believe in Jesus? What do they think about him being the only perfect one? What do they believe in? And why shouldn't they be able to go to heaven too?" She then dug deeper still: "How do you even know there is a God?"

Krista remembers a scene at five years old that helped her to challenge the way she saw the world. "I was playing in my front yard and was trying to see the world from an ant's perspective. I was actually able to get a couple of friends to do the same, but they tired of the game quickly. So I lay down and got my eyes as close to the ground as possible. Well, it must have worked because all of a sudden the blades of grass looked enormous to me. I was watching how hard those little ants were working and was amazed. I sat up quickly because the height of the grass was overwhelming to me.

"At that moment I had this vision of being part of something much bigger. What came to me (keep in mind I was five but it has stayed with me in detail because it was so clear and so intense) was that my house, my planet, was part of what made up a table or a chair in a giant's house, or that there could be a family similar to mine in my shirt. Well, this really intrigued me, so I approached my dad with the question 'Are we really part of something so much bigger that our planet would fit onto a giant's table?' He just laughed. His laughter was not mean; the question just caught him by surprise, I think. But that was the beginning of shutting me down."

Questioning assumptions, whether about the church or the world of an ant, can be more than an intellectual exercise—it can actually serve as a spiritual practice that helps to free the mind in order to see more clearly and immediately. Theologian Thomas Merton called this unraveling a "dark knowing," by which he meant it was mainly an "unknowing"—taking down rather than adding to.[14] The Buddhist Madhyamika method intentionally deconstructs core concepts, even of Buddhism.[15] The approach called negative theology in Christianity systematically suspends core beliefs, even the basic tenants of Christianity, as a way of arriving at the most profound knowing. Postmodern deconstruction helps us to see the origin of our beliefs and the structures of power and knowledge.[16]

The Mulla Nasrudin stories of Sufism are another example of exposing our assumptions. Nasrudin was a wise sage in the guise of a trickster. He would often put himself in ridiculous or unexpected situations in order to expose assumptions and shake up one's thinking. The following story will give the flavor: A passerby notices Nasrudin crawling on the ground apparently looking for something. "I've lost my key," Nasrudin says. The passerby stops to help. After the two men have spent considerable time crawling around carefully searching in the dirt, he asks the Mulla, "Where did you drop your key?" Nasrudin points some distance away and replies, "Over there, near the house." In disbelief, the helper asks him why in the world they have been looking for it over here. Nasrudin responds, "The light is better over here."[17]

If we listen earnestly to children's questions and experiences, even to the seemingly silly ones, children may help us to free *our* minds. We may be forced to ask ourselves, What *is* real? Who am I? Where is divinity—distant and angry or nearer than my own hand? Am I looking here just because the light is better? Media scholar and critic Marshall McLuhan said that when the assumptions by which we have been living suddenly turn out to be wrong, we experience a moment of "world collapse." Children collapse and rebuild the world naturally and constantly. Writer Umberto Eco's character William of Baskerville reflects on the process of knowledge building: "The order that our mind imagines is like a net, or like a ladder, built to attain something. But afterward you must throw the ladder away, because you discover that, even if it was useful, it was meaningless."[18]

The very collapse and inevitable rebuilding of our worldview is a spiritual practice as well. It is the parallel process of the inevitable cycle of death and rebirth that is so fundamental to life and the life of ideas. We join that rhythm intentionally if we can hold our conceptions lightly, always being open to new ways of being surprised by the sacred and new ways to build our understanding, whether about our identity or the nature of the cosmos. Rigidity is anathema to spiritual practice. Children's questions can help break the curse.

Through their questioning, children may help us see that *we* live by a series of assumptions taken as fact. If we are paying attention, their questions can challenge those assumptions and help us reconsider our understanding. They bring fresh eyes that may help us see more clearly. As a parent or teacher we return the favor by posing genuine questions about the nature of life and its meaning:

- *Big things:* "What do you think about God?"
- *Both local and distant influences:* "What would make your school, the world, your parents, the universe better?"
- *Ethics:* "How do you know what's the right thing to do?" "What would you do if you were the president, the principal, the parent?"
- *Who they are:* "What is the most important thing about being you? What's the most fun?" "If you weren't you, who would you like to be?"
- *New perspectives:* "What do you think the world looks like through an ant's eyes or a Martian's?" "What do you think your parents think about when you're not around?" "What would you do if you had a week to live?" "Draw what you think a terrorist feels like on the inside and tell me why."

Another way to unravel assumptions, especially when decisions are looming, is the Quaker "clearness committee," which turns questioning into a community activity designed for clarifying decisions.[19] A member of the community can simply call upon others to sit together and ask them questions about a concern or choice that is being faced ("Should I take this job?" "What should I do with my life?" "Should I quit the gymnastics team?"). The committee then poses questions back to the person who called them together. The committee is not there to offer opinions or advice but simply to pose honest questions and listen to the person's responses. The point is to free up the person's thinking and help him or her listen to his or her inner knowing.

We can try this at home. The only caveat is to be certain our questions are in the best interest of unearthing assumptions and helping the person hear his or her own voice, and not in the interest of influencing the outcome in some particular way. In many circumstances, adults can invite children to serve as part of the "committee" for them.

Thought Experiments

Philosophy is often thought of as a deadly serious (and sometimes dull) affair. But pondering may actually work best when we play—one of the things children do best. Playful and thoughtful questioning, like these lines from poet Pablo Neruda's *Book of Questions*, helps us to think outside the box:

Is 4 the same 4 for everybody?
Are all sevens equal?
When the convict ponders the light
is it the same light that shines on you?[20]

Such questioning allows us to turn the world upside down and inside out. The timeless author of whimsical children's books Dr. Suess knew how to do this. So did the Swiss psychologist Carl Jung, even as a child. "Often, when I was alone," he wrote, "I sat down on this stone, and began an imaginary game that went something like this: I am sitting on the top of this stone and it is underneath. But the stone could also say 'I' and think: 'I am lying here on this slope and he is sitting on top of me.' The question then arose: 'Am I the one who is sitting on top of the stone, or am I the stone on which *he* is sitting?'"[21]

Conceptual play and "philosophical whimsy" free us to imagine a world of endless possibilities.[22] We can draw out the imagination in all sorts of ways. When I do not have a bedtime story at my fingertips, my young daughter and I keep the spirit of play alive by jumping on the tail of each other's ideas to form a story. "Once upon a time," I say. "There was a gorilla," she continues. "With red hair," I add. "And the red-haired gorilla named Rudy was going to take a long trip," she says. And off we go into mystery—silly, unexpected, sometimes perplexing, but always opening to new questions. "Can gorillas have red hair? What are their families like? Do they like staying in the zoo? Do they make up stories too?"

That great playful ponderer of the twentieth century, Albert Einstein, knew the power of conceptual play. His great work was conducted in the laboratory of his mind, as "thought experiments." Essentially he asked questions like, "What if I ride on the head of a rocket and travel at the speed of light. How would the universe behave?" He understood well that "imagination is more important than reason" precisely because it allows us to transcend the way we see the world.[23] As philosopher Arthur Schopenhauer said, "The task is not so much to see what no one yet has seen, but to think what nobody yet has thought about that which everybody sees."[24] This leads not only to scientific breakthroughs, but to spiritual ones as well.

At five, Pat was hiding in the bushes near the driveway at his home waiting for some important visitors to arrive for a meeting with his parents. It was a visit for the adults, but he wanted to get a glimpse of the new car that he had heard they were driving. When they arrived, there was a sort of "to do" about the car, but soon everyone went into the house. Pat stayed there in the bushes for a while, just daydreaming. "I realized for the first time that my thoughts were my own and that no one knew them," he said. "That's why no one knew I was in the bushes. I played with that idea and then I wondered at the fact that I was there and not anywhere else—in another family and at some other time—but at this single time and space I was in and could not get out of. I tried to remember where I was before I was in this family. I couldn't; I could only remember going back so far and then nothing at all. And I pushed at that and somehow I saw a face whose neck vanished into space as if its whole body were the universe.

"Then there was sort of a flashback on a very difficult event, in which I was facing a high wall made of square logs that were all blackened with tar. I didn't fully understand it but I somehow felt it so clearly. But next there was an immediate flash in the distance, and the thought came to me that this time things would be taken care of properly, that the end was far off, that it would not be so bad. I left the bushes feeling that there was a greater reality than the one I saw around me that was involved in my life and that I was on my way regardless of my choices and wishes. It gave me the feeling of having a purpose other than any I thought up or wished for. Later, I thought that happiness would be the result of wishing for what was inevitably going to come my way."

Jenelle recalled bedtime on a summer evening at six years old: "It was still light out—the sun hadn't set yet—but I had a pretty early bedtime. I knew my friends were still outside playing, so I sneaked out of bed, tucked my nightgown into my jeans, and threw on my cowboy boots. I managed to sneak out the back door without my parents realizing. My friends were still out playing in front of a neighbor's house. It was a favorite hangout because it had great stairs to sit on.

"As I was standing on these stairs, one step above my friends, looking sort of down upon them, the thought occurred to me that this way of seeing—from above—was probably how God saw us. And as I played with this thought, I felt myself come out of my own body and see myself as Jenelle—this other person, this person whom I could look at for the first time. I was completely removed from the

'I' that I normally thought of as myself. I saw that I was more than I had thought I was.

"When I came back, I tried to tell my friends and asked, 'Hey guys, have you ever tried to see yourself like God sees you?' They didn't answer. 'You know, like take yourself outside your body and look at yourself.' Again, there was no response. To this day, I can remember peering over my own shoulder, watching myself with these friends, really questioning who I was, and knowing somehow that this was what it might be like to see with God's eyes."

Jenelle's comment calls to mind the following line by mystic and theologian Meister Eckhart: "The eye with which I see God is the same eye with which God sees me . . . one vision or seeing, and one knowing and loving."[25]

"Who am I?" "What are we here for?" "What will happen when we die?" "I might know later today." These questions and statements by children reveal that they do consider *ultimate concerns*—their place on Earth, the nature of knowledge, their being and their becoming. And their lives are shaped by what they uncover. As it was for great philosophers such as Plato, these questions are a spiritual pursuit. A child's pondering, puzzling over, and playing with questions are ways of entering a dialogue with mystery, with the spiritual. Children's natural openness, freshness, and candor make them remarkable natural philosophers.

Chapter 5

Seeing *the* Invisible

Shakespeare once wrote, "There are more things in heaven and earth than man has dreamt of in his philosophy."[1] His statement affirms the message of the mystics and sages that the world is more than meets the eye. Our universe is multidimensional and mysterious, and it exists beyond our ability to measure it or even, as Shakespeare implies, to imagine it. Virtually every spiritual tradition recognizes unseen worlds that are alive in our midst. Teilhard de Chardin, the Jesuit sage, had a glimpse into this world as a child: "I was certainly no more than 6 or 7 when I began to feel myself drawn to Matter— or more exactly by something that 'shone' in the heart of matter."[2] He perceived the invisible, and this was the impetus for an entire lifetime in pursuit of the spiritual.

Much to our surprise as adults, children are often aware of this hidden world. My youngest daughter sees shapes and colors around people and objects. A boy tells us that an angel comforts him before he enters surgery. A young child says she remembers her "other family" from when she "lived before." A boy falls unharmed from a three-story window and tells about being caught by "those guys dressed in gold."

We know the world is more than meets the eye. Science continues to disclose previously invisible dimensions to us. And the mystics declare that their own investigations reveal a world that is multidimensional, interconnected, alive, and evolving—and perhaps one that is increasingly transparent. So many credible figures across time and culture have described these other dimensions that it is difficult to relegate them to fantasy, delusion, or wishful thinking.

There are numerous maps of a multidimensional universe from both ancient and contemporary wisdom traditions that share commonalities. For example, ancient Kabbalistic writings contend that everything existing in our physical world originates in the nonphysical realm of the Sfirot. According to the *Zohar*, both the individual and the universe as a whole are composed of ten dimensions, the ten Sfirot, meaning "ten emanations" of light. Think of waves of light emanating out from a concentrated center—"a never-to-be-exhausted fountain of light."[3] Each of these waves represents a different dimension or level of consciousness or reality. Remarkably, more than two thousand years later, superstring theory from theoretical physics also suggests there are ten dimensions of existence that likewise emanated from a kind of supernal luminescence—the Big Bang. Physicists retrieve our familiar four-dimensional universe by assuming that during the Big Bang six of the ten dimensions curled up, or "compactified," while the remaining four expanded explosively, giving us the universe we see.[4]

In the East, the Hindu tenant "Atman and Brahman are one" means that the individual human and the Godhead are one and the same. We are "compactified," we might say, and the spiritual path involves realizing more of this innate divinity as we uncoil the multidimensional nature of ourselves and the universe. We do this by overcoming *maya*, or the illusion that the physical world we see is all there is. Similarly, Emanuel Swedenborg, the eighteenth-century scientist turned mystic, described the "law of correspondence" in which what we see in the physical world are correspondences of higher dimensions.[5] Creation is stepped down, like electricity, as if through a series of transformers to manifest as various levels of existence. Matter and the physical body are the densest manifestation of this energy.

A number of individuals have understood this multidimensionality in terms of different subtle energy "bodies," or levels, that make up an individual and, simultaneously, the universe. Imagine finer and finer sheaths of energy surrounding our physical form. These bodies, or levels of being, are frequently named the etheric, astral, mental, and causal, and there are various subtle spiritual bodies beyond these. The etheric represents the subtle energy that is recognized as the life force, or *chi* in Chinese medicine and philosophy, and is closely tied to the physical body.[6] The levels beyond this represent nonspace, nontime dimensions of existence, akin or at least analogous to the hyperspace of superstring theory. For example, the astral level represents a disembodied conscious, one in which emotions, for example, have their own reality and may actually be perceived as shapes, colors, and so forth.

We can image that our awareness makes its way between dimensions through a kind of wormhole of consciousness that may be entered spontaneously, in altered states like sleep, or more intentionally through such practices as meditation. For example, during out-of-the-body and near-death experiences, as well as the Dreamtime, as Aboriginals call it, consciousness leaves the dominant magnetic pull of the physical body and awareness opens in another dimension. Compelling evidence exists of individuals being able to perceive from vantage points (for example, the ceiling of an operating room or a remote location) that are not possible from their physical bodies.

In other instances we may tap into the even higher frequency of the casual body/reality in which we may perceive higher guidance that may be less individualized. We spoke about this in chapter 1 with concepts like the higher self. So when I use the term *seeing the invisible,* I mean that in some way children are tuning in to these more subtle levels of reality as they see visions, hear voices, feel energy, know things at a distance, and find insight and inspiration.

Multidimensional awareness does not usually arrive like a

meteor landing in our backyard; it is more often like a gentle breeze blowing on our face. What is revealed is subtler than a meteor, but no less real. Peering into the multidimensional world—the invisible—requires a sensitivity and openness to the limitlessness of consciousness that children seem to have quite naturally. For children, the veil between the worlds may be very thin. These experiences may, at times, be thought of as spiritual in that they (1) reflect an openness and expansion of consciousness; (2) show us more of who we are and what the universe is, and therefore shape our worldview; and (3) reflect a more direct, intuitive knowing that is so often the route toward spiritual insight.

Thomas Jefferson once said that only those who see the invisible can do the impossible. In these days of so much difficulty and so much possibility, when poverty and violence, environmental degradation, and collapsing political, economic, and moral norms seem nearly impossible to comprehend, much less to solve, we may need the power to see the invisible in order to accomplish the impossible. And children may help us to see.

Believing before Seeing

Seeing before believing is the credo of modern science. We are encouraged to believe something only after we see it for ourselves. For the most part, this works just fine, providing the kind of verification that helps us avoid foolishness and superstition. However, when it comes to spiritual matters, it is sometimes necessary to believe *before* we can see. More precisely, this means suspending *disbelief* in order to open ourselves to whatever is before us. This does not mean abandoning our critical mind or being a naïve convert to some idea or doctrine; rather, it means turning off our critical judgment for a moment in order to open up to possibility. This is the meaning of faith.

And what faith does is build a bridge between the known and the unknown that allows us to cross into new possibility—it opens our consciousness and allows us to see the invisible. Hugh's story, which follows, demonstrates the power of this openness.

As he entered high school, Hugh was a troubled and troubling underachiever. He was on the fast track to a disappointing life. However, his school had an unusual experiment at the time that involved periodically busing Hugh and a group of his peers to the nearby Princeton University campus, where students listened to presentations by distinguished physicists of the day, Einstein among them. The hope was that these scientists might have a positive impact on the lives of these difficult teens.

One day, after a long, dry talk by one of the physicists, a young girl sitting in the back of the lecture hall raised her hand and wryly asked these men of science what they thought of ghosts. After some chuckles, the first physicist stood up and with clear and definite certainty entirely dismissed any possibility of their existence. When he was done, the second scientist took his turn and with great authority rejected any chance of there being ghosts and cited a lack of any hard scientific evidence. When they had finished, Robert Oppenheimer, who was instrumental in the development of the atomic bomb and then a staunch opponent of its use, took his turn. He stood up, paused for a moment, and said, "That's a fascinating question. I accept the possibility of all things," and he went on to explain that "it is necessary to find one's own required evidence before accepting or rejecting a possibility."

For Hugh, this moment was a revelation that forever changed his life. Instead of closing down and accepting the world as prepackaged, Oppenheimer's perspective opened it back up to mystery, to the possibility of all things, and to one's responsibility to discover its validity for oneself. This gave permission for two things. The first was the openness to infinite possibility that comes from what poet

W. B. Yeats called "radical innocence"—that moment of suspending disbelief.[7] And simultaneously, there was the necessity to find out for oneself, to be true to one's own standards.

Hugh's inner life began a monumental shift as he came to define himself from the center of his own direct experience. He began to believe in possibility and mystery again, and to rely on his own verification rather than shutting down to conform to what others said was real or true. Hugh went on to become a distinguished, innovative, and also irreverent professor who helped open up multidimensional possibilities for others. More than fifty years later, Hugh vividly remembered Oppenheimer's response and the remarkable impact this had on his life. Essentially, this moment helped him to believe in the possibility of all things—to believe so that he could see.

Not long after the time that I was first introduced to my daughter's angel, my family and I decided to visit Asheville, North Carolina, for a weekend getaway. Several friends had told us that it was an interesting place, and we thought we would explore the area with our young girls, three and seven at the time. Two days before leaving, I received a phone call from a friend, who happened to mention a website that she thought was interesting, which was operated by a girl and her mom. I checked it out and found the page to be so unusual and to have such a genuine feel to it that I thought I would track them down sometime. Then I realized that they lived in Asheville. Within minutes I was speaking with Nancy, this child's mother, who invited us to come and visit with them during our weekend trip.

That Saturday we met at their home on a wooded hillside in Asheville. Nancy welcomed us. Her daughter, Llael, and I eventually sat down to chat, with Nancy nearby. Llael was a cute twelve-year-old at the time who seemed both self-assured and a little shy—not someone who appeared to have any hunger for the spotlight.

Without any fanfare, Llael told me about her three guides, who formed a kind of council and often answered her questions as a three-some dubbed STJ. The first guide was a gray wolf named Sanka. Llael explained, "She protects me, keeps me company, and plays with me, but mostly, she gives me information on almost anything. It's like she has access to the Internet of the universe. I met Sanka at Town Creek Indian Mound outside of Charlotte when I was nine."

Her second council member was a Native American called Tank-too-wa. Llael said, "He guides me in doing healing work. He came to me one day when I was putting a mud pack on my mom's back; then later he and I performed an Indian dancing ceremony to honor my remembrance of healing." She said that Tank-too-wa was willing to be her mentor and teach her if she wanted to study healing. She described her third guide: "Juangwa came to tell me he wanted me to get all the children like me together in the world. His mission is universal harmony." Since that time she said another figure has appeared to her: "Celentien is a seven-foot-tall angel who came to guide me in the ways of communication and to keep a clear channel for me at all times."

These descriptions are interesting, but they might also be the product of an active fantasy life. Some people might even worry about Llael being delusional. As a psychologist and longtime therapist, I am trained to assess mental status. Llael, like so many of the children and adults to whom I have spoken, confounds the psychiatric maps because she appears to be extremely psychologically healthy and well adjusted. Yet she talks of things that psychiatry would typically recognize as "delusion," a possible sign of schizophrenia, or, more mildly, fantasy or just an attempt to get attention.

However, what gave Llael remarkable credibility was the quality of her as a person and the quality of her answers. For example, during our conversation, I asked if her guides were available to chat. In the next few moments, Llael brought them "into focus" by relaxing and "concentrating on their energy." She then provided accurate and extremely insightful and private information about me that she had no way of knowing through conventional means. She was able to zero in and even offer insight into my own life with remarkable clarity. This was a very small part of our time together, but it gave powerful credibility to her story.

For Llael, each guide represented a different aspect of consciousness and provided a somewhat specialized kind of assistance, as she mentioned. Just before I left Llael and her mom, I asked if she or her guides had any insight into what I was doing there talking to her; I was not sure myself. She paused and again brought her guides into focus. She then said, "You are to write a book about children like me. Do the book for these kids and for your kids." I had no intention of writing such a book at the time, but if you are reading this, her instructions have been fulfilled. I have kept in close touch will Llael over the past several years and have grown even more impressed with her continuing ability to tune in to the multidimensional realms and with the quality of the information she offers. But I am most impressed with the quality of her as a person—the psychological, intellectual, and spiritual balance and maturity she embodies.

How unusual is Llael or any of the children with whom I have spoken? Llael makes the point that while there are certainly different levels and facets of development, multidimensional knowing is available to everyone. These children are not rare or even particularly unusual. While some children may have easier access, different styles, or greater degrees of profundity, all children have this capacity to see into the depths.

When a culture begins to recognize a particular human capacity as valuable, it will begin to see this dimension first in exceptional adults (like mystics and sages), then in prodigious children (perhaps like Llael), and finally it will be recognized in all of us. Llael said, "Sometimes I feel like what I experience isn't really another reality at all, it's just a more expanded view of this one." When she was fifteen,

I asked her what the difference is between somebody who, like her, has access to this invisible world and someone who does not. She said, "It's just about being open to it. For children, the big factor is whether they were allowed to express what they saw or felt and have it accepted. I think every child has that innate ability, but if it is just considered fantasy or discouraged by an adult, then it's not going to grow and they won't have that ability as an adult. Many adults would not even put another thought to it—it doesn't exist. But it's so much easier for children to believe, and you have to believe that it exists to be able to do it. Some people think this is strange, and if you have to believe it before you see it, then it's fake. The difference is openness. For me, I don't have to turn anything on or go anywhere; my guides are always right there."

Inner Senses

Cultural norms teach us to consider our senses as distinct from one another. We are taught to describe a good meal by its flavor, music by its sound. But childhood perceptions are not necessarily so distinct. The philosopher Maurice Merleau-Ponty told us that we are naturally synesthetic—our senses are naturally merged and fused. But, he said, culture has shifted "the center of gravity of experience, so that we have unlearned how to see, hear, and generally speaking feel, in order to deduce [what we sense]."[8] During moments of expanded awareness, such as some personal ecstasy or perhaps during meditation, nearly everyone can have synesthetic experiences, and young children have them often. We may see colors or shapes when hearing particular music; we may smell a flower and have a feeling in our body or hear sounds. "I heard flowers that sounded, and saw notes that shone," reports eighteenth-century transcendentalist philosopher Saint-Martin.[9]

Synesthetic impressions occur not only in perceiving out-wardly—a blue sky or the sound of a bird—but also inwardly, as with the birth of an idea. Mozart (remember, he was a child prodigy) de-scribed his process of composing in this way: "I can see the whole of it at a single glance in my mind, as if it were a beautiful painting . . . in which way I do not hear it in my imagination at all as a succession . . . but all at once."[10] For Mozart, musical inspiration came as an experience of seeing music—"a single glance," "a painting."

We can play with the richness of the multisensory knowing of children through inquiries such as, "What shape does that sound have?" "What sound does that tree have?" "Where and what does that song feel like in your body?" "What is the shape and movement of this food that you're eating?" We can suggest that they draw a piece of music; use colors to describe a flavor; move their body in the way that a color (food, sound, etc.) feels like in them; or draw an outline of a person on a blank piece of paper and then, while listening to a piece of music, mark the location, shape, color, and any other im-pressions they have in their own body on the paper. These can be playful games that help children explore the natural richness of their perceptions.

A clarification here: These invitations will not necessarily yield very interesting results if we ask the question as we are racing through breakfast on the way to school. It requires a playful and gentle space where it is safe to sound or look silly. Expanding perception in this way is a step toward an even deeper and richer world. William Blake, English poet and childhood mystic, tells us, "If the doors of percep-tion were cleansed, everything would appear to man as it is, infinite. For man has closed himself up, till he sees all things thro' narrow chinks of his cavern."[11]

Children often describe what we could call "inner senses" that access a multidimensional matrix. Six-year-old Meg announced to a visitor that she "saw colors around" the visitor. After some conversation about the colors and shapes that she saw, the visitor asked, "How do you see it?" "I see it inside here," Meg said, as she pointed to the center of her forehead. "You don't see it with your eyes?" the visitor asked. "Not really. I see it from my inside." What Meg described was the inner sense that is a parallel perceptual system to physical sight. It may be helpful to think about four general ways to perceive the invisible: seeing, feeling, hearing, and knowing. While we may have potential for all of these styles of knowing (and probably more), a child may have a natural preference or strength for one way of knowing over another, just as a child may be primarily a visual or auditory learner, for example, in the classroom.

Author and MIT graduate Pete Sanders suggests that these inner senses correspond to different locations in the body and that these senses can be enhanced by focusing our awareness at that location.[12] Just as Meg recognized, the inner sense of sight is identified with the middle of her forehead, or "third eye," as it is described in ancient Hindu tradition. Feeling—"I feel something is wrong with John"—which we explored primarily in chapter 2, is often localized near the solar plexus region of the abdomen. It may also be manifest as sensitivity in one's hands, such as when one can sense information through holding an object or through healing. One might feel heat or energy, or simply let one's hands move in ways that "feel right" when giving a massage. Hearing—that sense of an inner voice or sound—seems to be facilitated by bringing awareness to the temple region, located above the ears (it is interesting that we call this area of anatomy the "temples," like those buildings to which many have gone in order to hear and listen for "the word"). Sometimes we "just know" without an inner feeling, sight, or sound. This intuitive sense is associated with an opening at the top of the head, known as the crown chakra in Tantric tradition.

As parents, we can never be quite sure when our children will take us into their confidence. From very early on, Maia, our youngest child, would periodically say things that gave us pause. I remember sitting at the kitchen table when Maia was twenty months old and asking her whether she remembered being in "Mommy's tummy" before she was born. She immediately answered, "Yes." When asked what it was like, she paused, carefully looked around, and then said, "Pool!" pointing at the kiddy pool in our backyard. And when she was two, we were all silently watching a funeral on television. Maia, who had been viewing intently, suddenly pointed to the screen and announced, "Going home!"

We began to see even more through her eyes when Maia was five years old. She was at a large work-related party in the woods at a friend's home. Our friend had built a very big tree house overlooking a stream and decorated it with Chinese lanterns and Christmas lights—the perfect place for pixies like Maia on a warm and darkening August evening. Maia had been playing in the tree house and was coming down the slippery ladder. She fell. It was a long fall for such a little girl, perhaps seven feet, and then she tumbled down a very steep embankment, really a cliff, to the edge of the stream another eight or nine feet below. (It was probably a good thing we did not witness this. It would have been one of those images that gets seared into a parent's memory and wakes you up panicked in the middle of the night.)

A friend carried her over to me and explained what had happened. Maia was scared, but she appeared to be all right, except that her neck was very sore. We discovered that nothing was broken, but she walked around for the next two days with one shoulder hunched up nearly to her ear, and when she turned to look at something, she had to turn her whole body instead of swiveling her neck. The best diagnosis we could get was that she had sprained some muscles; we were very thankful that nothing more serious had happened.

After a couple days, we decided to take her to a massage therapist, thinking that this might provide a little relief from the pain and trauma. Both Maia and I went to the therapist's office, and I sat silently in a chair in the corner of the room while Maia lay on the table. At one point Maia was staring, apparently out of the window, for several minutes, and I wondered to myself what she was looking at. On our ride back home, we talked a little about how her neck felt and what the massage was like for her. She said it felt "good" and that she would be willing to do it again. I could see that her shoulder had dropped a good deal and she was able to move a little more freely. I mentioned that I had noticed her staring out the window while she was on the table and I wondered what she was looking at—a bird or something? She said that she hadn't been looking out the window; she was just looking at the picture on the wall.

After a short pause, Maia announced from the back seat of the car, "I do see faces around my bed at night." "What?" I asked, wondering if I had heard her correctly. "I see faces and people around my bed at night, and sometimes around your bed, too," she reiterated. "Can you tell me more?" I asked. She said, "I see them after the lights go out, when my eyes are still open. I see lots of colors and shapes, too. Sometimes I see them around people," she said matter-of-factly. "Do you see anything now?" I asked. "I see colors and lines around and behind you. Green dots in your hair and long sorts of colored strings," she replied.

I was shocked that she had never mentioned this before; I suppose we had never had any reason to ask. She continued to periodically and privately (she said that it's OK if I tell this) mention what she saw, ranging from shapes and colors to people and ideas. For example, one night lying in bed, she said, "I see things like snow on the walls. And colors and blobs of colors." She then asked me, "How much is two twenties?" "Do you mean forty?" I answered. "That's how many things I see right now," she explained.

Maia's perceptions may not be so unique. The week after Maggie, four, her older sister, Shannon, and Diane, their mother, returned from summer camp, Shannon woke up at 5 A.M. and gave her dad a hug on his way to work. Shannon was surprised to hear that Maggie was awake and went into the living room to see why she was making so much noise. Maggie was dancing and seemed to be trying to catch something in her hands. She said that she was seeing "lights sprinkling down" from the ceiling. She described them as "bugs on strings" that were "all colors" and related that she could catch them in her hands. As they talked more, Maggie said that as soon as she had woken up, she had seen "wires" of all colors wrapped around her bed. At first she had thought that she couldn't get out of bed, but then she had decided she could. She had also seen purple and green "hairs" coming out of her arms and pink squiggly lights coming out of her hands.

Laura, like many of the children to whom I have spoken, sees lights and color around people. Her mom says, "When she was three she would, without any direction or prompting, draw people with colors around them. And then she would interpret them and tell us precisely what the colors meant about each person. She would sometimes put a little black in mine and say, 'That's because you argue with Daddy.'"

Ellen discovered as a child that she could bring faces and colors into clear view if she would just stare, especially at a blank surface such as a white wall. She now works with others to help them develop their inner senses. She says, "I teach them how to stare; I'll have children look at a white wall and ask them to stare. Within a few minutes they see auras and a lot of them see faces and guides. If there aren't any fears or preconceptions, then it happens very quickly. They are often able to interpret what they see. It's like they have a wave of intuition that goes along with it. It's not blocked; it's just a sense of knowing."

There is a simple exercise to help children explore and compare their intuitive perceptions that has been used at the summer camp that I help to run. Children (and adults) have a piece of paper with a rough outline of a person on it. One person stands in the midst of the circle, and we might ask that person to hold a flower essence or to hold a thought in his or her mind or simply to be himself or herself. Group members are then asked to draw whatever each person senses—colors, shapes, words, feelings, scenes, and anything else that comes along. We separate children far enough from one another so that it is difficult for them to see each other's drawings.

When they are done, we ask them to hold up their pictures to show one another. This is a way to compare their perceptions and to notice similarities and differences. (In research, this is called "intersubjective validation.") While there is diversity in how each person sees and draws the world, there are also stunning similarities. Choices of colors, shapes, size and location of the colors, even words are often remarkably similar if not identical. This is a fun exercise that gives children an opportunity to compare impressions, to see how others see, and to honor their own and others' inner senses. I want to note here that perception is an active process as we filter, construct, and interpret what is perceived. Said another way, we are part of what we perceive; the "inside" and the "outside" blur.

But what is this light and color that children are seeing? The notion of light is used in virtually every spiritual tradition to describe the nature of spirit. We use words like enlightenment, illumination, radiance, and so forth, and claim, as in the Qur'an of Islam, that "God is the light of heaven and earth."[13] We read about a burning bush or a heart aflame, and halos are almost invariably painted around spiritual figures. The halo, often depicted as a gold or bright disc behind and above the head, is a representation of one's illumination, connection to, and embodiment of Spirit. Jesus is considered to be the Christ because he embodies this light.

However metaphorical, the use of light also has a literal meaning. One of the most detailed explanations is the four-thousand-year-old Hindu notion of chakras. Chakras are referred to in the Vedas, the later Upanishads, and most elaborately in a sixteenth-century text called *Sat-Chakra-Nirupana*. Chakras refer to wheels or discs of energy (like a halo) that vibrate at different frequencies and therefore produce different variations of light (colors), which are localized in and around various areas of the body. As mentioned earlier, the idea is that the physical body is the densest manifestation of intersecting energy fields or energy bodies. These fields are connected to one another through a complex network of energetic "threads." Chakras are generally thought of as transformers that allow life energy, or *prana*, to flow between different-frequency energy bodies and the physical body. Emotions, thoughts, intentions, and so forth are all energy in this grid, and children's perceptions of color, strings, threads, and blobs are perceptions of energy and information.

Jenna, a mother of three young boys, told about the colors and shapes that her five-year-old saw: "We were at a party at our church one afternoon. I noticed that Avalon was talking very intently to a woman who was a church schoolteacher, and I was wondering what he was saying to her. I didn't think too much more about it and carried on with the party until she came up to me and said, 'Oh, I just wanted to tell you that Avalon is so loving and amazing.' I had to chuckle to myself because he and I clash so much. We are so different and I sometimes forget to look for that loving side of him.

"Naturally, I thanked her and then I asked, 'Do you mind telling me what he was saying to you? You both seemed so intense.' She explained, 'He was telling me in great detail about crystals. He told me that each person has colors representing him or her and that these colors mean different things. He was telling me what each meant and what each person's crystal meant. It was in pretty remarkable detail, and I'm not sure I really grasped it all but it was pretty amazing.' He had never told me anything like that. I know I have to be really careful about asking about things like this with him because if

I pry him too much, he will clam up; but I'm beginning to learn just how amazing he is."

Science has come to realize recently that an underlying structure of things from molecules to mathematics is well represented by its crystalline or geometric superstructure: from quartz crystals in our watches to fractal geometry used for data compression in e-mail attachments, from the geometric form of DNA to liquid-crystal-display computer screens, from the structure of snowflakes to the ruby laser first developed by Bell Laboratories in the sixties, from the geometry of molecules to the remarkable information storage on a silicon crystal—a chip—that is the heart of the modern computer. Perhaps what Avalon, Maggie, Maia, and so many other children I have heard from perceive is an aspect of this sacred geometry of the world—the latticework of matter and consciousness that we are only beginning to unravel.

In a very practical sense, color has already been used to help children read. Some educators have found that if children place the right colored transparency over the material they are reading, their performance improves. Some even find that if they hold an image in their mind of a particular crystalline shape (diamond, cube, etc.), this enhances their ability even further. While we do not understand the mechanisms fully, we can speculate that the frequency and form of different colors and shapes correspond with and activate certain energetic and, in turn, neurological activity. The main point for now is that children may both perceive and be influenced by this invisible world.

In his autobiography, Jacques Lusseyran, a remarkably joyful man who was a teenage leader of the French Resistance in World War II and a survivor of Buchenwald, describes looking at his grandparents' garden in a small town in the French countryside. Their ride to the train that would take them back to Paris after their Easter holiday had just arrived. Jacques was in the garden sobbing. "I was crying because I was looking at the garden for the last time," he wrote. "I had just learned the bad news. I couldn't say how, but there was absolutely no doubt. . . . When my mother . . . finally found me and asked what the trouble was, I could only say: 'I am never going to see the garden again.'"[14] Three weeks later, as a boy of seven, he was permanently blinded in an accident at school.

But it was through his blinding that he learned to see in a new way—he learned to see *light*. One day several months after the accident, he said:

> I realized that I was looking in the wrong way. . . . I was looking too far off, and too much on the surface of things. . . . I began to look more closely, not at things but at a world closer to myself, looking from an inner place to one further within. . . . I was aware of a radiance emanating from a place I knew nothing about. . . . But radiance was there, or, to put it more precisely, light. . . . I felt indescribable relief, and happiness so great it almost made me laugh. . . . I found light and joy at the same moment. . . . For every waking hour and even in my dreams I lived in a stream of light. . . . I could feel light rising, spreading, resting on objects, giving them form. . . . I saw the whole world in light existing through it and because of it. . . . Light was my whole reason for living. . . .
>
> Light threw its color on things and on people. My mother and father, the people I met or ran into in the street, all had their characteristic color which I had never seen before I went blind.[15]

Jacques described a young girl he came to love: "I followed her by the red wake which traveled behind her wherever she went. I did not understand it, but no matter, since I was living it. There were times when the light faded. . . . It happened every time I was afraid.

. . . Fear . . . made me blind." Anger and impatience had the same effects, so did jealousy and growing anxious to win at all costs—they threw everything into confusion. Jacques explained, "I could no longer afford to be jealous or unfriendly, because, as soon as I was, a bandage came down over my eyes. . . . Armed with such a tool, why should I need a moral code? I had only to look at the bright signal which taught me how to live."

Jacques discovered intensities of hearing and feeling as well. For example, he related, "My hands discovered that objects were not rigidly bound within a mold . . . objects branched out in all directions. I had to move my hands from branch to branch [on an apple tree] to feel the currents moving between them."[16]

Like Jacques, children perceive the world in a deeper way than we may have come to believe. Their inner senses may reveal a world that is vastly richer than we may have imagined.

Faces in the Dark and Light

One night my youngest daughter had a friend spend the night. They were both tired, but they were still riding the momentum of a good day full of play. I took the usual steps of turning the light out, admiring the new glow-in-the-dark stars on the wall, complying with the requests for glasses of water and other "necessities"—"I need to go to the bathroom," "I have to put my plastic ponies to bed," "Can we have a night light?" Then another round of hugs and kisses and lights out again. I went downstairs, suspecting that they would chat a while longer. Soon another twenty minutes passed, and it had gotten pretty late for the little girls. I heard some conversation and thought I'd trudge up for the inevitable and final round of, "OK, I mean it; time to stop talking and go to sleep."

However, as I approached the door, I could easily hear them

talking. I'm not one to eavesdrop, but I could plainly hear my daughter's friend, Ashley, talking about seeing spirits. "One time I was at church and I felt a spirit come right through me; I don't know what it was but I felt it. I hear them sometimes, too. One time I heard my great-grandmother's voice tell me that she was always looking out for me and protecting me."

My daughter responded by saying that she didn't hear anything, but she saw people and colors. "Do you know the people?" Ashley asked. "No," Maia said. "What do they look like?" her friend inquired. "They look like different people. One was a little girl."

That seemed to trigger something in Ashley and she said, "One time I had a bad fall and felt something pick me up." I remembered hearing her parents' description of this very scary high-speed, head-over-heals-without-a-helmet crash that could have ended in disaster, but from which she walked away with just a few scrapes.

The girls went back and forth like this for several minutes. There didn't seem to be any sense of competition; they were just comparing notes. I was so appreciative of hearing this, but felt like I didn't want to eavesdrop any longer. I went in and reminded them how late it was and asked why they were still up. They let me in on their conversation and added new twists and stories before I finally got them off to sleep.

When children can actually share with someone who also sees the invisible, like Ashley and Maia, they have the great benefit of comparing notes and learning from one another. One of the things that children perceive is other people whom not everyone seems to see. For the next few pages, I will give some of the range of these encounters.

Descriptions like the following are surprisingly common. A friend of the family had died, and Julie went to Alison's funeral with her young boys. "We had a friend die last December," she related. "We saw the casket and the kids went to the funeral. Three or four days later Jamie, 3 1/2, went into my bedroom and said, 'Alison's in there; she's an angel.'"

Eighteen-month-old Sydney started mentioning "the lady" who was in their old Victorian house. Her mother says, "When we go into her room to get her up from her nap, as she wakes she goes *shhhhhh!* with her finger pressed to her lips. She says, 'Lady!' as she looks toward the small rocking chair in her room. Her eyes follow her rocking back and forth, although I don't see the chair move. She is not at all frightened. The lady apparently sits in the rocker in her room with her when she naps.

"The other day," Sydney's mother goes on, "Fran [an employee and friend] was cleaning out some photos from her desk. A picture of Lydia Hicks fell to the floor. Sydney walked over, pointed, and said very excitedly, 'LADY!!!!!!' Fran asked, 'Is that the lady in your room?' 'Yupeeee!!' The picture was of her great-grandmother, who lived and died in this house twenty years before Sydney was born."

Sarah, eleven, had spent time at her grandfather's house just a few days before the car accident that took his life. She and her grandfather had been really close. His death was so sudden that she had not had a chance to say good-bye. Sarah told me, "He was cremated and we had a funeral, but I didn't feel like I got to say good-bye to him. I felt like I couldn't see him again, and I was missing him very much. That night I was sleeping in my grandfather's room. The house was pretty full; the rest of the family was there. I couldn't sleep very well because I just missed him so much. I had fallen asleep for an hour at nine, but had been up thinking about him from 10 P.M. on.

"Around midnight, I had this strange feeling that there was someone in the room. I smelled 'Ben Gay' moving around the room. The room did not smell at all before this; I had been in the room since nine, and it didn't start to smell until after midnight, when no one else was awake. The smell was really weak at first and I just thought

I was imagining it, but then it got stronger and stronger. When he was alive, my grandfather wore a lot of Ben Gay. I just knew that it was my grandfather. Then the smell slowly faded away. I think he was just saying good-bye."

The most common metaphysical explanation is that when the body dies, the essence or soul carries on in some nonphysical realm. It is fascinating to hear accounts of near-death experiencers who, when considered clinically dead, describe themselves hovering above their body and then frequently seeing deceased friends, former pets, relatives, and sometimes beatific beings who greet them. Upon death some seem to move on and appear to evolve, and some seem confused and in shock.

Not all encounters with the invisible are pleasant. They can even be deeply disturbing to both a child and a confused parent. As one mother describes, "When my oldest son was a toddler, we lived on an island, and I used to pull him everywhere on a sled because we didn't have a car. He loved it and always rode happily. Often we'd explore little back roads that led here and there around the island. One day, though, we turned down a little road we hadn't seen before. We went a little ways without incident, and then abruptly he started to scream, rolled off the sled, refused to get back on, threw a full-scale tantrum, and generally behaved as he'd never behaved before, until I gave up and turned around—where upon he got back on the sled and rode happily again. His babysitter told me, when I described this strange event to her the next day, that a child had been killed on that little road while sledding, thirty or forty years before."

Beginning in childhood and continuing throughout her life, Ellen would see all sorts of nonphysical people. "Some were stuck and confused," she related. "There were times when they seemed to be looking for help, and they had a quality of fear or confusion or trauma in their face. But the beings who started appearing to me after my mother's death were angelic. They were teachers. I remember the first being that talked to me after my mother's death; he had scintil-lating light in his face. It was like his skin was illumined. He and other teachers I saw do look like people, but they are more energy and less flesh. When you see the face, you can see the movement of each particle. It's more scintillating."

Bill also saw angelic beings during an unusual night more than sixty years ago. Formerly a corporate vice-president and now a pro-fessional therapist, Bill recalled a moment from childhood that has served as a touchstone: the faces that he saw were comforting and beautiful. "I lived with my extended Italian immigrant family, four-teen of us living in a Chicago suburb," he described. "I awoke in the middle of the night. My bedroom had no electricity, so it was usually very dark. But when I awoke, it was very bright and suddenly the ceiling and the roof went away. Going out from my bedroom ceiling was a golden staircase leading up to this brilliance. I was called to come and look at this and be with this brilliance. So I started up the stairs. There was no railing; it was like a golden path with steps. There were these entities alongside the stairway to keep me from falling. (What I realized many years later when I started to read about angels and seraphim, and so forth, was that this was a hierarchy of angels leading to this incredible brilliance. Words like *beauty* and *purity* don't even begin to describe the feeling.)

"So I went up to listen and heard what life was about and what heaven was. And it was awesome and overwhelming to me as a five-year-old. And 'the brilliance' recognized that I was overwhelmed. There were no words but there was always—and it has been from this point on—a language that comes to me. For me it is in the form of a voice and words. I was not in my bed; I could look back down and see my room and my uncle who shared the bedroom with me—I could see him from above. I came back down the staircase and ended up in the hall by my parents' door. Throughout my life in times of difficulty I've tried to remember the lessons that were shown me as a five-year-old: that we're connected, that we're guided, and, mostly, that we're loved."

Children sometimes have imaginary friends. A child's doll, in moments of intense play, becomes a baby treated with great care. A stuffed animal becomes a friend to cuddle and talk to in the midst of a tough day. Maybe a child will have an imaginary friend who becomes a playmate. This rich play is a way for a child to experiment with all sorts of roles and situations. But sometimes the imaginary friend may be something more than imagination. For example, at 2 1/2, Laura had a friend who was invisible to her mother but whom she claimed to see quite clearly. Her mother said, "Laura called her friend Hana Peach. Hana Peach would come and play with her, and Laura would often tell me about her friend in great detail. She explained that her friend was a little Japanese girl. While Laura had never had any exposure to Japanese, years later we learned that *hana* means 'peach' in Japanese, and Laura always gave us both names."

As a four-year-old, Tammy had a playmate named Robert, whom only she could see. But Robert was completely real to her, different from her dolls or make-believe characters. Describing him, Tammy said, "What is strange to me is that I really saw three beings. Robert is the one who interacted with me the most. He was small, about my size. Even though he looked like a child, he didn't seem childlike. He seemed to know more. I could talk with him either with my thoughts or out loud if no one was around. Sort of just beyond Robert was a female who looked like an angel. She was floating and had a flowing white, gauzy gown. It seemed that she was observing and protecting both Robert and me. And just behind her there was another being that I sensed was more genderless and more formless. It seemed like each was standing behind the other, but it is very difficult to describe. The memory of it has never left me."

When Diana, whom we met in chapter 1, became a parent herself, she began to doubt her communication with her deceased father.

She wondered if she was just imagining this relationship that she had had since his death when she was twelve. One night she needed more proof: "At 10:30 I remember telling my dad that I needed a sign that this was all real. At 2:30 that morning, my daughter, Claire, who was not quite two but very verbal, woke up and was pointing into space. She seemed a little nervous and scared and kept pointing toward the spot. 'He's right here, Mom, he's right here.' This began to happen almost every night at bedtime. 'That boy here again, Mom,' she would say. Then she started saying that she also saw a dog: 'My dog here.' At one point, I felt the presence of my father, and Claire dropped her bottle and pointed to that spot. 'That boy here again, Momma.' she said.

"Just last night I was reading to Claire in her room. Suddenly I felt my dad's presence. Claire looked up and said, 'That big boy here again, Momma.' I put my hand in the air and my fingers tingled. I took her into her crib and she lay down and kept looking at that part of the room with smiles, saying, 'Big boy here now, Momma.' The next morning I took down a picture of my dad from the shelf. She smiled and laughed and said, 'That's that daddy.' I said, 'This is my daddy.' She shook her head yes and smiled and said, 'That's the big boy.' 'Is this who is watching you?' I asked. She nodded her head yes. I said, 'Where is he?' She walked back to the room with me in tow and said while pointing, 'Right there.' I said, 'Is he your friend?' She smiled and laughed and nodded her head."

Diana posed the question to her father in her journal: "Why are you here with Claire?" This was the answer: 'I want to be with her while she can still get to know me. She won't be able to be with me like this forever, and I want her to know me while she can. I just want to be their granddad for a while.'"

Beyond Time

In *The Four Quartets*, T. S. Elliot says, "To be conscious is not to be in time."[17] Children are often "not in time." Their sense of clock and calendar is quite different from typical adult time. Even for adults, we know that time is not only a consistent march into the future; we have moments that are better measured by quality and intensity, rather than quantity. Time may disappear when we get absorbed in a moment, or it may stretch into an eternity in the back of the car on a long trip: "How much longer till we get there?"

Beyond these normal alterations of time sense, some children also bridge the gap between present, past, and future. The most startling evidence comes from children's memories and recollections of times past and their precognitive knowing about the future. Physicists like Einstein, as well as philosophers and mystics, tell us that our linear, sequential sense of time is only one way of perceiving it. Time is relative to how fast we are traveling and is described as both eternal and immediate. It is almost too much for our rational consciousness to hold the paradoxes of time—for example, how can something both be about to happen and have already happened? We do not need to figure this out; we can simply take the direct experience of children to help us understand that time bends in a multidimensional world. Like Hildegard von Bingen, who would sometimes predict future events (and who began her visions as a very young child), children sometimes tell us about what is to come and what happened long ago.[18]

June said, "I knew that I was going away, but I didn't know when. I would see myself on a train leaving home and traveling to a distant city. This image would come regularly for several years. It just flashed through my mind when I was awake, but I wasn't sure what I was experiencing. What I saw and felt was not like going on a fun adventure, but it was a traumatic event. The vision felt devastating. This went on for years, but I never told anyone. And then it happened. My mother went into the hospital for TB, and I was sent away to live with relatives in another part of the country. I got on that exact train that I had seen so many times before, and it felt just like it had in my visions. My dream had come true, and I didn't get to see my mother for three years."

Children not only tell us about what will happen, but also apparently about what happened long ago. Theresa tells about her experience with three-year-old Nicole: "The other day, Nicole and I were eating breakfast and out of the blue she said, 'A long, long time ago when I was a little boy I could turn the light switch on and off all by myself.' I asked her what her name was then and she said, 'I don't remember right now,' but that she was eleven years old then and I was her mommy. After a few bites of toast she continued, 'And a long, long time ago when you were a little boy, I was your mommy, and Grammy and Papa and my aunt and uncle were there then.' I was just listening at that point and said something like, 'Oh, they were?' and she said, 'Yes, Mommy, we all take turns. Everybody takes turns.' So I said something to the effect that 'Mommy can't remember things as clearly as you can sometimes.'

"Well, she put her toast down, looked me right in the eye, and said, 'Mommy, I know everything you know.' At that point she seemed to engulf me, and I felt in awe and humbled and had absolutely no response. Nothing like being humbled with the truth by a three-year-old. It's so fascinating to really hear what she shares with me about people's 'colors' and her angels and the fairies."

Nancy and Llael (ten at the time), whom we met earlier in the chapter, were driving home from school and work on a local highway that had a train track parallel to it. Nancy explained, "She was commenting to me on something from the day when all of a sudden the train blew its horn right out the window directly opposite her. It was winter and dark already, so it took me a few moments before I realized that she was hardly breathing. It took a good twenty to thirty minutes for her heart rate and emotions to settle down. Llael told me she was watching her lover die in front of the train. She said it happened at Bath and commented on what a funny name that was. I told her that there is a town in England called Bath."

Ian Stevenson, formerly head of psychiatry at the University of Virginia Medical School, set out to look into historic documentation such as municipal records (of birth, marriage, death, hospital records, property deeds, and so forth) for evidence of alleged past-life events.[19] He would take a report such as Llael's accident in Bath, gather all identifying details he could, such as names, dates, and descriptions of locations and events, and research the records to find if an accident and death had occurred at that time and place. What he discovered was that he was indeed often able to find clear documentation confirming these events. His meticulous research provides compelling evidence that the recollections and emotional responses of these children correspond to events that happened before their lives. He even found that physical symptoms—a chronic sore throat, a rash on the arm, or even a birthmark—correlated with the location of an injury that occurred to a person in this alleged past life. We will explore this phenomenon further in chapter 8.

Karen's daughter, aged six, announced one day that she had died in a street fight from a stabbing. "She asked me, 'Mommy, what does this mean?'" Karen reported. "She said that she had numerous dreams and also waking visions of this, and she described the event in such detail that I was amazed because this kind of event is not common to our lives. It didn't really scare her—just perplexed her. She said it was like it happened to someone else, but somehow she thought it was herself."

Most of the world's population ascribes to the principle of reincarnation, and, according to a 1999 Gallop poll, approximately one-quarter of Americans accept this notion. While reincarnation is a center point of Hindu and Buddhist belief, it is also found across the world's spiritual traditions. The Jewish Kabbalah, in the *Zohar*, or *The Book of Splendor*, traces explicitly the cycle of death and rebirth.[20] Sufism, the mystical center of Islam, uses reincarnation as a cornerstone of its faith. Although the Christian church has spent considerable energy from the fourth century onward repressing the idea of reincarnation, even Jesus Christ is said to have made clear reference to it when he explained that the deceased Elias had come back as John the Baptist.[21] The Lebanese poet Kahlil Gibran captured the idea eloquently: "Forget not that I shall come back to you. . . . A little while, a moment of rest upon the wind, and another woman shall bear me."[22]

Children's awareness reaches into the past and the future in remarkable ways. There experiences may help us begin to fathom the mystery of time.

Rescues

One of the most sickening feelings for a parent is helplessly watching their child in the midst of an accident. Sometimes a child gets lucky and ends up with just a scratch and some tears. Chance or good luck seems a reasonable explanation most of those times, but in other moments, children show us and tell us that the invisible world offers direct and divine intervention. The following very typical accounts suggest the benevolence of a world we cannot see.

Ginger is a computer project manager and her husband a retired military officer. One evening before their daughter, Eryn, was two years old, she was playing in her room on the third story of their home. Ginger says, "I was upstairs with her until I heard the buzzer go off on the dryer down on the first landing. I ran downstairs to grab the sheets out of the dryer. In the meantime Skip [her husband] had just arrived home. He and I walked upstairs together toward the second landing. Skip had a nightly ritual where he would come home and Eryn would run and lunge at him. He would scoop her up and give her hugs and kisses.

"On this evening, we both saw something that defied the laws of physics. Eryn came racing out of her room. We were standing on the second-floor landing looking up just as she lunged forward off the third-floor stairs. There was no way either of us could catch her—it was an instant of sheer frozen panic where you feel so helpless. Suddenly, in midair, Eryn was propelled backward against the wall at the top of the stairs. We raced up the flight of stairs to see her sitting there grinning at something that we couldn't see."

John, three, had gone with his older stepbrother to visit some friends who lived in a third-floor apartment. There was a back door that led off the kitchen out onto a balcony. Within just a few minutes of their arrival, John managed to get up on a chair that was on the balcony, leaned over, and fell three stories, landing on the ground below. One of their hosts saw him just as he went over and immediately called 911 for an ambulance while the others raced downstairs. John was conscious and was told not to move. He wasn't crying, but he seemed frightened by all the commotion. The ambulance arrived quickly, and John was rushed to the nearby hospital. Remarkably, he didn't break any bones and had only a minor cut or two. His mother met him at the hospital, and once she realized that he was fine, she asked him what had happened. He said, "A man in a gold suit caught me when I fell," and he wanted to know who he was.

Nancy, a schoolteacher, says, "When my youngest son was four years old, he was on the back porch playing with his Matchbox cars. One of the cars went off the back of the porch and he went right after it. He launched himself headfirst off the porch, when suddenly his direction changed; he turned right side up and landed on his feet. Watching that was unbelievable enough, but then he said that he saw an angel grab him, turn him right side up and place him on his feet. He said the angel was kind of white, and looked almost like a statue."

Mark, an airline pilot, said that his five-year-old son fell from a third story window at their house. He related, "This was our worst nightmare come true. We were in complete panic as we raced downstairs. When we arrived at the spot where he had fallen, he was sitting on the ground, still a little surprised but just fine. He was looking around and asked where 'those guys' were. 'What guys?' we asked. 'The guys dressed in gold who caught me.'"

A Word of Caution

The mystics and the sages have often described their own ability to sense the invisible. However, a great many also offer a word of caution about these capacities. They warn that it is possible to become overly fascinated by these powers and lose our way on the spiritual path if we are not careful. For example, people who spend their effort on developing their psychic abilities without simultaneously developing compassion, intellect, emotional maturity, and personal responsibility may become preoccupied with their own achievement and, ultimately, destructive toward their own and others' spiritual growth. One twelve-year-old girl expressed an especially balanced way of seeing her ability of telepathy. She said, "It's hard to think what life would be like without it; I'm so used to it. But it's not the most important thing to me; I've got it and so I'll use it."

Developing spiritual potential means integrating and balancing all the different parts of oneself. If you are highly intuitive, you can develop your ability but not have a "together life." It is easy to find folks who are quite psychic, but whose lives are not integrated. If you have sensitivity, it is not so hard to get answers as it is to live by them. In the end, it is never our sheer capacities or our wondrous experiences that determine a spiritual life, it is what we do with them— what we learn and how we live—that is the measure of our spirituality. Profound events may be important milestones on our journey, and intuitive capacities may be a powerful and misunderstood way of knowing, but they become out of balance if not guided by love and wisdom. As so many of the sages and mystics have warned, any human power—physical, intellectual, intuitive—may ultimately be destructive if not guided by the energy of the heart.

By the way, here we are only touching the tip of the iceberg of children's inner knowing and of this multidimensional realm. I have been talking with children who demonstrate remarkable capacities for healing, describe complex technology that does not currently exist, claim to see fairies, describe lives on other planets, talk with God, and have all sorts of other remarkable experiences. Especially with children, there are more things in heaven and earth than we have dreamt of. Our task as parents and friends is to respect and try to understand what and how children see, and, most especially, to encourage them instead of judging them.

Part 2

Balancing Heaven *and* Earth

Chapter 6

Spiritual Parenting

We enter into a sacred contract with our children, whether they arrive with great planning and intention or they are unexpectedly delivered on our doorstep in the middle of our life. The nature of a contract, any contract, is to draw people together for a purpose. Throughout this chapter we will explore the essential nature of that contract as it relates to our role as parents and spiritual friends as well as to our relationship with our own inner child.

Jim and Krista had an unexpected introduction to a surprising dimension of their own contract when they heard their three-year-old explain the roots of their marriage through his eyes. At the dinner table one evening, their son announced out of the blue, "Heaven was really a fun place." After a few moments of silence, he went on, "You know, I'm glad I'm here." His parents replied, "We're so glad you're here, too." He continued, "Yeah, when I was in heaven I asked God to give me a telescope, and I looked down here. And I said I like her and I like him." Krista said, "Oh, really, that's nice. Daddy and I knew we were going to have you." He said, "Yeah, but this was before you knew Daddy. I helped to bring you guys together. I thought you guys would be really nice to me."

This revelation struck a very deep chord in both parents. Krista explained, "When Jim and I were dating, we had this uncanny sense of our son, who was not even conceived yet. We would talk about him all the time and we even toasted him in our wedding video. I guess it was pretty weird and not the kind of thing we might be likely to do. But we just had this incredibly vivid sense of him being around us throughout the time we were dating. What he told us that night at dinner made perfect sense."

Who are these children with whom we enter into a sacred contract? We often get a glimpse of children's unique personalities even as infants. The way they respond, the things they are drawn to, what they evoke in us all begin to demonstrate that they are their own unique beings right from the start. One mother describes how an unusual first meeting with her children helped her recognize even more deeply who they were. "I had a dream of who my children were before they were born. I saw these young adults and what they would be doing at that time. I saw my son as a young man working with a Chinese teacher. I didn't know what to make of this at the time, and I never shared the image with my son. Twenty years later I have to smile when I think of that image because my son is now studying Taoist philosophy in China."

She continues, "I had these images of my children, and from this I could see that they weren't *my* children. They were their own individual selves becoming my children. This was a revelation for me. And I think that one of the most important messages for parents is, 'Your child isn't just your child.' The questions then become, 'Why has your child come?' and 'How can you help them fulfill their purpose here?'"

When we recognize a child first as a complete spiritual being rather than merely as our growing offspring, a powerful shift occurs just as it did for this mother. What arises is respect and reverence for the uniqueness of this soul in front of us even though they may not yet have fully ripened as a human. Our children do not belong to us; they belong to their own soul and calling.

Kahlil Gibran tells us, "Children come through us but not from us."[1] We are the gateway through which children enter and explore the world, but they are not merely "ours." Through some unseen cosmic agreement, we serve as their sponsors, hosts, and guides. Perhaps our child is like a visitor from Mars or a teacher, an old friend, or a new playmate, who soon becomes family.

It is important to recognize that biological mothers and fathers and legal guardians are not the only parents. We share in parenting as teachers, relatives, friends, and neighbors. "Spiritual parents" come in all kinds of guises:

- A neighbor who takes a child to the library when she takes her own child, opening new horizons and stimulating a mind
- The elderly friend who provides a soft cookie and an even softer ear as she opens a soothing and compassionate heart to a child
- The coach or teacher who notices a child's effort and who, by simply saying, "Nice job today," affirms the child's worth and maybe his or her very existence
- The friend who sees that a child is capable of more and shapes the child's character by expecting more—good manners, kindness, having their homework done
- The relative who is honest with a child and thereby reminds him or her how to be truthful
- The teacher who validates the inner life by asking for a child's ideas and opinions about important topics
- The eccentric relative or friend who shows the child that it is OK to be just who he or she is

These are the simple day-to-day spiritual relationships that shape a life. They soothe and support, bring inspiration and imagination, and affirm a child's value so that the inner life can flourish.

What we know of resilient children—those who have grown up in very difficult, abusive, or neglectful situations but who have thrived nonetheless—is that they nearly always have had a "leg-up" person—a spiritual friend—someone who made a difference in their lives—who saw a spark in them, who noticed them, who offered a kind word or took genuine interest in their lives. All of us have the opportunity to spiritually parent in this way, and at times children need more than one or two parents.

Sometimes the main parent plays his or her role and fulfills the contract by giving the child something to push against. Through the child's eyes, the parent might even become more of a symbol (of authority or whatever) than a person. This is sometimes the perspective of adolescents as they struggle to individuate. Parents provide limits so that the children can clarify their ideas and beliefs, and find their own limits. In such situations, other "parents" or "spiritual friends" are especially important serving as other symbols—role models, kind nurturers, listeners, visionaries, wise elders, mirrors in which children can find their own reflection, and maybe even more demanding ogres ("I guess my parents aren't all that bad after all"). When we serve some small but significant part in a child's life, we become part of the child's family; we become kin.

In *The Education of Little Tree* by Forrest Carter, the narrator, a young boy who, upon the loss of his own parents, has been sent to live on a rural mountainside with his grandparents, explains the meaning of "kin" as his grandparents knew it: "'I kin ye,' it meant, 'I understand ye.' To them, love and understanding was the same thing. Granma said you couldn't love something that you didn't understand; nor could you love people, nor God, if you didn't understand the people and God. Grandpa said back before his time, 'kinfolks' meant any folks that you understood and had an understanding with, so it meant 'loved folks.'"[2] Perhaps it is our greatest task as parents and spiritual friends to understand the child. But understanding does not simply mean figuring something out; the word means to "stand among," implying that we hold and behold our children.

Beholding

The heart of understanding comes through what Thich Nhat Hanh calls "pure recognition," which means seeing without judgment.[3] This begins as an attitude of simple appreciation and a willingness to try to see the world through the child's eyes—to stand among. This is the practice of beholding, and it is a gateway to love.

For a moment, look at a child, whether in your mind or face-to-face, through the eye of your heart. Stare in a way that is not considered polite for adults, but in that absorbed way that children often stare. Let yourself fall into this child with openness, curiosity, and simple appreciation. The goal is just to see and feel him or her without judgment—pure recognition. You may notice the light in the room seems to change; your chest may warm or ache just a bit. You have reached into the heart of the child in the only way possible—through your own heart. You begin to feel the spirit of the child, to see him or her as perfect, radiant, and mysterious, in spite of that child leaving dirty dishes in the living room, or fighting with a brother or sister, or being mean in some way that shocks you. From this vantage point, the child is remarkable. In this moment, he or she loses all weight of being a burden or an imposition on you. The child transcends the gravity of who you hope he or she will be and instead emerges with the lightness of who he or she is in essence.

It is so easy to get caught in our judgments and frustrations as parents, but this simple exercise of staring can serve as a kind of centering prayer or meditation amid the bustle of parenting. Perhaps once a week or even once an evening, after our children have gone to sleep, we can behold them in this way. We stare with no goal except to see them with the fresh, soft eyes of appreciation.

Psychologist Ira Progoff tells us, "Love depends upon the capacity to reach beneath the surface of persons, to feel and touch the seed of life that is hidden there. And love becomes a power when it is capable of evoking that seed and drawing it forth from its hiding place."[4] Beholding the child in this way nourishes the seed of the child, even if we cannot fully see what it is or what it is to become.

Levi had been a handful for his parents. He was extremely demanding, often out of control, and a little emotional powerhouse who just seemed to overwhelm his family. He was only four years old. His parents tried one thing after another to help him and them survive his childhood. At the suggestion of a friend, they decided to have him tested by a psychologist who specialized in intellectually gifted children. His mother tells the story: "Right after we had him tested, we left Denver and drove to Colorado Springs, where we stopped for the night at a motel. But before we got into our room, Levi gave me a hug and said, 'I just love our family.' And I said, 'I just love our family too.' I was wondering what prompted his sudden comment, and then he said, 'Since we went to that place [the psychologist's office], it seems that you really want to know me now.'

"A little later that evening, we were all playing hide-and-go-seek in the hotel room, so you can imagine how many places there were to hide. So I decided I was going to get under the covers and hide like they were. Levi exclaims: 'Stop! Stop! Time out! Mom, close your eyes!' I said, 'OK, they're closed.' He said, 'No, really, keep them closed. I have a great surprise for you!' He went through the whole thing of really making this a big deal. 'Close them! Are they closed?! Are they really closed tight?!' Finally, after building and building this up, he said, 'OK, mom, here's the surprise! Here it comes! OK, Mom, you can open your eyes!'

"He was standing over me with that incredible spark in his eye. And it was like looking at Levi, but it felt like someone bigger and different, and it seemed that there was a silver light around him. He held his arms out to me with a big smile, no words, then he covered his hands over his heart and said, 'It's *me*, Mom!' That was his surprise.

I was totally overwhelmed. Tears came to my eyes, and I felt like I was seeing him in a whole new way. I hugged him and said, 'Thanks; I'm really sorry it took me so long to get to know you like this. I'm going to do the best I can do to help you with whatever you need to do.' And he looked at me and put his hands on my face, and this little four-year-old said, 'Thanks, Mom, I really needed to hear that.'"

Understanding makes the other *kin*, it makes the other "loved folks." Our greatest offering is to have the presence and allow the space for our children to show us who they really are.

Waking Up

Parenting becomes an intentional spiritual discipline when we practice the art of understanding. This requires more than *showing up* for our life and the life of the child; it means that we *wake up*. Waking up means being present and mindful—watching and feeling the child, ourself, and our relationship. Presence allows us to be more aware of what is called for in a situation and to engage deeply and spontaneously in the relationship. The opposite of this is to be disconnected, distant, unaware, self-absorbed, distracted, numb, and caught in the whirlwind of our own thoughts, reactions, and agendas.

If we are distracted when eating a good meal, we will hardly be able to taste the food. We will have fueled our body in the most basic way, but we will have missed the texture and smell, the color and taste, the care of preparation and the marvel of abundance. When we really are awake and take the time to savor a meal, it nourishes more than our body—it sustains our soul. Even after the food is gone, we may draw sustenance from the felt memory of that flavor, the soothing of the warm tea, the sense of belonging as we sit with our friend or family. Artist Julia Cameron says this about paying attention: "The quality of life is in proportion, always, to the capacity for delight.

The capacity for delight is the gift of paying attention."[5]

When we are awake as parents and friends, we get the full power and gift of our relationship with children. We are deeply nourished by it and, in turn, provide nourishment for our children in the form of our earnest listening, thoughtful responses, and genuine meeting. Such presence is described in many traditions and has been referred to as "mindfulness." To be mindful is to be nonjudgmentally aware in the here and now. Mindfulness includes the ability to witness the contents of our consciousness—our thoughts, feelings, impulses, and so forth—without getting lost in thought or habitual and mindless reactions. It is not so much learning to do something as it is undoing the habits of mindlessness.

This practice does not require sitting meditation or years of training. It is activated by simply taking a breath and being aware of where we are right now, in this moment, without being overly attached and therefore overwhelmed by our thoughts and other reactions. Through this gentle awareness, we create more spaciousness and spontaneity in our consciousness, instead of being driven by a mind on automatic pilot. As we hear our own parents' voices rising within us or find ourselves withholding our love as a message of disapproval or feeling helpless as we are taken emotional hostage by some tiny tot, mindfulness invites us to pause inwardly, take a breath, and perhaps ask ourselves, What's that about? Is there a better way through this? What's the real lesson here? Where am I right now?

This practice is very simple and remarkably powerful. I remember a week some years back when my wife was out of the country and I was trying to juggle my work, her work, and our two young children and all their activities. It was to be the longest period of time that I was alone with our children. By the end of the first day I was already tense, resentful, and very curt with them. Something would have to change drastically, or it was looking like a miserable week was in store.

After putting the children to bed, I did manage to be still for a few minutes and ask myself, What's really important during this week? How could this go better? I realized my expectations for my work were unrealistic and unnecessary during this week. I then stripped away my own agenda for getting anything except what was absolutely necessary done and decided that the number one priority was to just be with my children.

The next day felt so completely different that I still chuckle about it. After a dreadful start, we ended up having a glorious week. I enjoyed them so much and fell more deeply in love with them than I thought was possible. I loved being with them in this way and secretly looked forward to the next time my wife would go out of town. What felt to me like an absolute transformation was possible simply by my pausing for a moment and being present to the here and now. The opportunity is available to all of us at every moment.

Mindfulness does not take us away from action and engagement with the world, but allows us to be fully present in our action, whether eating food or helping a child with homework. As awareness develops and we simply and honestly observe and tolerate our own reactions, we also gain a tolerance for others. We come to appreciate their uniqueness and lead with compassion rather than judgment. Fundamentally, being awake is an act of respect, and it sends the message that the child is worthy of our full attention. We respect the child enough to listen and understand him or her.

Respect can be expressed by how richly, honestly, and deeply we respond to a child's questions and often how willing and well we are able to pose more questions in return: "What do *you* think?" And it is not only our responses, but also the way we establish our requests and demands that conveys respect. Respect comes when we explain why something has to be done, not just that it has to be done. "Because I said so" is a disrespectful and ineffective response and sets up a power struggle with the child. Explaining the purpose of something gives the child a bigger picture. Blind obedience is ineffective for most children today; explanations help them learn how the world works and elicits their cooperation.

Explaining the "why" often gives them the sense of meaning that allows them to move forward and find their agreement with your request. Sometimes the why is quite specific and logical, but other times our reasons defy reasonableness. Sometimes the best explanation we can offer is just to let children know that this is the way that people on this planet operate. Beyond explanation, we can also ask for their help: "I'm tired and really need your help today." This elicits a partnership through honesty and information rather than through demanding compliance at every turn. Of course, nothing works 100 percent of the time, but I am still amazed at how the energy changes with this kind of request. And sometimes it is not what we say but how we say it.

At eight years old, my daughter explained to me how a request could be more effective, that is, how I could elicit her cooperation instead of her resentment. After some ranting on my part about some earth-shattering transgression on the order of leaving toothpaste all over the sink, she offered this feedback to me: "When you talk to me like that [ranting], it hurts my feelings. If you are upset about something, you can tell me but please don't yell at me. It hurts. I get it without you yelling."

Spiritual parenting implies that we are present not only to the child, but also to ourselves. Presence allows us to realize that unexamined anger moves us backward and that our own expectations may get in the way of the child's life. We can begin to see parenting as a practice of our own spiritual growth—it truly is a spiritual path. We practice presence when we ask ourselves, Where am I now, in this instant? Why am I so upset about this? What is triggered in me? Does this have anything to do with my own parents? How am I withholding my love to this child and even to myself? How can I be of service to this child? How can I be gentle and loving with my own inner child?

As parents, it is often the hangover from our own childhood—the parenting *we* received—that we are challenged to either overcome or honor. Through presence we practice the art of centering ourselves so that we can act from our highest spiritual aspirations and our biggest heart, rather than from our automatic habits. Many of us have to reparent ourselves in order to do better for our children; otherwise we simply repeat what was done to us. As one mother told me when I asked her what was most significant about being a parent, "It was realizing that I had to be the one who broke the cycle of abuse in my family. I had to do something better to my daughter than what was done to me. It was my responsibility. And I did it! When Leigen has her own children, she will have to overcome other things I probably did wrong, but she won't have that abuse to overcome." The child is helped and the parent heals.

The Inner Parent

We never parent alone. Beyond whatever partner or community we may have, the child is our partner in parenting. At the most fundamental level, the baby tells us when he or she is hungry or uncomfortable by crying. And messages come in all sorts of other ways as well. Sri Aurobindo, the Indian sage, told us that there is an "inner teacher" or inner parent within each of us. This is the part of us that knows what we need, that is wise, that directs the seed toward its blossoming, and that is connected to the wisdom of the universe. He suggested that the greatest offering of a teacher or parent is to listen to the inner teacher of the child through the ear of his or her own inner teacher, intuition. It is as if there is a conversation between these two inner teachers.

Carl Rogers, the influential humanistic therapist, described it this way: "It seems that my inner spirit has reached out and touched the inner spirit of the other. Our relationship transcends itself and becomes part of something larger." This is exactly what is realized between parent and child when we listen for the inner teacher. The message may take the form of a glimpse, a feeling, or a hunch of something to do or say. As Rogers said, "When I can relax and be close to the transcendental core of me, then I may behave in strange and impulsive ways in the relationship, ways which I cannot justify rationally, which have nothing to do with my rational thought processes. But these strange behaviors turn out to be *right*, in some odd way."[6] As we wake up, we are increasingly able to hear the inner teacher though that small voice of our intuition.

While insight often arrives spontaneously, we can activate the energy of this intuition through our intent. A parent simply needs to pose the question, What is the best I can offer here? This is an invocation, a prayer to the inner teacher and whatever guides the universe may provide. We then must listen carefully for the response. There is a familiar old story of a devout man who is stranded during a flood and who prays to God for help. A makeshift raft floats right under the tree and he elects not to leave. "I'm waiting for God to help," he reminds himself. A man comes by with a boat and offers to help. "No, thanks, I'm waiting for God to deliver me," the stranded man replies. Next, a helicopter comes by and dangles a ladder for the man to grab. Again, he declines, knowing that God will answer his prayers. Finally the waters overtake him and he drowns in great shock and disappointment, believing that his prayers have been ignored. Upon meeting God in the afterworld, he complains about his fate and cannot understand why God did not hear his prayers. God responds, "Who do you think sent you the raft, the boat, and the helicopter?" Oops.

The answers to our prayers and questions come in unexpected ways. We have to be awake enough to hear and see: a neighbor uncharacteristically mentions a new book that seems to be a bull's-eye for a problem we have; a telephone call from a friend offers some spontaneous advice; a child tells us what is called for in his or her own way; a spontaneous impulse arises to change our diet; a dream arrives in the middle of the night; a still, small voice whispers insight; or maybe an angel appears directly to a child. We need only to ask and stay awake enough to listen.

Holding

While each parenting contract is unique, the bottom line seems to be nonnegotiable. Our responsibility is to behold and to "hold." Holding means to provide the safety and the clearing that allow children to find their way in the world. The impulse to provide safety and nourishment to our children is instinctual; it is part of our animal nature, just as it is for mice or ducks. That deep place where we are connected to the earth gives us the messages we need.

Before our first child was born, my wife and I could feel the impulses rising in us to provide a safe nest for our little hatchling. We went to classes, we read, we bought the safest car we could afford. We still did not really know what becoming parents would be like, but we were ready to take the leap, and we were both excited and a little nervous. Throughout the pregnancy, I had this strange worry that seemed to anchor my anxious uncertainties about parenting in a single concern. I just could not figure out how I would ever know if the baby was the right temperature—if she was a little chilly, or too hot. She would not be able to speak, so how would I tell? And when I asked, the answers I received were never very satisfying. A nurse said, "Oh, you'll be able to tell." The doctor said, "Whatever you're wearing will be about the right weight for the baby." Not good enough! How would I know?

I think this worry was like my new-parent-anxiety lint trap. It seemed to capture all my worries about parenting in one little fairly harmless-looking question. This kind of anxiety is just a sign that we are feeling the primal instinct to nurture and protect. It is not to be avoided, but instead honored as part of our connection with creation. After my daughter was born, the question disappeared. I did just seem to know, and I also knew to "ask" her by holding her close and feeling her body. At whatever age, holding means that we stay in touch enough to feel each other's warmth.

Holding implies more than physical safety and sustenance. If we are distracted, angry, only going through the motions, what message are we sending? We comfort the psyche and soothe the soul by how we hold a child. Can the child fall asleep in complete trust and safety in our arms? If we can hold in this way, we teach them to trust and we teach constructive surrender. And at the same time, can *we* surrender to the peace of holding a sleepy or sleeping child? We hold and heal ourself as we hold that child. A young child holds her baby doll; we hold her. We soothe and heal one another.

Family rituals and routines are a way of holding. Family meals, bedtime stories, back rubs, a family joke, special foods and special places, celebrations, rites of passage such as weddings and funerals, walks, even chore time, all provide a sense of dependability that help children feel at home. Yet it is easy to overlook the importance and meaning of these little things.

As bedtime approached for his four-year-old son, Francis would start singing an old song, "Good Night, Irene," as the signal that it was time for bed. He would scoop up the child and carry him toward the bedroom as he was singing. One evening, Francis was distracted by some problems at work and forgot to sing the song. As he was tucking his son in bed, the child had a concerned look on his face and, with a very serious tone, asked, "Dad, what happened?" "What do you mean?" Francis replied. "You didn't sing 'Good Night Onion Ring' tonight."

The little things are like glue that holds us together; they serve as touchstones for our lives. And the safety does not just hold, it also teaches. We demonstrate responsibility through our reliability; we teach trustworthiness through our dependability. We create a container of safety not only by a lock on a cabinet door or a safe car seat, but also and especially by our energy. Children are especially sensitive to the energies of others. They may pick up another's moods or thoughts and sense subtle energies in a variety of ways.

One child told her mother about the shapes and colors that she saw. Jane had had a difficult day in a demanding week. She had been wrestling with conflict with a frustrating coworker. While she had physically left work several hours before, she was still feeling the resentment and still fussing about this coworker in her mind, although she had tried not to show any of this to her daughter. Just before bedtime, her young daughter said, "Mom, what's the matter?" "Nothing. Why?" "You have black spots on you and dark lines coming out of you. It looks bad and I don't really want to be near it."

We can create safety by generating a kind of force field through our intention. We may call upon all sorts of protection in the form of prayers. We may also create a sphere of safety through imagining protection as a gold ball surrounding the child or perhaps calling on an angel of protection. Thoughts and intention are energy. While science cannot yet directly observe or measure thought, it has already well established its power (for example, the evidence on the effect of prayer and healing that we discussed in chapter 3). We do not need to wait for more evidence to use the power of our intention.

Michael was in second grade and had had a difficult childhood so far. He had been severely deprived and abused as an infant, and his aunt and uncle were now raising him. He was still struggling in school, but he had come a long way. One day, very sheepishly and in private, he told his teacher, Mrs. White, about an angel that came to visit him regularly. His teacher said, "It was easy to tell by his voice and his demeanor that this was very important and very real to him. Almost daily for several weeks, he would mention that he would see this angel. One day he spontaneously blurted out, 'Look, Mrs. White, there's that angel!' He was staring outside. We had huge windows, floor to ceiling, in our classroom. I said, 'Michael, can you describe him to me?' Still looking out the windows, he looked down at the ground and then he looked up—way up, like twelve feet high. Michael said, 'He has a sword in his hand, he is whitish, he's strong.' He added a moment later, 'He makes me feel safe.'"

While Michael's angel, like my daughter's, arrived unexpectedly, in a time of need we can invite children to find their own source—an angel or another healing, wise, or protective image—through the gateway of their imagination. "Is there a place that you can see in your mind that feels safe?" we might ask as we comfort them at their bedside or in a ride in the car. We could suggest, "Close your eyes, if it feels OK to, and imagine someone who would be able to help you with this problem," then ask, "What would this person do; what might they advise you to do?" "Ask and ye shall receive," the Bible instructs.[7] Sometimes a parent's job is simply to help the child to ask and then be still enough to listen.

We also hold and protect children by listening and trusting them. Di and her family were at a big national event in which, among other things, there was a demonstration of army parachutists. "We got there early and got settled in a good position to see everything. Right from the start, my older child said he did not like where we were standing. I was surprised because we were right at the edge of the circle with a great view of everything. We ended up moving because our son, then two years old, was fidgeting like crazy and the show had been delayed. When we returned, we settled at the other side of the circle, and our young son stopped fidgeting. It was not as good a spot because we were farther away, but by then others had settled down where we had been before. The show finally started. Within just a few minutes two of the parachutists ran into problems and landed in the crowd in the exact spot we had first settled in, and two young boys were severely injured."

Holding On and Letting Go

How tight do we hold on and when do we let go? When do we guide and when do we get out of the way? Parents who offer too many and too rigid limits or those who offer too few do not do their children any favors. Children reared in these extremes suffer from lower self-esteem and all the problems tied to it. But in that broad middle ground, parents can give healthy limits and liberating freedoms. Whether we are dealing with a child learning to walk or one going off to college, the challenge is to provide the right balance between protection from the world and freedom to explore it firsthand. We do not need our children to grow up to be "good," compliant, and dependent; they need to grow toward mature independence.

While parents can be rigid and unyielding, they can equally be afraid to set limits. They may back down because they are exhausted or perhaps afraid of being taken emotional hostage. Children's spiritual, social, and psychological development depends on their ability to control themselves. Reasonable and consistent limits not only help them to live in society, but they especially help them to learn to control their own impulses and gain mastery over themselves.

Self-discipline develops when we cannot have what we want right this second— ice cream, a new toy—and we learn to deal with it. We may throw a tantrum at first, but in time we develop more control and patience over our reactions. We learn that it is not the end of the world if we do not get everything we ask for; some new delight will come along in time. If as parents we rescue children prematurely from their frustration or give in to their tantrums—

"Oh forget it. Here's the ice cream"; "OK, if you're going to make that big of a deal, go ahead and watch TV"; "I'm just too tired to fight with you; have it your way"—we reinforce manipulation instead of self-mastery. As the German author and mystic Goethe wrote, "Whatever liberates our spirit without giving us mastery over ourselves is destructive."[8] It is also self-indulgent, narcissistic, and downright irritating.

Sometimes children are so powerful that it takes a special effort and creative strategy to hold the line and elicit cooperation. Suzanne discovered that a particular explanation to her young powerhouse daughter made a surprising difference. Some days it seemed that no amount of arguing, consequences, threats, logic, or anything else seemed to be enough to win over her daughter's agreement, until one day she spontaneously reminded her daughter, "I'm the parent this time and you're the child." Her daughter suddenly stopped and seemed to be letting this sink in. She immediately calmed down. It was as if she was reminded of who she was and what this sacred contract was about. Suzanne would use this explanation from time to time to break the deadlocks that would periodically arise. And it worked.

In addition to limits, children learn through freedoms. In the next sections we will explore five freedoms that are foundational to children's spiritual growth. We can also note here that these are not only relevant for the child in front of us but also for the child within us. As we consider these five freedoms for children, we can also consider offering them to our inner child. We will talk more about the inner child in chapter 9 as well.

Freedom to Play

Children learn especially through their free play with the world. Fredrick Froebel, the nineteenth-century creator of kindergarten, emphasized that play is very much a spiritual activity; it is the "self-active representation of the inner [nature]"—the spiritual nature.[9] For

Froebel, the purpose of the kindergarten was not to give children a head start in information acquisition, as it has been increasingly co-opted to do. Instead, it was an opportunity for playing together in order to bring out their inner seed, or soul. Play enables children to find and define themselves. Without sufficient free space, especially psychological space, it becomes difficult to play out our inner natures. Play is the holy work of children. And as adults, play can help nourish our own spontaneity, vitality, and simple joy. Do we give both our children and ourselves space to be playful?

Freedom to Pursue Their Own Interests

Our interests, passions, and the direction of our play may reveal a sense of our character and calling. Psychologist James Hillman takes up this question in his exploration of the lives of many famous individuals, from Ella Fitzgerald to Eleanor Roosevelt, who seemed to demonstrate their calling from a very early age.[10] Their genius pushed itself into embodiment as they found themselves driven to perform or to help others, or whatever the deep impulse was. In this sense, "growing up" is actually better described as "growing down"—bringing one's calling and character into the world. Without the freedom to pursue authentic interests and desires, the self tends to be overly shaped from the outside rather than drawn forth from within.

Parents can offer not only freedom, but also assistance in pursuing children's interests. Speaking about the environment in which child prodigies and human potential in general can develop, researcher David Feldman described the response that parents of exceptional children gave: "They possessed an unusual willingness to act immediately on requests or other signs of interest, virtually regardless of time or place."[11] It often means taking a time-out from the parents' agenda in order to explore the child's curiosity or question—any question.

And for our own inner child, what are the curiosities and

longings that we have postponed but that our inner child wants to pursue? Sometimes only when death approaches do we allow our secret longing—a trip to a special place, a reconciliation with an estranged friend, taking up painting—to be pursued. However, there is no need to postpone our life. It is best lived right here and right now.

Freedom to Experiment and to Make Choices and Mistakes

In science, an experiment does not succeed or fail, it just gives results on which we develop our understanding, build our theory, and construct new experiments. The same attitude helps to free us from the fear of making mistakes. Restricting children's ability to make mistakes, spill their milk, or fall down on their own cultivates self-doubt, a lack of self-initiative, dependence, and timidity. Giving them age-appropriate choices, even little ones ("Which shirt do you want to wear today?"), helps children develop skill and confidence at choice making that grows into discernment. Even if today's choice leads to a fashion disaster or a moral quandary, it can help the child develop self-responsibility and perhaps a keener sense of self-awareness.

As adults, can we make choices and take risks from our own center, an "internal locus of evaluation," rather than relying so much on others' reactions? Are choices made from fear and fashion, or from some place deeper down?

Freedom to Have Their Own Feelings, Thoughts, and Imagination

When something is scary to children, we negate their feelings when we say, "Oh, no, that's not scary." Instead, we can simply acknowledge and try to understand their fear and help them work through it. The need for privacy—for one's own feelings and thoughts and fantasies—balances the need for connection and protection. Even in the midst of abusive situations, the inner imagination can save the life of the child's spirit. The great sages and mystics remind us—

sometimes from their prison cell or cloistered retreat, and always from an inner silence—that much more than outer freedom nourishes the spiritual life. It is intellectual and emotional liberty, honesty, and stimulation that sustains and frees the child. The imagination is coaxed out with unstructured and unscheduled time, rich stories, and daydreams. It is invited when a child can sit, with no agenda, under a tree, or ponders his or her world for a few moments (without the lure of a computer game or TV), or even simply lingers in bed for a few minutes mulling over the previous night's dreams. Attending to the inner child means letting our imaginations soar and facing our feelings honestly.

Freedom to Betray Their Parents

As parents, we are powerful figures in a child's life, so powerful that we can sometimes overwhelm the tender stalks of the child's budding psyche. At times, we may need to expect and to even hope that the child will betray us. The betrayal of which I am speaking does not smack of selfish indulgence or insensitivity, but one that is driven by integrity. We may unknowingly be the oppressor, imposing our own projection or expectations on the child. And while expectations ("You need to take your dishes up to the sink") and standards ("Hitting your sister is not acceptable"; "No TV before homework") are valuable and provide helpful guidance to a child, when expectations for behavior slide into demands about who the child is and should be, this turns to imperialism: "You should be like this." It can mean that in some way we are withholding our love and tyrannizing the child. We can then expect to be betrayed. We open a space for the child's growth when we give up our projections of who we want them to be and instead hear and see who they are.

Now, I do have expectations for my children, but if they can listen well enough to themselves, they will join with those expectations that resonate and they will betray those that do not. If I listen well enough to the betrayal, I will even learn how I have tyrannized them with my own fears and unfulfilled wishes. Author Oriah Mountain Dreamer writes: "I want to know if you can disappoint another to be true to yourself; if you can bear the accusation of betrayal and not betray your own soul."[12] This is the lesson of authenticity and integrity for children. Their most fundamental spiritual task is to become who they are, just as it is for us as adults. This begins by facing, owning, and gently accepting who we are.

Who Is Teaching Whom?

As parents and spiritual friends, our side of the sacred contract is to hold and behold, doing our best to understand why this particular child has come and how we can help him or her fulfill his or her purpose here. But what do *we* get out of this parenting business? Sometimes it can feel like the contract is one-sided: we give and give to exhaustion. Children are an imposition sometimes, they do interfere with our plans, they can feel like a huge burden, and they can be excruciatingly difficult, demanding, impossible, expensive, and inconsiderate. But our sacred contract as parents is always a *mutual* agreement. We give and we receive, and if we are paying attention, the relationship draws out learning for both of us. I wonder sometimes what this whole parenting business is about. Who is actually parenting or teaching whom; who is the one who's learning the big lessons? Consider the following:

- Children learn how to brush their teeth correctly; parents learn patience.
- They learn to tell time; we learn sacrifice.
- We help them to open their lunch box; they open our hearts.

It is difficult to find anything (except maybe death) that gives us the powerful spiritual lessons that children do. We will pick up the question of what children teach us in chapter 9.

Chapter 7

A Spiritual Curriculum:
Ten Sources *of* Power *and* Perspective

What should I be teaching my child about spirituality?

How can I prepare this child to live in the world while keeping his or her delight alive?

How can I help children balance heaven and earth?

These questions, and others like them, emerge as we consider our role in the spiritual life of our children. Children are inherently spiritual beings. Their challenge is not really to reach up and transcend the world. Their challenge is to embody the divine in flesh and soil, here and now—in other words, to *grow down*. Nourishing their spiritual life does not mean adding on as much as it means drawing out that spirituality.

These days, messages of materialism, fame, money, competition, greed, violence, and sex swirl at children's fingertips with the click of a mouse or the remote control. Constant streams of messages, many of which are crafted (by advertising wizards) to shape consumer desire, bombard them. School also offers all sorts of messages—a hidden curriculum—such as the value of compliance, competition, and one right answer, and that authority and truth are to be found outside of oneself in the teacher or textbook. Religions offer concepts of a supreme being and humans, sin and salvation, doctrine and dogma. Any and all of these images and ideas may shape a child's worldview, values, and character.

As thoughtful parents, teachers, and friends, we try to be conscious of the diet of ideas that is offered to our children and provide alternatives to what is presented by the mass media. We may emphasize certain virtues (honesty, respect, charity), teach the Golden Rule, focus on the eightfold path of Buddhism, live by the three gems of Jainism, recite the Ten Commandments and any number of other worthwhile principles. In fact, as parents and teachers, we might want to make our own list of the values and principles we hold as most important and see how well our lives and messages express them to children. What are the virtues and principles that we want to teach?

But in trying to teach spiritual virtue, how do we avoid becoming overly moralistic, repressive, or simply embarrassingly superficial? At times moral, spiritual, educational, and political agendas may encourage moral immaturity through reliance on outside authority rather than nourishing one's own internal moral compass in dialogue with external codes and authorities. This demand for compliance without deeper understanding is "dangerous" according to Indian mystic Sai Baba, results in "arrested growth" according to author and poet Ralph Waldo Emerson, and even risks, in the words of philosopher Alfred North Whitehead, "soul murder."[1] It is a big deal.

A spiritual curriculum involves more than following rules, posting commandments, or memorizing a few virtuous words, however sage they may be. One of my daughters came home from school the other day and declared that she had been selected for recognition in the character education program. "Great. What is this for?" I asked. "So that you can get an award from the principal," she said. "Yes, but why were you selected?" I asked. "I don't know." "Was there something in particular that you were recognized for?" I probed. "Oh, yeah, there was a word—op-something. I don't remember." "Do you know what it means or why they selected you?" "No, not really. But we did get to go on the [closed circuit] TV."

Well, I found that the word was *optimism*, and she is indeed a good example of an optimist. But we see how ineffective the teaching of values is when we turn character into a commodity—just another word to memorize. The information download model is insufficient to cultivate anything that resembles character or spirituality. There is no shortage of good, guiding principles and yet the world continues to struggle with moral dilemmas, incredible violence, prejudice, and poverty. The challenge is not so much to find the right list of principles but to live them, to let our lives be a living expression of spirit.

Religion is an institutionalized approach to spiritual growth formed around doctrines, rituals, and standards of behavior. Spirituality is the very personal and intimate expression of our relationship with the Divine. The ten suggestions that follow nourish personal power and perspectives that may help us to embody our spirituality. These are not rules or regulations but are instead ways of empowering that deeply felt impulse that is the innate spirituality of children. You may not agree with all of these or may find others that seem more relevant to your own notions of a spiritual life. Modify, delete, and add as you see fit.

These ten principles are not meant to replace individual religious, cultural, and family conventions. Individual differences are the magnificent colors of human life, and the opening to spirituality has infinite gateways. The particular doorway in is not as important as how deep we are able to go. These ideas tap the deep structures of human life that cut across religious and cultural particularities and get played out at every stage of development. A child's work (like the task of any spiritual quest) is to explore things for him- or herself. These tools help children develop the power and the perspective to plumb the depths firsthand and find their own way by means of their continual connection with Spirit rather than automatically complying with convention or an unquestioned external authority.

Many of us wrestle with these ideas (like finding our voice or identifying our calling) in adult life, and maybe if we are lucky, we develop some mastery or understanding in midlife or beyond. In fact, my hope is that these ideas might be equally relevant to adults, whether we spend great amounts of time around children or not. Revisiting our own innate spirituality through the eyes of children may help catalyze our own spiritual growth as adults. And as is true for so many adults, I suggest that today's children are ready and hungry for these questions and considerations right now.

These are not instructions that we hand to children and expect them to absorb. They are intended to orient us toward noticing and nourishing the inner landscape of a child's life directly and indirectly. Parenting (teaching, befriending, etc.) is a process of mutual development. You cannot help the child very well unless you are working on your side of the equation. These are ideas that a parent, or perhaps a teacher or friend, digests and then uses in spontaneous moments while throwing a ball in the backyard or taking a drive in the car, and perhaps in more scheduled conversations at bedtime or at the dinner table, as well as in a formal setting or exercise such as in a classroom assignment. Parenting and growth in general are largely improvisational; they require that we are awake enough to offer the nourishing idea, pose the thoughtful question, or seize the insight at a moment when there is an opening—a soft and fertile spot for the seed to take root.

The following ten sources of power and perspective help to bring a spiritual life to Earth. They are not doctrines or rules (there are plenty of these out there already), but instead they provide touchstones for parents and friends in the midst of a teachable moment with a child or even with ourselves. Instead of providing answers, these ideas tend to ask questions—such as "Who are you?" and "What are you here for?"—that help to activate and open our life to the sacred.

Who Am I?

On the hillside of Mount Halcyon in ancient Greece, many came to visit with Pythia, the pythoness, also known as the Oracle of Delphi. Whether devout or desperate, they came because they sought insight and guidance from one who could see further than they. Pythia would take a deep draft of the volcanic vapors that leaked from a crevasse in the earth, then look into the future or into the heart of the seeker and offer her words of wisdom. The quality and utility of the advice was uneven—sometimes helpful and meaningful, other times cryptic and confusing. But there was one piece of advice that was absolutely consistent at the oracle. Inscribed over the entryway at Delphi are two words: "Know thyself." First and foremost, "earth school," this earthly learning environment, invites and requires us to discover who we are.

As easily as we teach them about the world around them, we can also invite children to explore their *inner* landscape. But how do we help children (and adults) to know themselves? There is no need or no way to force self-discovery in a child. Children, just like the rest of us, open gradually, through their play, exploration, and inter-action with the world, by following what they love and noticing what they do not, through experimentation with an idea, and through wrestling with an old friend or a new hairstyle. They learn what they do well and what makes them angry. Through play and interaction, they draw themselves out. We help children know themselves first and foremost by accepting who they are and providing the free space to play, to imagine, and to experiment with the world. This is also exactly what is required for our ongoing growth as adults.

Thomas Merton tells us that "the purpose of education [we can add parenting, too] is to show a person how to define himself au-thentically and spontaneously in relation to the world—not to impose a prefabricated definition of the world, still less an arbitrary definition of the individual himself."[2] Posed and pondered honestly, questions and dialogue do not breed narcissistic preoccupation or a prefabricated image of the self, but instead offer an unfolding revelation toward an authentic life. Self-knowledge is a fluid and flowing affair—we create ourselves as we go. We activate self-knowledge and intrapersonal intelligence when we invite children to look inward at their thoughts, values, and feelings—those things that constitute the inner world. All sorts of little questions help children look within: "If you were an animal [car, flower, etc.] what would you be and why?" "Draw a picture [of you, something you like, etc.] and please tell me about it."

The way we frame a question for a child will affect the richness of his or her response. Young children know especially through their *bodies*, and so questions for them (as well as for any of us) might sound something like this: "What is happening in your body when you're angry [happy, tired, sad]?" or "What do you hear [taste, touch, and so on]?" We might ask them to make a drawing, a sound, or a face to express what their body is sensing. In time, children integrate their *emotions* and can handle questions like "How do you feel about that?" As they develop further, their sense of *independent will* grows. We can tap that capacity with such questions as "If you were that character in the story we're reading, what would you do?" *Reasoned reflection* and values become anchored in time and can be evoked with questions such as "What do you think about that?" or "What do you love and what do you not even like?" or "What would you fight for and why?"

Children of nearly any speaking age can complete simple sentence stems, and they often surprise us with their degree of self-reflection and their deep and radical questioning, as we explored in chapter 4. At the dinner table, on a long car ride, or in a personal journal, family members might complete sentences such as the following:

A question I have is _____.
Something I want to remember when I grow up is _____.
I wonder about _____.
I feel _____ when _____.
I am thankful for _____.
Something I have trouble with is _____.
Sometimes I feel _____.
When I'm at my best, I am like a _____.
Something I want to remember about today is _____.

By comparing impressions and inviting clarification, we see what we have in common and how we are different. Through dialogue within and without, we meet ourselves and the world.

There is another dimension of self-knowledge that the great traditions name. Ramana Maharshi, one of India's spiritual leaders, whose own momentous revelations began as a boy, invited his students to perpetually consider only one question: "Who am I?" He found that relentless and honest pursuit of this question leads to a deep realization of the masks that we wear and the illusion of our separateness from one another.[3] If we go far enough into this question, he said, it allows us to see the limitlessness of our deepest self—the divinity that is our true nature.

As we explored earlier in the book, children often have a direct recognition of interconnection with this larger nature. Haley's angel, for example, could be thought of as an aspect of her higher self, Emerson's inner man, Aurobindo's inner teacher, and so forth—all ways to name that part of us that comforts, counsels, and connects with the larger currents of the cosmos. Children and adults can recognize this larger nature in everyday moments, maybe as a still, small voice or an angel, but also as recognition of injustice, a feeling of awe and bliss, or in a moment of tender connection and compassion.

The revelation of our larger nature is available even, and maybe especially, to children. When we value and take seriously children's intuitions, ideas, and experiences, and invite them to consider their own answers directly through contemplation, prayer, and pondering, the larger nature may emerge naturally. As we encourage them to look within for answers ("How can you deal with your sister in a better way?" or "What would your favorite wise person do?"), discern value or truth ("What do you think is the right thing to do?" or "Do you trust that person?"), or comfort and heal another ("Can you send a prayer to Grandpa?"), we reinforce that connection. If, on the other hand, we are always providing answers, dismissing the inner life as simply immature, or failing to see children as capable of such depth, we shut down that connection. "Knowing thyself" begins as a courtship with our interior and ends as communion with the world.

To Thine Own Self Be True

To *know* who we are creates an obligation to *be* who we are. In William Shakespeare's *Hamlet*, Polonius, Hamlet's intended father-in-law, captures the heart of authenticity and integrity when he offers this advice: "This above all, to thine own self be true."[4] Theologian Martin Buber recounts an old Hasidic tale that offers the same message: As an old man nearing his own death, Rabbi Zusya said, "In the coming world, they will not ask me: 'Why were you not Moses?' They will ask me: 'Why were you not Zusya?'"[5]

But there are plenty of messages that tell children that who they are may not be appropriate or desirable. Parents' expectations of who a child should be, advertising that tells them how they should look, peer pressure to act in a certain way, school systems that tell them not merely *what* they should know, but *how* they should know it, and religious dogma that places emphasis on such notions as sin can fragment the child and fuel shame, insecurity, and self-judgment.

One person in researcher Edward Robinson's study describes a painful scene from her own childhood: "I was sent to Sunday School and later to church. . . . 'The miserable sinner' aspect of orthodox religion had a large influence on my thinking between the ages of five and nine. I hated it, and felt more and more strongly that it somehow blasphemed against the beauty, light, and all-embracing fusion of God, man, and matter, which I thought I saw all around me. At the age of nine, I leapt up in the church service, unable to bear the 'for there is no health in us' intoning any longer, and shouted that God wasn't like that at all: that he was nearer than one's own hand. And I was hustled out in a flood of tears."[6]

Instead of "Know and be thyself," the message sent to children is too often more like, "Hide and deny yourself because you should act or look or think like this, not like you do." But the more children shut down, the more they suffer. They (and adults) may think that if they hide or deny parts of themselves that they believe are unacceptable, they will be better off. But the process of growth works just the opposite. What we resist persists. And pushing something away takes energy and ultimately creates shadow in our psyche.

Carl Jung coined the term *shadow* to describe the hidden parts of ourselves, good and bad, that we have either repressed or never fully realized. These are ultimately undeveloped potential. Shadow is created when we stand between ourself and our own light. Jung wrote, "Everyone carries a Shadow, and the less it is embodied in the individual's conscious life, the blacker and denser it is. At all counts, it forms an unconscious snag, thwarting our most well-meant intentions. . . . If it is repressed and isolated from consciousness, it never gets corrected."[7]

When we own unacceptable or difficult parts of us, their choking grasp begins to slip and frees energy that has been spent keeping those splintered parts of us at bay. The paradox of growth is that we transcend our limitations by owning them; we transform ourselves by being who we are. We grow by making the darkness conscious. No matter what else children must bear in their lives, they must bear themselves. The dark thoughts, shuddering fears, embarrassing acts, and nagging desires need not be shunned, but must be welcomed. Rumi, the twelfth-century Sufi mystic and poet, said it this way:

> *This being human is a guest house.*
> *Every morning a new arrival.*
> *A joy, a depression, a meanness,*
> *some momentary awareness comes*
> *as an unexpected visitor.*
> *Welcome and entertain them all!*
> *Even if they are a crowd of sorrows,*
> *who violently sweep your house*
> *empty of its furniture,*
> *still, treat each guest honorably.*
> *He may be clearing you out*
> *for some new delight.*
> *The dark thought, the shame, the malice,*
> *meet them at the door laughing,*
> *and invite them in.*
> *Be grateful for whoever comes,*
> *because each has been sent*
> *as a guide from beyond.*[8]

The spiritual path is not one of fragmentation—of leaving parts of ourselves out—it is about bringing parts together. The symbol, the sacred geometry, is the circle, representing wholeness. We stay true to ourselves by bringing into this clearing of honesty all the elements of ourselves, all the black holes and the small light, the darkest dreams and the shimmering hopes. When we do so, we stop wasting time and energy discriminating against, hiding from, and fearing ourselves.

We nourish the child's integrity when our messages both spoken and silent are, "You don't have to be anyone but who you are. Be flexible, explore, and try things on. See what fits and what doesn't, but most of all be yourself and be honest with yourself. Bring yourself into the world." As parents, we can ask ourselves, How do I want my child to be different than they are? What's that about? And how am I sending that message to them? Do I withhold my love and affection when I disagree with them or something they've done? And as with most things, we teach mostly who we are. To the extent that we can face our own shadow, our children will have a model for accepting their own.

What Am I Here to Give?

The task at earth school is not only to uncover who we are, but also to find (and create) what we are here to do, what we have to offer. We might even say that the job is not just to be "good," but to be good for something. And that something already lives within the child as a seed. Our lives come with visions, a calling, purpose, a sacred contract. We have something unique that is ours to offer the world, whether it is our particular expression of loving-kindness or a special way we see the world, like an Einstein or a Picasso. The challenge is for children (and adults) to find and align themselves with the tug of their calling. Sometimes we hear a religious person speak of a calling that led him or her to minister in some way. But all life purposes, from becoming a schoolteacher to being a caring friend, are spiritual offerings. In Hindu tradition, the notion is called Dharma. It means that we have come here to contribute to the world in some unique way.

A child's purpose does not typically come as a preset career or vocation. It has more to do with certain qualities, characteristics, and capacities. Any number of careers or situations may allow a child to express his or her purpose. A calling is more about the way we are able to listen and empathize with another person—for example, about the way that we bring delight into a room, have an ability to be calm in a crisis, or see the big picture in a complex situation.

The purpose is not only given, it is coconstructed, and the child must assume responsibility for creating his or her expression of it. Purpose is a process, an ongoing discovery, and it is crafted and clarified by our choices each day. When we use our personality to align with our calling, we honor our purpose. We have talents, desires, and fantasies, and through circumstances and choices our life takes shape. Sometimes the shape of our purpose begins to form very early and is recognized as a talent—child actress Shirley Temple and musical genius Wolfgang Amadeus Mozart come to mind. At six, Marshall Ball, a boy who writes remarkable poetry but who cannot speak or walk (you met Marshall earlier), recognized his calling quite clearly:

I see my self as a teacher
that knows about God.
Good thoughts come to me
and they teach.

I hope to gather thinkers
to give them my thoughts about Love.
Love to clean their ideas.
That cleaning might loosen the love
in their hearts.
Good thinkers take LOVE to heart
like gold in the evening wild sun.[9]

More typically it takes time for a calling to ripen. We catch little glimmers in the form of a vague tug, anger at some injustice, an obsession, a love, a curious affinity for someone or something, a fantasy. Eleanor Roosevelt had a very gray and angry childhood. Both her parents, who were largely unavailable to her to begin with, died before she was nine. She was withdrawn, hostile, and isolated, yet she kept a fantasy alive that provided the clue to her purpose. She wrote, "I carried on a day-to-day story, which was the realist thing in my life."[10] Eleanor's story involved her imagining that she was the mistress of her father's large household and a companion in his travels. James Hillman offers this interpretation:

> Their [her fantasies] caring and managerial content was purposeful preparation for the dutiful life she would later live. The fantasies were invented by her calling and were indeed more realistic in their orientation than her daily reality. Imagination acted as a teacher, giving instruction for the large ministering tasks of caring for the welfare of a complex family, of a crippled husband, of the state of New York as the Governor's wife, the United States as its first lady, and even of the United Nations. Her attending to "Father" was a preliminary praxis into which she could put her call, her huge devotion to the welfare of others.[11]

Like most issues in parenting, we cannot force children toward their calling. Putting pressure, especially on a young child, to decide on a career or life path is generally unhelpful. Asking, "What would you like to be when you grow up?" may give some clues as to their nature, but may not always clarify the calling very much. Instead of trying to push the child here or there, we, as parents and teachers, can first respond to the child's own interests, questions, and curiosities, taking time out from our agendas to attend to theirs. Second, we can expose them to a wide variety of circumstances and people—taking piano lessons, hammering nails in the garage, traveling, witnessing a death, seeing a show—that may resonate with the seed of a calling.

While we need to be prudent about overstimulating the child (sex, violence, etc.), it is the unfiltered richness and depth of the world that has the best chance of resonating with a calling. The more real the situation is, the better. "Should my child attend the funeral service with me?" a thoughtful parent might ask. I would probably (there are always exceptions) say, "Yes," unless you expect the child to be terribly distracting to others. "Should I take a route home that will avoid the homeless folks sitting along the street?" I would say, "No," so long as the journey seems reasonably safe. Life is to be met firsthand. As Alfred North Whitehead wrote, "The second-handedness of the world is the secret to its mediocrity."[12] The more real the experience, the more it resonates down to our cells and our souls, and that is where our calling lives.

Calling emerges in some mysterious alchemical mixture of seed and circumstance. Life works so exquisitely that it provides the outer situations and inner curiosities that offer us just what we need. When she was eight years old, a girl and her father came upon an injured elephant in her native Thailand. With grave concern, she asked her father where they could take the elephant for help. He answered that there was no such place. The elephant died in apparent suffering, and the tiny girl suffered right along with this giant. Thirty years later, she amassed a team ranging from veterinarians to truck drivers and financiers to form the only hospital in Thailand devoted to elephants. She still suffers along with her very large friends, but now she can help with that suffering. She created an outlet for her calling.

Joseph Campbell used the phrase "Follow your bliss" to describe a compass for living our life.[13] This was not meant as an excuse for superficial self-indulgence ("That feels good, so I'll do it"). It means following those currents within that bring deep fulfillment and deep satisfaction even when it may be difficult or involve pain or sacrifice. When we find and align with these deep currents, our lives are empowered in a profound way. Krishnamurti, the Indian sage who was recognized as a spiritual adept as a child, said that when you find "what you really, with all your heart, love to do . . . then you are efficient without becoming brutal."[14] Our lives become organized from the inside out, and we tap our authentic power. Pleasure and the relief of pain drive us to get nourishment, have sex, and seek security. Joy, justice, and deep fulfillment are telltales that drive us toward our spiritual life. We help children when we encourage them to practice listening to and choosing from the center of their bliss. They begin to see the consequences and learn the different feelings one gets from making choices from bliss, from that feeling of rightness and alignment, rather than from the feeling derived from more superficial indulgence.

When we say yes to our calling, synchronicities abound. The world says yes back to us. Life does not necessarily become all sunshine and light, and we do not always get what we want; but it seems deeply right for us, and we seem to get precisely what we need.

Children pursuing what they love today or keeping alive a rich fantasy (like Eleanor Roosevelt did) may be in preparation for a glimmer of their purpose tomorrow. They need only play these out and see what unfolds. Our callings and visions are not static, but alive, like a plant. They can grow and meander into fresh shapes throughout a lifetime. Maybe the heartwood of the impulse feels the same. "You must do something to make the world more beautiful," Miss Rumphius is told in a children's book named for her.[15] She ends up sprinkling her neighborhood with lupine seeds and telling beautiful stories to her granddaughter and her friends. Perhaps there is a sense of being a teacher in some way, like Marshall, or a healer who finds an elephant to nurse, or maybe the child is one who naturally brings tender compassion and hope to those who need it, without even being fully aware that this is his or her gift.

What Am I Here to Learn?

Earth school provides both a chance for us to contribute through our life purpose and also for us to learn life lessons. What have you come to learn? Courage, delight, the right use of power, or maybe patience and loving kindness? We may have big lessons:

- Greed's lesson is often generosity and trust in abundance.
- Restlessness and irritation invite a deep breath toward patience.
- The antidote to judgment is often tolerance for others and for oneself.
- Hostility opens an opportunity for forgiveness.

And along the road, there are all sorts of smaller lessons such as learning to tell the truth, the impact of courtesy, or how to say no. When life is seen not so much as a competition with others that leads toward success or failure, or as divine punishment or reward from the gods, and instead as an opportunity for learning—earth school—it becomes easier to accept and even welcome what life brings us. This small shift in perspective can have a huge effect on our sense of optimism and emotional balance. Being cut from the basketball team, having a friend move away, or being hurt in some way is not failure or punishment, but instead an opportunity to learn. We are healed, transformed, and made stronger by what we learn from a situation, especially a difficult one. The victim becomes a survivor when he or she learns from the ordeal. We heal not to be safe once and for all, but so that we may be wounded again in some new way and from it learn some new lesson.

In parenting, we help when we give children the space to fail and to feel. We can let them have their feelings, and while we are naturally on the lookout for danger, we do not rescue them prematurely from the lesson or from the pain. Once the tears or anger of a tough situation subside a bit, we can frame the issue by exploring the feelings and seeing what there is to learn. We might ask a child, "What would you do if you could turn back the clock?" or "What would the best person you know—a hero—do now?" or "If you could teach someone about this, what would you tell him or her?" Or maybe we have a helpful story from our own life or a children's tale (for example, "The Boy Who Cried Wolf") that may help put the lesson in perspective.

Playing off Shakespeare's insight that "all the world's a stage," [16] we can suggest to the child, "Pretend that what just happened was a movie or a play that you were in, one that was written specifically for you. How well did you play your role? What is the moral or lesson in the story? What could the next scene be?" This begins to engage creativity and makes us players rather than bystanders or mere victims in our own lives. We might even be able to laugh at the scene, or at ourselves—not always easy to do, but always helpful.

The lull after anguish is among the most teachable moments in a life. The direction for parents and children is toward a shift in perspective that turns off the road of blame, victimization, and resentment to one that asks, What can I learn from this? Paying attention to this question is the tuition at earth school.

At four years old Lynn had a dream that she was in a very big and special chair. The message was that she was so special, even though her life at the time was very difficult. Nine people, who seemed more like angels, came to her through a mist of glittering light. Each brought this special girl a special gift. The first offered art and music, which have become so nourishing to her life. The next brought love, the next kindness. In time, the last gift was presented: it was pain. Lynn was confused and couldn't understand why pain would be a gift. "Why are you going to hurt me when you tell me that I'm special?" she asked. They explained that through pain you learn lessons; pain is actually a gift of learning. "You'll see," they said. And so she has.

Sometimes suffering is the first grace precisely because it helps us to learn and pushes us to grow in some way. Suffering is transformed when we move from the illusion that this life is punishment to accepting the gift of learning. Our sins are already forgiven, Jesus told us. Buddha's enlightenment was to recognize that suffering is illusion. Forgetting who we are, and that we are here to learn, makes us the jailer in our own prison. As poet Ranier Maria Rilke wrote, the point is "to live everything," including the pain.[17]

One way that many wisdom traditions make sense of our lessons is through the law of cause and effect. The bottom line is that through our choices we create effects. The Bible tells us, "What ye sow, that shall ye reap," and "With what measure ye mete, it shall be measured to you again."[18] This is such a fundamental and fascinating principle for children to explore firsthand, such as when they see that their genuine and freely given kindness usually brings kindness back to them or when their resentment and hostility boomerangs. This is not an excuse to blame the victim, but instead to begin to consider that our actions have consequences. From Galileo's time onward the principle of causality—that every action has a reaction— has focused the scientific search for causal mechanisms in nature's mode of operation. Hindu and Buddhist traditions talk about this on the human scale as the law of karma.

Karma especially means that here and now we are sowing seeds. Are the thoughts we hold generous or jealous, and are the actions we take based on fear and selfishness or love and abundance? A hostile thought or a kind act sends out a ripple into the universe that eventually comes back to affect us. Gandhi said the root of violence in the world is *himsa*—the intent to do harm that is within our minds.[19] We can help children by asking them to notice their intent, helping them to see its consequence, and suggesting that they think about alternative intentions. When we walk down the street or face a difficult person, what is in our mind? Are we sowing seeds of love, understanding, and forgiveness, or hostility and hatred? Asking children to notice what is in their thoughts and then giving them the encouragement to set a more constructive intention, like sending love, empowers them beyond the obsessive loop of fear and mere self-protection. The primary lesson is to take full responsibility for choices, especially the choice of our intentions that serve as the seeds whose fruit we harvest.

In Eastern traditions, karma is believed to carry over from previous lifetimes and is the reason given why we may be drawn to or repulsed by certain people. In this view, while we may not remember our life before, there is a resonance that we may experience. That particular connection and warmth, like we are old friends, or perhaps that feeling of hostility or deep-seated resentment that we cannot quite understand, is explained as the karma that exists between us. The notion is that we are meeting again in order to nourish each other's learning. Eastern traditions imply that we tend to reincarnate in groups, that is, we have been with many of the people around us before. There may be a spiritual agreement with this person (perhaps your spouse, child, neighbor, or whomever) to work something out in this life to support each other's learning. While we sometimes think of a difficult situation and especially difficult people as obstacles or petty tyrants, they are like Lynn's ninth gift—growing pains.

Finding My Voice

As a young boy, Black Elk had visions that would shape his life and the life of his tribe. But in and of themselves, the visions were not enough. Black Elk reported that for a person who has a vision, you do not get the power of that vision until you walk it out on the earth for people to see.[20] The challenge for parenting is not just to help our children (and ourselves) to find their purpose or know who they are, but to find the means to express it, to bring the vision into form, to find their voice. By voice I mean the confidence, skill, and power of creative expression.

The fundamental nature of spirit is creation; creativity is its human counterpart. Alfred North Whitehead said that creativity is the ultimate category, the category necessary to understand all others.[21] The Divine becomes manifest in the moment of creation: the birth of an idea, a piece of art, the conception of a child. Joining the push and the pulse of creation means that we find and express our visions in the world. We walk them out for people to see, as Black Elk would say. We create our life and in so doing we both receive the power or, "medicine," of the vision and simultaneously give that medicine to the world.

Children have a natural drive for creative expression. They love to draw, play, build with blocks, make up silly words and songs, build a world in a pile of sand. The boys who are our neighbors build all sorts of jumps and ramps for their skateboards out of scraps of wood and even highway debris. My youngest child, with the aid of a new glue gun, started spontaneously to make people, fairies, and tiny household essentials (beds, dishes, cloths, etc.) out of sticks, flowers, and all sorts of little objects. This natural abundance is not rationed out, but overflows. This is the nature of creation and of Spirit itself—diverse, overflowing, endless, abundant beyond measure—the one in the many. As the ancient philosopher Plotinus wrote, "Spirit not only engenders all things; it is all things."[22]

Often children's visions run far ahead of their ability to express them: "I can't really draw a good pony." But in their minds they can *see* the good pony. And that defines precisely the tension and lesson of finding our voice. The challenge is to find ways to bring that pony into the world and all the ponies—the ideas—that are to follow. Maybe the child takes dance lessons or learns to write and to read. He or she practices painting pictures, masters a sport, learns the timing of telling a joke or the rhythm of telling a story that heals. Maybe he or she makes up colorful words, learns to articulate an argument, or sings songs. The parent helps by giving encouragement, opportunity, and constructive feedback when it is asked for.

If children do not find and develop the art and craft that can lead to mastery and virtuosity of expression, finding ways to walk the visions out, not only do they not get their full power (medicine), the visions back up and clog their consciousness—it can make them sick. Frustration can grow into hostility and anger, depression and demoralization: "Why bother? I can't do this or that well enough"; " I can't write"; "No one will hear me"; "It won't make a difference."

A spiritual life calls upon us to look within and bring to the planet what we find. In the Gnostic Gospels, Saint Thomas tells us, "If you bring forth what is within you, what you bring forth will save you. If you do not bring forth what is within you, what you do not bring forth will destroy you."[23] This is a delicate matter when a child's visions are big: world peace, compassion, unity, healing, and the like. Sometimes the big vision becomes the purpose or theme for our life. It is not satisfied by a single object or act. Instead, our work is to make our life a living expression of that vision.

Imagine for a moment that on one side is the vision—the idea. On the other is our ability to express it. That ability is like a pipe that the vision gets funneled and filtered through. The tension between a big vision—a big, beautiful pony—and our ability to express it usually requires the discipline to learn new tools or better ways to use the tools we have—writing, speaking, dancing, typing, carving, and so forth.

Sometimes we have talents and tools that are ready to be used. Linda sang opera for her family as a three-year-old; her voice was loud and clear until she got the message from the adults around her that this was not appropriate for a child. It took her more than thirty years and a near fatal accident to find her voice again. These days, her voice takes the form of writing (and she sings in the shower). At four, Sam knew how to put mechanical things together. Marshall, whom I introduced earlier, found his voice when his parents tried resting his elbow on their hands so that he could point to letters on an alphabet board.

There are times when we have to help children work on the other side of the equation and adjust the vision itself. We may have to help children be strategic in their approach and holographic in their understanding. They may need to make a small facet of their vision their focus. We can help them see that a small and near piece contains and is connected to the large and the far, just like a single cell in our toe contains the DNA necessary for the whole body or a small piece of a holographic image contains the entire picture. Ralph Waldo Emerson said it this way: "Man is surprised to find that things near are not less beautiful and wondrous than things remote. The near explains the far. The drop is but a small ocean."[24]

Let us say that a big vision is the recognition that we are all interconnected—a vision of unity—and there is a need to get others to recognize it too. To give voice to that vision, we help the child by finding a little and local drop of that whole ocean. Our advice for a vision of interconnection, for example, may look something like this: "Maybe you can connect with one person who doesn't seem to know that they're already connected. Is there one person in your school who seems disconnected, alone, unpopular? Maybe you can find a way to connect with him or her. You smile at the student today, say 'hello' tomorrow, ask a question one day, or have a short conversation another day. Sit next to him or her at lunch." A goal may not be an end, but is a direction. The big visions of spirit find voice in the little stories of our lives.

As parent or friend or teacher, nurturing the voice is sometimes as simple as an invitation to the child to share his or her viewpoint. A young high school student told me about how the simple and earnest invitation of a teacher helped her to find her voice again. She explained, "My teacher wondered what I thought, what was important to me. He actually thought this was important, that I was important. And after years of getting the message that what *they* thought was all that was important . . . I began to trust and listen to myself. It was like being reintroduced to someone I forgot was there—me. That spring, I started talking more in class and joined the chorus, which I had been too afraid to do before."

Longtime creativity expert Paul Torrance suggests five things that a parent or teacher can do to nurture the creative flow:

- Treat unusual inquiries respectfully
- Appreciate novel ideas
- Demonstrate that another's ideas have value
- Provide opportunities for self-initiated learning . . .
- Provide periods of nonevaluated learning[25]

What stifles creative expression and hushes the voice are messages like this:

- That's not logical!
- Don't be silly.
- Follow the rules; stay within the lines.
- Don't make mistakes.

- Stop playing around.
- There is only one right answer.
- You don't know anything about that. Let the adults do it.
- Be practical.
- Avoid ambiguity.

A symbol for finding our voice is the bell of a trumpet that funnels, filters, and amplifies the voice. The heart of the message to a child looks something like this: "Sing the song that sings in you. Go ahead, make your mark—on your paper, in your mashed potatoes, on the sidewalk, in your life."

Mastering Myself

To be free is a discipline. Liberty allows us to choose our actions as we wish, but it does not mean we choose in a way that necessarily frees our soul, deeply satisfies us, or enriches the world. While we hold external freedom (rights and liberties) to be extremely important in our society, it is the growth of inner freedom that is a hallmark of spiritual development. Inner freedom means we control our impulses rather than being controlled by them. It begins with the use of the will, which throws or holds back our weight, our heart, and our action in one direction or another.

Sometimes the power of the will allows us to push through some threshold of pain or frustration. When we have a demanding problem to solve or an arduous (a long uphill on a bicycle) or unpleasant ("I have to clean my room, again!") task to complete, we practice self-discipline by hanging in there a little longer, giving ourselves over to the task, avoiding procrastination, and not bailing out ("I'll find the answer in the back of the book or ask Mom for help"). Taking a deep breath and working through the initial frustration or discomfort is a sign of maturity. We help children develop this capacity when we present the right level of challenge—not too easy, where interest is lost and attention wanders, but not too hard, where frustration leads to helplessness. For example, if a book has more than 10 percent unfamiliar words, it may be too frustrating for most children to keep reading. We help children when we hold them accountable for appropriate goals, like cleaning a room or finishing their homework before play.

Beyond the love of family and friends, few things influence how we think of ourselves—our self-esteem—more than the development of mastery, our self-efficacy, and nearly any kind of mastery will do. My very young friend Anna recently learned to tie her shoe. Each time she comes to visit, she asks whether I want to see her tie her shoes. She can do this thing called shoe tying, and if she can master this, she assumes rightly, she can probably master other things.

In the midst of a struggle with a challenging shoe or anything in their life, we can remind children to take that breath, take a fresh look, and then we can provide the support for them to follow through on their own or with minimal help. Many years ago, I ran a program for children who had math anxiety and were desperately struggling with or completely avoiding math in school. What made the most positive difference during camp was not teaching them math concepts. Rather, it was helping them to control their initial reactions ("Oh no! It's one of those word problems: 'If a train is traveling at sixty miles per hour . . .' I can't do that.") and teaching them how to pause and then to refocus in order to give them a chance to work though problems with encouragement and just a little help from a teacher or fellow student. The problem was not really the math; it was their emotional and mental reactions. They were blinded by the headlights of that train coming down the track at them. Once they learned to refocus by taking a few deep breaths, learning how to relax, and just noticing rather than getting lost in their automatic doubts and feelings, they could do the math and find solutions. Their math anxiety disappeared. Many actually came to enjoy math, and their school performance and their confidence soared.

Along with pushing or breathing through some threshold of discomfort, our will can help us to hold ourselves back (for example, not eating all of our Halloween candy in one sitting). Effectiveness in earth school requires a certain degree of self-restraint. Self-discipline comes when we cannot have what we want in this second—say, Halloween candy or a new toy—and we learn to deal with it. The power of self-discipline enables children to avoid getting caught in their own drama, their own little whirlpool of existence ("I must eat all my candy now!" or "This problem is impossible! I hate it!"), so that they may live in the whole river of life. By the way, these everyday examples—math problems and Halloween candy—remind us that the spiritual work is precisely in the everyday struggles. Earth school provides the curriculum for spiritual growth.

Seeing Our Future

"In the beginning was the word"—the idea, the logos, the thought. And from the thought sprang all of creation, or so the story goes. This means that the world is created out of consciousness, as so many mystics and sages tell us. As Vaclav Havel, a playwright who became the first democratically elected president of Czechoslovakia, said as he reflected on the dramatic changes in his country, "If we have learned one thing about this revolution, it is that consciousness precedes being."[26] The idea, the shift in the mind, is the seed from which all things spring. The world is created from the idea. The world embodies our consciousness; the world *is* consciousness.

The tool here is manifestation; it is about the power of the mind to create the future. It is not only about working hard toward the goal; it is about being crystal clear and bringing it to life first in our mind. Whether breaking through the Iron Curtain or performing at the peak of our capacity, intention shapes our world. When we are in "the zone" or "the flow" of peak performance, we are absorbed in the task at hand, our sense of time alters, and our focus becomes power-fully centered. In Sanskrit, this is called *ekagrata*. This is not unfamiliar to even young children, who may find themselves so totally absorbed in finishing a drawing or at play that they do not hear our call for dinner.

Single-pointedness is harnessed when children take their natu-ral ability for *absorption* and tie it to their *intention*. For the task at hand and also for a goal down the road, intention means maintaining a clear focus. Energetically, our intention is like a triangle that points to the goal. If we have doubts, fears, reactive thoughts ("I can't do this" or "I wonder what my score will be"), it splits and diffuses the energy of our intention. We have lost ekagrata and therefore lost the full power of intention to create our goal. Whether it is a martial artist breaking a board or a gymnast focusing on her beam routine or a third grader learning her spelling words, success is, in large part, determined by clear intention and focus.

Like many great performers, Greg Louganis, winner of five gold medals in Olympic diving, trained hard. A key part of his training was his intention. First, he had a goal to be the best in the world, and this set creation in motion. Next, as part of his practice he would imagine himself walking up the ladder and out onto the platform. He would take a deep breath and then visualize himself pushing off into air, feeling every rotation and the pull of gravity, seeing the perfect line of his body as it broke the plane of the water, tasting the water, hearing the crowd cheer as he came up for air, and feeling the deep satisfaction of perfection.

Positive mental rehearsal, whether directed toward a flute per-formance or a math test, trains the mind to serve our goal and invites the universe to help out. It does not replace studying or practice, but it can take performance from mediocrity to mastery. Ignatius Loyola, founder of the Jesuits, captured two ways to focus our intention when he wrote, "We must pray as if all depends on Divine Action, but labor as if all depended on our own effort."[27]

Intention is a kind of affirmation. But affirmation is not accomplished by saying things like "I want this or that" (a gold medal, a new bike). This may tend to affirm our wanting rather than the outcome itself. Instead, the practice is to see our success, to create it in our minds, like Louganis did, in order for it to manifest in our life. In the beginning there is the word, the consciousness, the faith. It is about finding a vision and a focus and following the dream. We help children when we encourage them to frame their affirmations clearly, simply, and positively.

One mom describes how her four-year-old daughter seemed to be remarkably able to manifest what she wanted in all sorts of strange ways: "Katy and I were at Disneyland waiting for the rest of our group to get out of the Indiana Jones ride. It was shortly after dark on a summer evening. Disneyland sells these fiber-optic flashlights. Many people had purchased them, and Katy wanted one very badly. She kept asking for one and I repeatedly told her no, that I didn't even have any money. But it was clear that she was still absorbed by these magical-looking lights.

"As we were waiting in the exit area, two little girls about four years old and a dad approached, with the girls carrying the coveted flashlights. Katy had been watching the girls intensely. One of the girls approached Katy and handed her the flashlight. They wordlessly engaged in a game of sorts, watching each other play with the flashlight. I repeatedly told Katy that the flashlight belonged to the girl and that she must be sure to thank her and return it. Katy tried several times to give the flashlight back, but the girl wouldn't take it. When I finally took the flashlight over to the dad, he said that his daughter insisted on Katy having it. It was all very surreal, and I know this sounds silly, but it seemed as if Katy had somehow wordlessly gotten this child to give her the flashlight."

Part of the skill and balance of intention is the capacity to let go, to *constructively surrender*. We can keep our eyes on the prize (the note on our notebook that reminds us what we are shooting for, the clear vision in our mind, the prayer at night). But paradoxically, we must ultimately give up our attachment to the outcome and let the world do what it does best: create. If we anxiously or obsessively try to control every detail and force something to happen or only accept the outcome in the way we demand, we may end up blocking the creative flow. The power of will is insufficient for the spiritual journey. It takes us part of the way and then we have to trust and let go. Surrender reminds us that this spiritual life is bigger than we are—it is a mystery by which we are humbled. Surrender is falling backward and letting the universe catch us.

We use the power of intention when we pray, and not only for ourselves but especially when we serve others. Prayer is an invocation to the universe. Our consciousness serves as a magnet and a funnel to coax the forces of creation and healing in a particular direction. As we talked about in chapter 3, prayer seems to work best when (1) it is tied to the energy of love, and (2) we ask for the best as the universe sees it, rather than as we have predetermined it. We pray for the highest and the best healing, and let the universe figure out what that means. Remember in chapter 1 how Adam the dog taught Laura just to send him love and light? That is a kind of prayer that focuses consciousness without having us get tangled up in the details.

Where Am I Now?

Take a deep breath and ask yourself, Where am I now? Are you lost in thought? Worried about the day ahead? Wrestling with the knot in your stomach? Floating outside your body? A part of us, what we shall call our "I," notices the content of our consciousness. From this "I," we see from above the rise and fall of our thoughts and feelings. This "I" is a "still point of the turning world," as T. S. Elliot called it, the center point around which the activity of our outer environment whirls.[28] While finding this still point is often the goal of some meditation practice for adults, children have this capacity and can develop this witnessing of consciousness from an early age.

While modern Western science has developed technologies for the control of the external, material world, contemplative traditions, both East and West, have focused instead on the development of internal technologies. This is what the Dalai Lama calls Mind Science.[29] These awareness practices help us to use the mind, rather than being used by it. Ralph Waldo Emerson wrote, "Our thoughts first possess us. Later, if we have good heads, we come to possess them."[30]

The goal is to witness the contents of our consciousness and to recognize and interrupt habitual patterns of mind and action. As we mentioned in the previous chapter, Thich Nhat Hanh calls the activity of watching our mind "pure recognition," by which he means recognition without judgment.[31] Christian mystic and theologian Meister Eckhart refers to this as "detachment."[32] The point is to welcome equally all thoughts and feelings that arise by simply witnessing them without judgment or attempts to chase them away. Such mindfulness does not disengage us from the world or imply avoidance of action, but rather allows us to become fully present in our action because we are not controlled by automatic reactions.

The development of this witness consciousness is a lifelong skill that can be nurtured when we simply ask children to notice the flow of their feelings, sensations, and thoughts. This is not reserved to moments of meditation (although meditation has proven to be extremely enduring and helpful because it provides a structured practice through which to develop and refine awareness) but may occur at any moment. This is the place in which we see how upset we are or how much we enjoyed something, or where we simply notice the stream of our thoughts.

Compassion for others is nourished by tenderly witnessing ourselves. As we bring a gentle attitude of kindness, acceptance, and nonjudgment to whatever arises, we stop judging ourselves so harshly. And if we can be more accepting of ourselves, then we are much less likely to project our fears or hostility onto another person. Let us say a child is anxious or upset about something. After helping him or her to discharge some of the energy with some deep breaths, releasing noises (*AAHIIII!*), and maybe shaking his or her arms or legs or jumping around, we might ask the child to just watch the upset, notice where he or she feels it in the body, and just breathe through it without getting attached. Every thought or feeling can be imagined as a bubble from the bottom of a sea, and if we can just watch it float up without grasping for it or trying to stuff it down, it will burst and disappear when it hits the surface.

Witnessing combined with intention leads to an increased power to recognize and deploy attention in a way that is most useful for the situation at hand. For example, while a math problem may require a tightly focused attention (though not too tight!), generating possible ideas for a story is more openly focused. Enjoying a piece of art or a spring day may be best accomplished with the "soft eyes" of appreciation that open to wonder. When we are floating in the lightness of a daydream, we may find pleasure and unexpected inspiration. Five-year-old Denise discovered the power of shifting attention through crying and relaxing. She explained, "When you cry, it makes the pain better. Pain doesn't hurt as much if you just relax. You must relax your sores." One day a sore spot bothered her on her back. She said, "I found out how to stop the pain. See that bright shiny leaf out there? If I just think about it, the pain will go away."

The foundation of shifting our attention to the situation at hand begins with our being able to notice, to witness, and to feel the content of our consciousness. Inviting children to tune in to their senses and their bodies is a natural route to practice attention: "What does that feeling [or thought or headache or whatever] look like in your body? What is its color, shape, texture, hardness, sound, movement?" This type of exercise can help children develop their witness consciousness through recognizing, for example, that they *have* a feeling but they are *not* the feeling.

Often just a simple and honest question from an adult helps to activate this witnessing. I once asked a boy of fourteen, who was having a very difficult life, how much of the time he was angry. "Ninety percent," he said. While this surprised me, I learned later that his answer had shocked him. In this moment, he saw himself and how he was spending his life in stark clarity, and it did not sit well. Years later, he said that this simple look within provided a revelation that helped him to get control over his life and face his anger rather than just being angry. Witnessing gives the child a little distance between him- or herself and the sensation, thought, or feeling so that he or she can play and work with it without being overwhelmed by it.

Psychologist Eugene Gendlin wondered what made psychotherapy successful—what happened when a client was really healed and helped?[33] What he discovered was that those who made significant growth were able to tune in to and become aware of a bodily "felt sense" of their problem. From this research, he developed a technique called "focusing." It turns out that this is an easy-to-use approach that can develop witness consciousness and identify and release blocks in adults and children alike.

You can try this at home. Very briefly, his fundamental exercise begins by relaxing and bringing awareness to your body in order to locate a felt sense of an issue or concern. Invite your small friend (or just do it yourself for starters) to settle into a comfortable spot, maybe a big stuffed chair or a good lap. Then ask the child to ask him- or herself, What is the thing for me right now? or How is my life going? and then to direct his or her attention inwardly, perhaps in the chest or stomach, and see what comes to awareness. Suggest that rather than entering into it or getting lost in what arises, the child can stand back from this "thing" and acknowledge that it is there—"Yes, I can feel that"—in order to get a sense of what all of this issue feels like.

Next, ask the child to find a "handle" or "quality word" (sticky, murky, hard) and to go back and forth between the word or image and his or her felt sense of it. Encourage the child to look for a fit and to allow either the word or the felt sense to change in order to find the best fit. Then we can ask, "What makes this problem so sticky [murky, hard, and so forth—whatever one's quality word is]?" advising, "Receive whatever information comes your way, staying present and open."

Once the child has found a fit or gets a match or there has been an inward shift, he or she will often notice a give or release of blocked energy. These simple instructions provide an effective and easy way to practice awareness and identify and release emotional blocks. Imagine the personal power that children can have if they are able to release such energy regularly and easily.

For children (and adults), feeling the felt sense in the body and finding the right distance—not so close that it feels like it is all of them and not so far that they can hardly recognize it—develops the power of their witnessing mind. The lesson is that "I have feelings, thoughts, and sensations, but I am not these things. I'm more than that."

Elsewhere I have suggested the practical value of these kinds of approaches for improving performance, character, and depth of understanding in the classroom. Educators interested in techniques and justification for introducing methods such as this in schools might want to consult my article "Opening the Contemplative Mind in the Classroom."[34]

Hearing the Inner Voice

Children know the world through their senses and their growing rational mind. These are power tools that enable reasoned arguments and careful observations, and ultimately affect choices and beliefs. And they need fostering and refinement. (Unfortunately, basic logic and critical and creative thinking, naturalistic observation, and sensory awareness are often underemphasized in schools in favor of amassing facts.) But in addition to reason and the senses, children can also know the world directly through intuition. As we have discussed throughout this book, they have intuitive access to surprising information and powerful wisdom.

We can think of intuition as serving three general functions. Intuition's most basic task is to provide information about our safety. When we have a "funny feeling" or a "gut sense" about someone or something, that is often our intuition trying to get our attention. (Socrates's inner voice, which he called Daimon, would offer such warnings.) As it stretches further, intuition can also provide creative insight and information. This might be the flowing of a creative solution or a new idea. In addition to messages related to safety, guidance, creativity, and problem solving, intuition also serves even larger purposes. That is, the current of spirit can move through us in a more impersonal way. We play our sacred part in the mystery of life as if we are a hollow reed through which Spirit flows. Remember three-year-old Alissa's healing message to a stranger: "You have to let your daddy into your heart."

As we mentioned at the beginning of the chapter, we are so often taught to look outside ourselves to the biggest authorities or the latest fashion trends for answers and direction. Children are bombarded with outside information, but the spiritual journey turns inward toward that deep current through which our life flows.

There are two primary internal voices to which we can listen. The first is the chattering mind that is so familiar—the ego's voice. It offers all sorts of commentary and judgment ranging from worries about the past to advice about the future. Sometimes one or another dimension of this voice seems to dominate, and we hear that self-criticism, judgment of others, or maybe fear. This is the ego-generated voice that is simply a part of being human. It tends to prejudge experience and operates from self-interest, limitation, and fear. The other voice, the "inner voice," lives deeper down. This is recognized throughout the wisdom traditions as the still, small voice, inner teacher, Holy Spirit, inner light, genius, or guardian spirit, as we have considered earlier.

Children often have a natural access to this inner voice, as we have seen it take shape in the form of Haley's angel and Alissa's insight, and through so many other children from whom we have heard. However, as the ego grows, its own voice generally grows in strength. Without reinforcement, access to the inner voice may become overwhelmed by the ego's chatter or by external authorities. But with encouragement and practice we can keep access to the deep inner voice alive and well.

Three general dimensions are helpful in using the inner voice as a source of guidance: focus, opening, and discernment. We can pose a question or *focus* on an issue for which we seek clarity: What should I do about . . . ? Writing down a clear question beforehand or stating the question clearly out loud or in our mind concentrates the power of our intention like a laser. The clearer the question or issue, the more intense is the beam. Sometimes we help concentrate energy by asking such things as, What is the better choice here? or What seems true or right? Once we have focused clearly, it is then, paradoxically, helpful to let go, trusting that an answer will come. It is important to avoid being attached to the outcome. We constrict the intuitive flow when we demand that the information be in a particular form, package, or direction. Letting go of a desired outcome for this moment moves us past the problem solving of the ego and intellect in order to hear the deeper tones of the inner voice.

Next it is necessary to stop and be still, taking time out from our normal processing in order to *open* to the inner voice. Developing the witnessing capacity mentioned in the previous section—Where am I now?—helps to build awareness and slow the chatter down. In order to open to the inner voice we might then simply take some deep breaths, as we settle into a still and wise place within. Sometimes relaxing and moving in our minds to an inner image of a special spot—perhaps under a giant tree, at a soothing beach, on a mountaintop, or with a special friend like Haley's angel or Alissa's dolphin—can help us open to that wise inner space. Sometimes reading inspired writing activates the wise self. Breaking our usual routine of listening to the ego's chatter sometimes takes the power of a scheduled time-out in the form of a daily or weekly meditation time, especially as we grow. Even once a week for fifteen minutes of "wise silence" together can help reinforce the inner voice. At other times we may simply take a moment of pause in order to ask and listen to those deeper currents. The bottom line is taking a time-out from our usual inner chatter and outer stimulation to be still and listen deeply.

Discerning the difference between the inner voice and the ego's voice is not difficult once we know what to look for. Even when the ego-generated voice sounds reasonable and logical, it will typically prejudge a situation with a tone of self-interest, lack, and fear—fear of missing out, being hurt, or all types of things. By contrast, the inner voice generally feels more generous rather than self-interested, works from abundance and limitlessness rather than lack and limitation, feels more peaceful than fearful, and is open-ended rather than prejudging. With just a little practice and awareness, we grow more confident and recognize the differences between these voices.

In addition to the qualities just mentioned, the inner voice is often accompanied by a felt shift, a feeling of things falling into place and a sense of flow. It often emphasizes a way of *being* rather than simply *doing*—for example, holding an attitude of openness or forgiveness rather than specifying the precise action. If we do not get the message the first time, the inner voice often will present the idea again and again.

The inner voice can also arrive in unexpected ways. It may speak through a dream, in the face of an angel, as a flash of an idea, or as a gut feeling, a word or phrase, a moment of synchronicity, or a spontaneous impulse to act in some way. Some people get chills up their arms when they are tuned into the flow in a particular way. Others may hear a little buzzing in an ear. When I asked Haley how she and her angel communicated, she said, "It's kind of like thoughts and pictures all together. Mostly I just know what she wants to tell me."

Listen with Your Heart

The lights had just gone out, and Lucy's eyes were searching for light in the dark bedroom. Suddenly there was a glow in front of her, and she could feel tingles over her body. Between the light and Lucy appeared a little boy with freckles. Off to his right was Lucy's grandmother, who had died a year earlier. As Lucy described, "It was like my grandmother and the boy were shadows of the light. They were part of it; they couldn't be without it."

Lucy became very frightened. "What do you want? Why are you here?" she asked. Her grandmother moved toward her and Lucy reached out to touch her, but her hand seemed to pass through her grandmother, and the light seemed distant and unreachable. Her grandmother then spoke to her, "It's OK. Calm down. I want you to just listen with your heart."

This settled Lucy down and then suddenly she saw that there were more people between her and the light. As she tried to listen with her heart, she could hear them singing; all their voices were harmonizing with one another. The vibration of the music was like words and feelings all bundled together, and she could feel these vibrations coming into her body.

Then she saw that there was a man in the back of the group, his head held low. Without words, she understood that he wanted her forgiveness for something he had done. She said, "I didn't know who he was or what he had done to me. But he was so sad about what he had done I could feel it right into my heart. Because I could feel how sorry he was, it was easy to forgive him. And when I did, they moved to the other side of the light and disappeared. And then the light was gone."

The wisdom traditions tell us that if there were only one thing we should know about the spiritual path or one piece of advice for us to heed, it would be that both the path and the goal is to be in our hearts. Christ's message was love; Buddha called this compassion. To have love and to offer compassion are what make us both fully human and fully divine. This takes us beyond narcissism and self-absorption to realize our inescapable interconnection with the world. Rabindranath Tagore tells us that "love is freedom: it gives us that fullness of existence which saves us from paying with our soul for objects that are immensely cheap."[35]

Listening *with* our heart is not to be confused with listening *to* our heart. Listening *to* our heart means paying attention to our feelings and sensations about something. This is important for staying in touch with the flow of our feelings and sensations, and it balances the life of the intellect. But listening *with* the heart turns the focus outward, toward others. It means that we listen in order to under-stand, to appreciate, and to love. Nothing more and nothing less.

As we explored in chapter 3, there are two way of seeing: one prejudges and puts things in categories, and the other meets and ap-preciates. The former separates us from others; the latter moves us closer, toward empathy and compassion. At any moment, children can listen with their heart by simply being quiet for a few moments, taking a deep breath, and gently bringing awareness to the area of the chest. Simultaneously we can invite children (or ourselves) to call forth something they appreciate (a favorite moment, a friend, and so forth) or a feeling a joy. From this place, their attention can then turn to whatever is before them—perhaps a conflict or a new person who has crossed their path. As children and any of us listen and live through our heart, whether through an act of unselfish ser-vice, genuine giving, or deep understanding, we really see into the soul of the other, just as I ucy did, and move toward communion and community.

In closing this chapter on power and perspective and as we are faced with both tiny and terrible conflicts in our world, I want to note that the wisdom traditions tell us that the greatest power is not force but love. From watching television or listening to the news or even being on the playground, it would be easy to get the message that might makes right and the strongest ultimately wins. But the sages and mystics tell us something different. They tell us the power of love and compassion is the force that must balance and guide might. Without it, power turns to brutality. With it, we find an ethic toward right action—an internal guidance system that keeps us centered. The Jesuit sage Pierre Teilhard de Chardin describes the power this way: "The day will come when, after harnessing the ether, the winds, the waves, the tides, and gravitation, we shall harness for God the energies of love. And, on that day, for the second time in the history of the world, man will have discovered fire."[36]

Chapter 8

Difficulties *and* Discernment

*H*ow is a child's life affected when he or she meets an angel or sees a ghost? What is the response when a child asks big questions about life and meaning or feels overwhelmed by the suffering of another? What happens when this secret world meets the "real" world of a classroom or religious institution? Are today's children somehow different and therefore presenting new challenges?

Children who have spiritual questions and experiences are susceptible to the pitfalls of grandiosity, depression, boundary problems, spiritual bypassing (focusing on spiritual considerations to the neglect of more basic psychological or emotional development), and other difficulties, just like adults. Playground politics, making friends, getting along with parents, and fitting in at school can be demanding enough for a child, but having spiritual experiences and questions brings even more complexity to their lives. This chapter explores the challenge of being a child (and an adult) who has spiritual awareness and examines what parents, teachers, and other friends may do to help.

This may be a challenging chapter in many ways. These are not easy or tidy issues, and they manifest in unique ways in individual children. What I hope to offer is an understanding of what goes on beneath the surface of symptoms. Symptoms may be similar—depression, for example—but the originating issue may be quite different and sometimes pretty "far out," as we will see. Since each child is unique, we cannot give the three magic things that will help every child. But once we have a better understanding of the roots of a child's concern, we can begin to shape our response and explore ideas for helping. What I most hope this material will do is help parents, teachers, therapists, pediatricians, and other friends of children deal with their own fears, discomfort, and confusion, so that they can then, through their own new understanding and insights, be of service to these children and learn from them.

Too Little or Too Much

Before getting into a range of specific problems that children encounter, I first want to talk about two of the most fundamental and culturally embedded concerns confronting children's spiritual lives. These are our *making too little* and *making too much* of children's spiritual moments—and they are equally dangerous. The more common danger is that children's spirituality may be ignored, dismissed, or pathologized. This entire book is an attempt to correct that bias. To begin, we will explore a few of the unchecked assumptions and practices from education, psychology, and religion that prejudice us against recognizing the spiritual life of children.

Too Little

Children may be judged as "too sensitive" when they cannot tolerate adult attitudes and actions or when their compassion overflows. A child's serious questions about life and meaning may be dismissed with responses like "You're not old enough to understand." It is easy for a child to get a message that these things of most importance to him or her are not OK to talk about, that life is about surfaces and not the depths—it is about what we are told to know and not what we know for ourselves, about what is *out there* rather than what is *in here*.

Perhaps nowhere has this approach been more consistently reinforced than in conventional education. Jacques Lusseyran's reflections on his own childhood are entirely relevant to today's educational practice: "I couldn't understand why the teachers never talked about the life going on inside them or inside us. . . . The world is not just outside us but also within. . . . To accumulate knowledge was good and beautiful, but the reason to acquire it would have been more meaningful, and no one spoke of that. I could not help thinking that in the whole business someone was cheating somewhere."[1] Today's typical downloading approach to education emphasizes filling up the child from the outside in rather than balancing the outside with the inside. In such an approach, it is the inner life of the child—that place from which spirituality grows—that is cheated most of all.

Psychology has generally assumed that children cannot have genuine spiritual experiences. Of course, most of psychology has not even acknowledged or concerned itself with spirituality. In fact, as of this writing there is no contemporary developmental psychology textbook that even mentions children's spirituality. Children are considered merely immature, without sufficient ego and intellectual development to have anything that might be called meaningfully reflective and spiritual. Children may conjure up a funny image of what God is or they may be able to repeat a prayer they have memorized, but for the most part they are not assumed to have spiritual impulses, feelings of compassion, or questions of meaning. But these conclusions are based, in part, on the erroneous assumptions that spirituality is dependent on mature linguistic and rational capacities and is akin to religious *knowledge*. Essentially, the assumption is that we can only know Divinity when we can think and talk about it logically.

At the same time, religious thinkers have often blurred the distinction between the spiritual and religious. One common error is that a child must have understanding of the tenets of a particular religion in order to be considered "spiritual." The intimate spiritual experience, what William James called "personal religion" as opposed to "institutionalized religion," has been a point of suspicion in the West for a very long time.[2] As one person in physician Annette Hollander's study said, "I found out it was O.K. to listen to talks *about* Jesus [in church] but not to be talked to *by* Jesus."[3]

These religious and psychological assumptions emphasize logical thought and language over feeling, and "God talk"—how a child thinks and talks about God in relation to a particular religious doctrine—over spiritual experience. Ultimately, these assumptions logically preclude any possibility of children having a spiritual life. Based on these beliefs, children have to wait until adolescence or adulthood, when they have sufficient cognitive capacity and religious knowledge, for genuine spirituality.

Underlying this linguistic, rational, and religious orientation is an emphasis on particular ways of knowing while excluding others. Carl Jung described this difference as the *feeling* function versus the *thinking* function, or what has been called *aesthetic* versus *theoretic* modes of knowing.[4] Language and reason develop word and concept, what nineteenth-century philosopher Jean Paul Richter called "finite knowledge," while feeling and intuition open to "infinite knowledge."[5]

However, there has been a general devaluation of feeling and intuition in Western institutions (education, developmental psychology, religion) in favor of the theoretical and linguistic. In light of the bias toward rational-linguistic-religious understanding, children's spiritual life is often dismissed. But as I have tried to show throughout this book, consideration of spirituality lives beyond words, beyond rational ways of knowing, and beyond predetermined concepts of God. Children may not have fully developed their capacity for *finite* knowledge but they have surprising access to the *infinite*. As psychologist Gordon Allport said, "The religion of childhood may be of a very special order."[6]

Documents like the *Malleus Malleficarium*, better known as *The Witches' Hammer*, written in 1486 by two Catholic monks from Germany, insist that mystical experiences, moments of ecstasy, visions, and "voices" are the mark of satanic influence.[7] Such documents have institutionalized misunderstanding, repression, and persecution of those having spiritual experiences. For example, Joan of Arc, who first heard her inner guiding voices as a teenager in her father's garden, would not deny the reality of her voices and was executed because of her refusal. We can see in this the seeds of the Spanish Inquisition, the Salem Witch Trials, and all sorts of less well-known persecutions. These ideas have affected not only religious attitudes but have thoroughly permeated modern secular life, as evidenced by the prejudice and fear that so much of the culture has toward mystical experience at any age.

Amazingly, we still have a hangover from the fear and misunderstanding that *The Witches' Hammer* perpetrated. At five years old, Kristin asked her dad, a minister, an innocent question: "Dad, you want me to tell you about when I was an Indian?" She began to explain in great detail what she was seeing and how real it was for her. "I was an Indian and lived in the side of this cliff, and I was sick and there was a man on a white horse and he . . ." Her father became quite upset and stopped her, saying, "No honey, the devil put thoughts in your head. Jesus came once, so you don't need to do that." She persisted in trying to tell him how real this memory was to her, and he said even more firmly, "No, honey!" and walked away. "This was the beginning of shutting me down," Kristin related. Only when her own son started to express his inner knowing did she begin to reawaken her own.

The rise of scientism and psychiatry have made it even less reasonable to have a source of inner guidance. Contemporary psychiatry tends to dismiss such moments as mere fantasy or, worse, as a sign not of divinity, but of pathology. The result has been a stunning repression of our ability to meet the Divine. Traditionally, if Moses were to enter the psychiatric consultation room, he would be diagnosed as delusional. Mohammed would be categorized as schizophrenic for his meeting with the angel Gabriel. If Jesus were to have an intake interview, he would likely be offered antipsychotic medication. Few would debate that there is real pathology and suffering that benefits from diagnosis and professional care; that is not the issue. The problem is when we misinterpret epiphany as pathology. This usually happens when we prejudge the surface of a symptom rather than digging to its root.

Thanks to the work of some thoughtful experts, the primary diagnostic manual for psychiatric disorders has added a category, "Spiritual Emergency," to describe crises of meaning and experiences that have a spiritual flavor.[8] Children's experiences reflect natural emergence and not necessarily an emergency, but we are beginning to recognize that the spiritual is central to our well-being, not a marker of our pathology. The Joint Commission on Accreditation of Hospital Organizations is now requiring that assessment and treatment plans for patients, including mental health patients, include spiritual considerations. This is a very mainstream recognition that spirituality is central to our healing and wellness. As of this writing I am helping to integrate spiritual considerations into the clinical assessment and treatment approaches of a local hospital's mental health staff who work with children.

Too Much

Beyond dismissing children's spiritual life, the other general danger is that we make too much of their spiritual experiences, overemphasizing or leading them in a way that makes them feel pressure to perform for others in order to win approval. A grandson of the famous psychic Edgar Cayce, described his own experience as a child when psychologists came from all over to see if he had inherited his grandfather's psychic abilities. He saw these visits as very intrusive and revealed that he was even bribed by a researcher to say that he saw strange colors and lights. He said that all he wanted was to be left alone and live a normal childhood. When children are used to fulfill our unfulfilled hope or exploited for our own gain, whether on a baseball field or with spiritual experiences, we distort their development.

Sometimes in an attempt to honor and respect children, we go too far and put them on a pedestal. When children are elevated to this height, it may become more difficult for adults to set limits, understand the children's immaturity, and recognize their range of needs. Because a child may have access to wisdom, wonder, and compassion does not mean that he or she is mature or without the need for guidance and instruction. We know that children can be distinctly unwise, naïve, impulsive, and self-indulgent—in other words, children. Development progresses along more than one line (physically, cognitively, emotionally, etc.) and is asynchronous (especially noticeable in gifted children). This means that while children may be expressing profundities of the wisest adults in one moment, they may be emotionally like a four-year-old when it comes to sharing toys, like a ten-year-old in relationships with friends, and like a thirteen-year-old when it comes to the self-discipline required to finish their homework.

Having expanded awareness and access to the deep currents of the stream of consciousness does not mean that we always make sense of it, listen well, or act on the information or insight. After all, even as mature adults, we often behave unwisely. We cannot expect children to have it all together, and therefore, as parents and teachers, we should not be afraid to parent and teach—comfort, guide, set limits, and try to understand the unique needs of each child.

From the height of a pedestal, children have a great balancing act to play out in their lives. If they fail to live up to expectations that others hold for them—which is very likely—they have a very long way to fall. The adoration and pressure of many child movie stars is a good example of how expectations and pressure can lead to crises. We see so many who as teens or adults have serious addictions and distorted relationships, and even attempt suicide.

When it comes to spirituality, sometimes a similar kind of attention and elevation reinforces the idea that the child is "more special" and thereby encourages a kind of "spiritual narcissism"—"I'm more spiritual than you"—instead of the kind of mutuality, respect, and humility that spiritually wise souls teach—"I'm special and so are we all." Without this respect and concern for others, the developing ego of the child will use whatever it is given for its own gratification and to demonstrate its superiority. Inevitably, this sets the child up to swing between delusions of grandeur and depths of inadequacy. Spiritual capacity (like any knowledge, experience, or talent) is dangerous and confusing when it is co-opted by the ego for self-glorification. It is most natural when it is used for learning, opening, and serving.

Spirituality is about the whole of our life, not just isolated moments, ideas, or skills. When adults overemphasize certain experiences or capacities—like seeing an angel—children may get the message that it is not them but their skills or experiences that are worthy and worthwhile. A child may make more of their experiences in order to fulfill a parent's expectations or to compete with a spiritually sensitive parent as a way to seek approval and attention. But experiences and capacities are secondary to how we use what know. The goal is not to have big experiences; it is to learn and to live with big love and big wisdom.

Making too much of special abilities or insights at the expense of basic well-rounded development may bypass natural developmental tasks in favor of some more glorious or shining path. This "spiritual bypassing," as mentioned earlier, is a common pitfall on the spiritual journey.[9] The inflation of special abilities has the potential to be used as an excuse to avoid dealing with more mundane—but essential—

demands such as developing friendships, dealing with fears and limitations, and playing well with others.

Barbara, a parent of a young girl, captures a sensible balance point between the "too much" and "too little" extremes. Of her daughter, she says, "I don't want to push her; I want to follow her toward it [the spiritual]. I don't want her to say things like 'I'm seeing a spirit' or whatever just to get a reaction. Instead, I want to be open and responsive to her, not afraid to ask her questions, but treating what she says as if it were like finding a new bug in the yard or a painting she brought home from school. I want her to show me, talk about it, and explore it like anything else in her life."

Balancing Heaven and Earth

There are all sorts of problems and difficulties on the spiritual path, including various crises, confusions, and opportunities. In what follows, we will consider a range of more specific problems that children face. However, there are plenty more concerns and helpful suggestions than I can mention here. Please feel free to write me about what you have encountered and what has helped the children you know. The more we understand these considerations, the more they can be dealt with as "normal" development, thereby avoiding the repression, confusion, shame, and pathologizing that create layers of avoidable problems on top of the original challenge.

The Divine Creates a Demand

"It all began with the crash of a car against a brick wall and the small knee of an eleven-year-old boy caught in between," Jungian psychologist Robert Johnson described. Robert's leg was pinned against the wall of a building he was entering to buy a Coca-Cola. The major artery was severed and he was rushed into emergency surgery. It looked like he was going to make it. However, after surgery, he was lying in his hospital bed slowly bleeding to death. The sutured artery had broken loose, but no one realized it. He reported,

> I set my feet against the downward spiral and determined not to die, resisting it with all my willpower. But at a specific moment I crossed a divide . . . and suddenly I was in a glorious world.
>
> It was pure light, gold, radiant, luminous, ecstatically happy, perfectly beautiful, purely tranquil, joy beyond bound. I wasn't the least bit interested in anything on the earthly side of the divide; I could only revel at what was before me. . . . It was all that any mystic ever promised of heaven, and I knew then that I was in possession of the greatest treasure known to humankind."[10]

But Robert's return from the "golden world" was very difficult. He struggled to find beauty, meaning, and purpose on this side that could compare with what he had seen on the other. He tried to make sense of what he had seen and to reconcile the golden world that he glimpsed with the gray world that he found too often in his daily life. He found himself balancing a lifetime between heaven and earth.

A glimpse of the Divine creates a demand in us. When our consciousness opens to the depths of the spiritual, we are moved and changed, and it can be difficult to find new footing—a center point where we can balance the worlds successfully. For example, in P. M. H. Atwater's research on children's near-death experiences, one-third of children studied turned to alcohol within five to ten years after their experience. Over half dealt with serious bouts of depression. A staggering 21 percent actually attempted suicide (this number compares with 4 percent in adult near-death experiencers).[11] Confusion, guilt, shame, lack of understanding, and family members who felt threatened contributed to the difficulty in balancing the worlds.

Although she did not have a near-death experience, Elaine saw moments of profound wonder and perfection not unlike Robert's golden world. She said this of her childhood epiphanies: "It's like a gift and a curse all in one . . . of being pulled to seeing something else . . . having these wonderful experiences and yet, 'Oh, I have to keep on with the day-to-day,' the mundane. No one else was talking about these experiences, so I felt like I never fit in. My mother used to say that I was like a little old lady when I was a child."

After Black Elk had a vision at age nine, recounts his friend Standing Bear, he, too, seemed to have aged in some inexplicable way. Standing Bear remembered "riding together and talking and he [Black Elk] was not like the same boy. He was more like an old man."[12]

Terry describes her glorious childhood visions: "The moments of connection were so wonderful, so intense, ecstatic, sublime that they made the other times just pale by comparison. These experiences kept sort of detaching me; I kept having an image of a new background to my background. As a child, these experiences happened just matter-of-factly and I thought, *Well, this is how it is.* And it was amazing. There was no judgment.

"When I got a little older, I became aware that other people weren't experiencing the same things, or at least they weren't talking about them. I never had a negative experience except what I would do to myself afterward. In time, I came to use my bliss against me: *I'm strange. I'm weird. No one is talking about this stuff.* I made myself wrong. Those experiences were wonderful, but because my family told me what I should and should not be seeing, these moments became confusing. I kept thinking, *Is this illusion, just a game?* When you get a glimpse of it, you just can't jump back into daily life and pretend you haven't seen something else. Now I'm able to use it more."

For Terry, learning to mindfully observe her life rather than just reacting automatically to it has helped her balance the worlds. She says, "Witnessing helps. It's like being on the center hub and things are moving slower than on the outer part of the wheel, yet you are experiencing the outer wheel as well. I don't get so stuck in reacting to any one thing."

When the truth we see with our own eyes and the truth that we are told about are two very different things, it creates tremendous confusion, as it did for Terry, which can lead to anxiety, guilt, and self-judgment. If a child's experiences are met with derision or dismissal, or described as the work of the devil, he or she has to split that part of him- or herself off in order to fit in and try to be loved. This leads to tremendous repression and the creation of a shadow that can haunt for a lifetime. When we deny what we see and what we know, we live against ourselves. We live a lie and we suffer because of it.

The antidote to this alienation is really pretty simple. Finding others (in person or in stories) who have also gotten a glimpse of the spiritual is like finding an oasis in a desert. When a child finds someone who can relate to and understand the depth of the vision, or at least who wants to understand, he or she no longer feels alone. Once the gift is accepted and the judgment and shame fade, the task then shifts to finding ways to express what was seen, perhaps through art, music, poetry, and especially the way we choose to live in the world. Sometimes the golden moments inform a life's calling by shaping a career or a faith. Others try to make this life more like the world they glimpsed by bringing love, beauty, or justice to the world in their own unique way. Once we learn to trust our experience, we can stop judging and repressing ourselves, and let the gold shine through our life.

I Don't Fit

The parent of a seven-year-old boy describes his infancy as very difficult: "When he gained command of language, he would regularly say that 'this life is too hard,' or that he 'wished he would have not been born,' or that he 'should have picked a different time to come here.' This just broke our hearts, but it began to help us see what a tough adjustment this life can be, especially for highly sensitive kids."

Another mom says of her five-year-old son, "If we don't understand him the first time, rather than explain he gets vaguely annoyed and says, 'Never mind.' My son often tells me that he shouldn't have come back right now and that he should have stayed away longer. I think with these kids we have to be gentle and guide them with love and patience. They get very frustrated at having to learn things over again. I wonder how we would feel if we woke up one day in the body of a child."

The sentiment of these little children is not uncommon and can even lead to the extreme of considering suicide. This reflects how difficult the transition to this life can be. Such sensitive children require more support, assurance, and space to find the unique ways that their gifts can grow, those things we discussed in chapter 6.

Most of us are experiencing a world that has speeded up. We can expect instant communication, overnight delivery, and a hurried race through the day. But some children are frustrated by the slow and plodding pace of words, classrooms, and maybe adults in general. Einstein said it hurt him to slow down to write. Some children tend to think in visual and spacial images and in leaps and circles rather than in steps and lines. Their minds move fast and grasp wholes more easily than parts. If we, as adults, are not able to keep up with them, they may be frustrated and withdraw ("Never mind"). Children with an especially intuitive style of knowing may "get" things at a glance. They perceive a packet of information—energy—immediately and may determine the value of something very quickly. For example, they may instantly assess the desirability of a television show as they click through the channels or the trustworthiness of the person standing in front of them. The inner assessment may sound something like this: *This is irrelevant to me. . . . . This doesn't [or does] have much to do with my purpose on Earth. . . . I resonate with the feel of this. . . . I just know.*

Sometimes a child's insight and style of knowing is a threat to a teacher and/or parent. For example, having a child know the answers or move quickly without linear steps may be a frustration for a teacher who is trying to walk her class through the sequential steps of solving a particular problem. In situations like this, the problem is not so much the child's per se, but one of fit between the child and the classroom. It can be difficult for children to slow down enough to fit in. In a context of a highly homogenized school curriculum and tightly structured teaching styles, many children have trouble finding a rhythm of learning with which they can join.

According to the Centers for Disease Control and Prevention, 9 percent of current American public school boys have been diagnosed with attention deficit disorder.[13] These epidemic numbers say as much about the school system as they do about individual children. A child may need to move toward the school—everything from medication to behavioral management to loving support is used toward this end. But the school needs to move toward him or her as well by reconsidering the assumptions of what "normal" thinking and learning are and how many educational practices are built on the erroneous idea that "one size fits all"—that all children should be able to learn and think effectively in the same way.

Trial and error in parenting and education may be inevitable because the innate style of thinking or being of these children seems different, out of phase with what we take to be normal. Sometimes experimenting with simple changes may help children find a fit. Anything from the color of their room (has the child selected it?) and the arrangement and flow of furniture to their diet, sleep schedule, and the posture and conditions under which they study may affect their ability to be effective and feel at home in this body and this world.

Children need to find outlets for the pace and depth of what they see, to develop capacities for self-expression. They need to find their voice, their sense of purpose. They need to be told the big picture and be respected for the way they know. Most children are appreciative of getting the big picture. We show respect by filling them in on our adult rationales and involving them in decisions that affect their lives. If they offer an alternate way of doing something— from homework to cleaning their room to walking down the street—consider it their creative attempt to find a way that works for them, rather demanding that they comply with your way.

There are other ways that children can be out of synch. Some are extremely sensitive to touch, movement, sound, and sight, while others may be underresponsive to these same stimuli. Karen goes through times when she cannot stand being touched; Alan seems to first "freak out" and then shut down around noises that might not bother you or me. These problems have come to be grouped under the term *sensory integration dysfunction*. There is currently quite a lot of information out there on this type of sensitivity, so I will not go into it further here except to suggest that children who perceive multidimensionally do not always process sensory data in a typical fashion. We may need to take special care and have more flexibility with such children.

Children who move so differently are among the most challenging to teach and parent. It is especially important to develop community in order to gain support for yourself as a parent. This means nourishing yourself so you can nourish your child. As with all children, it is also helpful for your child to find community—friends. When a child finds someone who has a similar rhythm, style, or a mission in life, there is recognition, a kind of frequency lock that can make it easier for him or her to be here.

Feeling Everything

A great many children and adults have told me about being so sensitive and open that they end up feeling confused, or tugged by feelings or thoughts of others, or just plain overwhelmed by the deluge of feelings that wash over them. If you are empathically sensitive, I suspect you will instantly recognize what I mean.

Seventeen-year-old Sarah tells about a surprisingly typical circumstance of being a kind of psychic sponge: "I'm an empath, and I hate school. I walk around and people walk in and out of classes, and I get everything from them—their anger, frustration, even happiness or joy. But it's no fun. I'm not a big fan of crowds . . . but I'm working on turning the empathy on and off."

June, who said she was extremely sensitive to the "vibes" of others, dealt with this sense of being overwhelmed in her own way. "I became a loner," she said. "I didn't understand why at the time. I was naturally tuning into so many things, and I didn't know what I was tuning into or what to do with it, and I became a very moody child. I don't know why I picked up all different people's feelings, but I did. Plenty of times I would be down and I didn't understand why, and then I'd realize I was picking up other people's moods. My escape was sleep. I would sleep long hours to keep away from all those feelings. I didn't know what else to do."

A psychotherapist might have diagnosed June as depressed. It is hard to say how many children withdraw like June in order to compensate for their empathic sensitivity. Along with moodiness, withdrawal, and feeling overwhelmed, some children try to manage their sensitivity by creating a kind of barbed perimeter around them with a hostile personality or even aggressive behavior. They try to keep others away so they do not pick up so much from them. Others may turn to alcohol or drugs to try to numb out. However, these do not create an effective boundary; the children just cannot feel as clearly. Without knowledge of what is happening, children grow up coping by defending against feeling instead of knowing the world directly through their intimate meeting with it.

Especially for children who are deeply empathic, it is hard to be in a home that does not feel safe. If there is frequent conflict or lack of genuine attention and affection, it is hard to feel welcome. A hostile or inordinately chaotic environment causes a child to contract for protection, act out the hostility in some way, or dissociate from the body so they do not feel so much. On the other hand, consciousness does gravitate toward safety, beauty, caring, and gracious warmth.

Families operate as systems. If something is happening in one part of a system, the other parts will be affected. Children are sometimes the emotional barometer for their parents' relationships. How might the child be manifesting the energy of the family? Are they taking on Mom's depression or acting out the unspoken conflict between Mom and Dad? Does their lostness or hostility reflect the anger or hopelessness of the family? Are they working hard to be the "good child" in order to fulfill Mom or Dad's unfulfilled hope, or are they serving as a scapegoat to release tension in the system? Empathically sensitive children are particularly adept at responding to the dynamics of the system, sometimes at the cost of their own freedom. We help to unwind unhealthy roles when family members, especially parents, attend to their conflicts and difficulties directly. Doing our own work as parents frees our children from trying to do it for us.

There is another related problem that occurs with empathically sensitive children. When children know things about others or about things that are to come, sometimes they, especially young children, misinterpret information as responsibility. We know how common it is for children in the middle of a divorce to assume that they have contributed to the parental woes. They often think that if only they were "a better child," the parents would stay together. The same type of self-blame and sense of responsibility can occur when a child has a precognitive experience—knowing something is going to happen before it occurs, or knowing something at a distance, or knowing someone's feelings or intention directly. They may think that they should have said something, that they should have intervened, or that, in some magical way, this was their fault. They may believe that knowing about it means they *caused* it.

Researcher Samuel H. Young offers an account of Jenny, aged seven, who was riding in the back of the car when she asked, "Mommy, if a man in a big truck, a man who can't speak English, bangs into our car and doesn't hurt us but smashes the car, do we have to pay to get the car fixed?" *What an odd question*, her mother thought, and went on to explain what insurance was. It wasn't long before their car was indeed hit by a man who didn't speak English, driving a dump truck. No one appeared hurt, but Jenny was hysterical and was taken to the hospital to check for injury, including possible head trauma. No injury turned up, but through her tears she finally said, "It was my fault!" "What was your fault?" the physician asked. "I knew the accident was going to happen and I didn't tell Mommy."[14]

This "magical thinking" can be a tremendous source of anxiety, guilt, and confusion in a child. Helping children recognize the difference between knowing something and being responsible for its occurrence is part of mature discernment. A simple conversation with a child about this topic is often enough to help them release the guilt and form a new understanding.

This whole theme of "feeling everything" is related to the nature of boundaries. Because developing appropriate boundaries is central to several major concerns, I have included some direction for managing boundaries toward the end of this chapter.

What's the Point?
Children have questions and crises of meaning. They can ask those tough philosophical questions about the point of life, and they

often hunger for a purpose, as we have discussed. Unless these questions are addressed genuinely, children may find little point for being here. Agitation may lead to anxiety, even desperation or hopelessness.

An articulate young teenager told me, "I'm not sure that I really belong here. I know there is more to it [life], but no one is talking about it. I can't be the only one who sees it. Everything seems like a game. How can they say one thing and do another? How can they be so dense? I just feel betrayed; the adults don't seem to get it. How can they act like that? They are supposed to be adults. How can my family act like that? Since third grade I've kept a bag packed under my bed in case I get the courage to run away, but to where? Is it different anywhere else? Doesn't anyone understand? What's the point?"

This is a child hungry for spiritual sustenance. At least three sources may help provide that nourishment: a spiritual friend, a story, and the Divine itself. For a child struggling with deep questions of meaning, someone who has also asked the big questions can be a source of affirmation. Honest and open conversation about the meaning of life and the nature of spirit can be like fresh air: "I think life is about . . . I think that after we die we . . . What do you think?" A spiritual friend is especially helpful to offer understanding and guidance, and to pose more questions: "When have you felt closest to meaning, spirit, God, in your life?" "When have you felt whole?" "What do you think life is about?"

Socrates drew out meaning and the wisdom that lies within by posing questions rather than offering answers. We can do the same or maybe we can find a spiritual mentor for our child. This is the traditional role of elders, godparents, and the wise men and women in a community. These folks are still around; sometimes we call them therapists, rabbis, ministers, grandparents, and so forth. Of course, simply because people have a title or credentials, it does not make them wise. They may be pushing their own agendas rather than listening for our children's. But I suspect we can each think of a few folks who seem wise and a few moments when our own wisdom rises to the surface in the form of a juicy question.

Spiritual stories (*Siddhartha, The Alchemist, Lord of the Rings*, etc.) and rich ideas about life provide another source of nourishment on this quest for meaning.[15] Books like these often offer a lesson, but most importantly, they tell us that we are not alone—other people also ask these big questions, seek purpose, and feel like an outsider.

This style of spiritual seeking—searching for meaning—often involves a mind that is constantly reaching out to try to grab that meaning. This provides a powerful focus, but sometimes a kind of obsession or desperation goes with it. One of the great spiritual lessons is the counterpoint to reaching, searching, and grasping. It is the capacity to *receive* divine love. We have spoken of facets of receiving as willingness, constructive surrender, listening, and trust. We are reminded of the invocation "Ask and ye shall receive"[16] and of allowing the life force—the Tao—to carry us. Meaning sometimes comes when we work it out, but it also arrives when we are willing to let it find us. There really is no universal way to teach this idea of receiving divine love, but maybe by entertaining the possibility, by practicing little moments of letting go, of simple appreciation, and asking for help, we soften the landing field for grace and learn to recognize our direct connection with the Divine.

There is little passion or relevance in finishing homework, cleaning a room, or being nice to an aunt until meaning and mission are clarified. But when children are able to explore meaning through a story, a conversation, or a glimmer of insight or grace that touches that deep longing within, suddenly there is hope and energy to sustain them. When they can create meaning and link up with their mission, life comes into focus, the world magically gets aligned, and there is inspiration to carry on. They become different human beings.

Spaced Out

Ellen, a professional in her forties, recalled her own childhood: "I was always called a 'sensitive child' because I felt things so deeply and saw a lot of things, especially in the dark. I saw faces and colors every night when I went to bed. I slept with my light on for many years because as soon as it was dark, the visuals intensified. I was primarily raised by my father, who was a physicist, and I can remember telling him that I could see molecules because I didn't have another name for the color and the energy that I was seeing. And he would kindly explain to me why that wasn't possible, but he didn't understand what was happening. So I felt isolated and frightened; I thought that something was going wrong with me. I was seeing things that other members of my family couldn't. I could see this all along, but I remember feeling particularly anxious around six or seven because I realized that no one was talking about this, no one was saying, 'Oh, yeah, I had that experience.' So I just learned to keep it to myself.

"School was difficult for me because I tended to be unconsciously focused on what people were feeling. I had this tremendous empathy for someone who was having a hard time, and in the midst of feeling, I would miss the math lesson. I remember my fifth-grade teacher. I would just commune with her as I was sitting at my desk and she was at the blackboard. I would be staring at her, as all the other kids were, and then I would go into this other dimension where I would know what was going on inside of her and inside her life. It really is that feeling of moving into the energy, feeling oneness. But of course I was missing the math lesson. I think I was the kid who would look out the window and feel oneness with all of life and be called spaced out. It became difficult because I was being told not to see this way but instead to see in the way the adults wanted me to."

What would we assume if we have a student or a child who seems spacey like this? Children who perceive multidimensionally may be viewed as slow learners, autistic, attention disordered, on drugs, or all sorts of other labels because they have not learned the accepted way of seeing the world. Children like Ellen may operate in multiple worlds, but without support and understanding they may end up shutting up, shutting down, or getting labeled. They do not need to be "cured"; their own unique ways of perceiving need to be honored. Even if we do not fully understand what is going on, we can try to help them find ways to keep their uniqueness alive and at the same time find balance in the world.

One of the first principles of being spiritual beings on Earth is that we live in bodies. Our bodies anchor us here on the planet, and rather than being an obstacle to spiritual growth, as has sometimes been assumed, the body is the pathway given. Bodily sensations may help us to recognize moments of expanded perception. Things like unexplained headaches, ringing in the ears, "spaceyness," dizziness, and stomachaches are sometimes hints that children are perceiving interdimensionally. In some cases their perceptions are not especially anchored in the three-dimensional world. They may instead be tuned in to a teacher's emotions (like Ellen), to world trauma, or to floods of ideas, or they may notice colors and shapes or all sorts of things that most of us do not see, perhaps that we can hardly imagine. Their perceptual style allows them to focus on different dimensions of reality. This can provide them with remarkable information, but it can also make it harder to be in phase with the three-dimensional world that is often taken as the only reality.

One challenge is to find the right proportion of being anchored in one's body, so as to be effective in the physical world, without closing off access to the depths that exist beyond our three-dimensional plane. Simple physical activity—a walk, swim, whatever they are drawn toward—can help children to feel grounded and present in their bodies. Drinking water, having a massage, and eating well all tend to ground us. Stretching, taking a few deep breaths, sharing in a big hug, letting out a loud moan of release, singing, activating any and all of the senses, sometimes changing their diet, and being outside can all help children to more deeply inhabit their bodies.

Basic grounding exercises can be practiced with children by inviting them to take a few deep breaths and bring awareness and feeling into their feet and their bottom, perhaps imagining themselves growing roots like a strong tree or resting like a pyramid on the earth. We also help children to ground by being grounded ourselves. We can practice this in the car or bus on the way to school, at home before a meal, when fears arise, or in any moment when our presence is required.

Helping children gain awareness of where their energy is can help put them in control. We can simply ask, "Where are you now? In your head? Flying around? Thinking about the future or the past? Now draw your attention to your body." We can take them through a body scan, starting at one end of the body and bringing awareness through the levels of the body, noticing where it feels tight, open, numb, or alive, for example. We can ask them to bring more attention, warmth, light, or whatever is called for to the part of their body that seems to need some help.

Expressing and sharing their perceptions can bring children into the open for validation and clarification. Asking them to draw a picture or use other media to express their perceptions can be especially powerful and revealing. We might also invite them to share with us through questions: "What are you seeing? What does it feel like? Have you seen anything like this before? What do you think this means?"

Being in the body in this way does not take away from the multidimensional perception; it instead helps children to be more present and effective in this world, too. And perhaps the biggest obstacle to being open and present is fear.

Facing Fear

Fears and other difficulties may be immediate, imagined, or vaguely remembered, but all fear can be acknowledged, talked through, made space for. It is insufficient to try to talk a child out of his or her fears. Even the fear of a scary dream can be a powerful lesson. At about eight years old, one of my daughters woke up in the middle of the night with a very scary dream. Sitting at her bedside, I asked her to tell me about it. "It's too scary," she protested. After a few more requests, she described being chased by some people who almost caught her before she woke up. I asked her to describe the details—how she felt, where she was, who else was there, and so forth. Once she talked them out, she was able to calm down some and soon went back to sleep. But before she did, I suggested that if something like this happened again, she could turn, face the creature or person, tell them to stop, ask them what they want, and then tell them to leave. "You might also find a special way to leave them behind," I said. "Do you think you can try that if you have another scary dream?" "Maybe," she said. "You'll be surprised what you can get them to do," I offered.

Two nights later she had another dream, but this time we did not hear about it until the next morning. "I had that dream again!" she said, as I was getting her up for school. But instead of being frightened, she was actually excited. "This time I remembered I was dreaming. I stopped and turned around as we were running, put my hand out, and said, 'Stop!' They did! Then I asked them what they wanted. They said, 'I don't know; nothing, I guess.' They didn't look so scary or big. Then I told them to go, to leave me alone. And they started to walk away. Then I flew away on a hang glider." This lucid dreaming was remarkably empowering for her, serving not only as a way for dealing with a nightmare, but as a metaphor for dealing with the fears that might come along during the daytime.

This same formula for facing fear will work in all sorts of domains, from dealing with a dream to a difficult acquaintance, to our own feared shadow—a disowned part of us—and even to an unwanted ghost. Face and acknowledge what confronts us; ask what it wants, what it has to offer, or what there is to learn; ask the universe for help; set limits perhaps by telling it to move on. In a Jungian sense, the shadow that we fear wants to be acknowledged, and then it can integrate or withdraw.

Beyond more typical fears, some children have phobias, obsessions, deep inexplicable longings, and knowledge of places or events that seem unlikely, if not downright impossible. Psychiatrist Ian Stevenson, along with other researchers, has suggested a link between alleged past-life memories and physical and psychological symptoms.[17] (We touched on this in chapter 5.) Whether or not this definitively points to past lives or some other explanation does not matter. Children are deeply affected regardless of how we explain it.

Nicole said, "I've always been cautious of bringing up my son's fear of being in a car during a storm. I have to warn people of it if they take him anywhere, but I never explain why. Even when he was just a baby he would scream and cry if we were in the car and it was thundering and lightning. I didn't think anything of it, just that it scared him, until one day my son let me in on his secret. Before he turned two, he told me that he had died in a car accident during a big storm back when he was six. He told me more about it over the next two years and gave me many details. He says his mom—that wasn't me—died too. This hasn't been brought up since he was four until two nights ago, when he told me that he hoped we don't die in a storm like he did the last time he was six. He'll be six in a couple of weeks."

Parent and author Carol Bowman was surprised when she learned the roots of her six-year-old's fear. Chase would become hysterical at loud booming noises like Fourth of July fireworks. One day while Chase was sitting on Carol's lap at home, a friend and hypnotherapist simply asked her son to relax and tell him what he saw when he heard loud noises that scared him. Chase then spontaneously told about fighting in a trench and being shot in the wrist with a bullet during wartime. Since infancy Chase had had severe eczema on his wrist and no amount of medical treatment had made much difference. Since his recounting his soldier story, the rash disappeared and has never returned.[18]

Trying to talk someone out of a phobia is like trying to talk a dog into giving up its favorite bone—it just will not happen. Whatever the source of the memory, it has become part of the programming of the subconscious mind. Anytime the memory is triggered (by a noise, a scene, or a person who looks or feels familiar), the program kicks in and we react. It appears that children have easy access to these realms of consciousness. With only minimal prompting, these types of memories will rise to the surface. Rather than something to be avoided, symptoms themselves are messages saying, "Come look here."

When children experience distressing symptoms, we can then simply invite them to relax, take some deep breaths, close their eyes, and feel into the experience, then ask them to describe the scene that is before them. Maybe they find themselves on a battlefield like Chase or facing some other difficult situation. Looking at this while feeling safe sitting on a parent's lap or in one's own bed is often an effective way of facing the fear directly.

Some folks find it helpful to use a guided visualization to find the way to this level of consciousness. Here is one that can be easily used with children. We can invite them to "Find yourself on a lovely path in a special place. Feel the ground under you, hear the sounds, smell the day, and feel the comfortable temperature of the air on your face. As you walk down this path, you'll see yourself approaching some steps that lead downward into a large round room with any number of doorways—you may find a few or a great many. Let yourself be drawn to the doorway that is most helpful to you right now. Open the door and, while remaining in the hallway, peer inside. Watch the scene unfold as if you were watching a movie. Try to describe what you see. You can fast-forward through any parts you want. Take the time you need. Is there anything you can learn that will help you? Is there anything you can let go of, forgive, or heal? Remember that that was then and this is now. When you've gotten what you've come for, you can close the door and return up the stairs and back down the path you came on. When you've reached the place where you started, open your eyes slowly and we can talk about this further."

Through going inward in this way, it is surprising to see how quickly a new perspective or a sense of release is gained on an entrenched problem. Sometimes this is enough to make the appropriate separation between this life and a particular memory. At other times more visits are required. Seeing the root of the issue and letting it go can release the grip of this subconscious programming.

How can we tell the difference between fantasy and past-life memory? Carol Bowman answers the question. First, she makes the point that both fantasy and past-life recall provide potentially useful information. Children's fears, worries, and passions may be expressed in fantasy play, and therefore it may be helpful to listen and watch for themes that might give us insight into their world. Past-life memories may also have some additional charge to them. Bowman suggests four general qualities that are typical of past-life recall: (1) matter-of-fact tone, (2) consistency over time, (3) knowledge beyond experience, and (4) corresponding behavior and traits (for example, a phobia, a particular talent, or a physical symptom that matches the incident). If you are interested in this topic as it relates to children, Bowman's book, *Children's Past Lives*, is the most comprehensive.[19] For a compelling autobiographical account you might also consider author Barbro Karlen's *And the Wolves Howled*.[20]

Working in the Dark

The majority of spiritual encounters that I have heard about from children and experienced myself are "positive." But what are we to think about children's (and adults') tales of a ghost that they see in their room, a spirit playing tricks, or a scary, even malicious, entity? Do children encounter energies that are not so benevolent and wise?

If we walk along a busy city street, we are likely to find folks who are ready to help us if we are in need and also those who are willing to take advantage of us. Among the crowd, there will be wise and generous souls as well as those who are small-minded and selfish. There will be some who want to play, some who want to give, and others who want to take. From the description of children and from the mystics who see into the invisible world, the same appears to be true in the nonphysical realms.

What are we to make of Michael, a nine-year-old boy diagnosed with autism who would hardly ever speak? He was watching the computer screen when his mom visited our ChildSpirit website. Michael got very excited and insisted to his mother that he needed to contact us. She said, "I can't understand this. He never responds to anything or anyone like this and has never wanted to contact anyone."

Michael wrote a letter to me, a part of which I want to share: "I want to tell you I like to swim in the sea. I am a fishy and Michael the fishy flies in the sky up to the clouds . . . and to the moon. I like to fly. I like to sit on the floor under the table and I like to play ball with me and you. I have good and bad people in my head. The bad people tell me not to talk, not to touch me, for no one to touch me. [They tell] the good people to be quiet." What do we make of his sudden insistence on communicating, his flying, and especially these people in his head? Fantasy? Beginning schizophrenic hallucinations? Or something else?

Professional consultant Frances Fox, who has had intuitive gifts since childhood, says, "The children who say that there is a monster in the closet, who need to sleep with the light on, and many who play with imaginary friends or hear voices have contact with the spirit world. Hardly anybody tells them that it's real, and if they are told that it's real and the parent is a 'New Ager,' they're told it is a nice angel. But there are also essences that don't have such great intention. This is a planet of light and dark, of duality, and to only teach about one side is to deny an aspect of reality. You don't have full choice if you don't have adequate information."

The bottom line is that not all visions, voices, and visitors are created equal. Just because "someone" does not have a body, it does not mean that he or she is trustworthy, has good information, or is smarter than we are. The radio receiver in our car or at home picks up various types and quality of information—from angry call-in shows to traffic reports to hard-sell advertising to music to world news and so forth. Not all channels provide information of equivalent quality or relevance. The same is true in accessing the invisible world. Many traditions warn of trickster spirits whose only task seems to be to upset the applecart for the sake of a prank (and sometimes for a humbling lesson). As we have heard, children describe ghosts who seemed quite lost or even predatory, while on the other hand some children talk about great beings who show them love. The challenge is to develop discernment through considering what the offering is and what we do with it. Does the offering from the invisible world

- encourage self-aggrandizement or service?
- fuel the ego or the soul?
- heal or harm?
- seem right in your body, in your heart, in your rational mind?
- provide distraction, distortion, delusion, or clarity?
- offer judgment and shame, or love and connection?

- cause you to feel like you need a shower or like you have just taken one?

Dialoguing with ourselves, with trusted others, and with these "voices" gives us the chance to develop discrimination; shutting them down gives us nothing.

We may also want to see if there is anything within the child that may make him or her vulnerable to the seen and the unseen world. Frances Fox says, "Unresolved trauma and unresolved issues are anchors for negative energy. They break our energy grid, which creates an opening for negative energy. The antidote is having an acceptance of everything you are. Don't try to throw it away or push it out, which breaks your energy field, but simply accept it. If you've done something awful, accept it; if you're afraid, accept it. The truth may be that 'I did such and such and that I'm ashamed of it, or that my parents beat me up, or the truth is that I hate this or that.' The more that you accept, the clearer you are and the less anchors you have for negative energy to stick to. Truth does cure all."

But even energies that we might typically judge as "negative" may also be here to teach us. Here is an example of how even what appears to be very dark can be a life-changing gift: Liz, at six, was seeing all sorts of things in the dark. She also had a regular visitor at night who was not very pleasant. She saw him as a man who was "a little scary." Her encounters with him were preceded by her reports of seeing a green and purple monster in part of her room. Liz's parents started to notice an unpleasant smell in the room, like really dirty socks. Her parents spent hours tearing the room apart and cleaning trying to get rid of the smell, but it would come and go unrelated to Liz's dirty laundry or the condition of her room. They couldn't figure it out.

Then they started feeling something unpleasant sometimes when they entered the bedroom, a kind of gut sense of some disgust and fear. When this smell and the feeling seemed present, they would discover that Liz would often masturbate. In and of itself this, of course, is no reason for concern; it is normal for children to masturbate. But in this case it seemed excessive and also remarkably tied to her reports of this visitor; it was as if a wave of energy wafted over her. Was this some invisible sexual predator? they wondered.

As parents, it would be easy to completely "freak out" over this whole scene. As you read this, you may even start to feel a kind of contraction. But these parents hung in there and tried to work with it. For a parent who acknowledges an unseen world, the first inclination is probably to try to banish this being, protecting this little girl at all costs. The parents said prayers and got advice on ritual cleanings. These seemed to help a bit, but it did not seem to solve the problem. The visitor would return, as did Liz's moodiness, irritability, and self-doubt. Then they asked a question to themselves that proved critical: Was there something for Liz or for all of them to learn in this?

The answer to this question is multifaceted. First, the fact that she was seeing the invisible was important. Perhaps she would use this perception to help others understand those influences that swirl around us. For now they needed only to honor that she did see and make it safe for her to talk about what she saw.

But what about this visitor? Why had he come, and what was his offering? And how were the parents to get rid of him? Sometimes the parent just needs to rescue the child, to grab him or her out of the path of oncoming danger. But most of the time our best approach is to offer coaching from the sidelines, or in this case, the bedside. What if the lesson were for Liz to protect herself, to learn to claim her power and discern what she wanted near her and what she did not, despite any lure?

In this case her parents asked Liz how she felt about the visitor. "He scares me sometimes," Liz said. "Do you want him to stay away or be near?" her mom asked. "I want him to move away," said Liz.

"OK, let's ask the visitor to move away or leave if you want." "You mean to say it?" Liz asked. "I think you could either say it out loud or in your mind," her mom replied. Liz concentrated for a few seconds and then said, with some surprise, "I did and he left."

Was the gift of this visitor for her to learn to face fear and learn her own power? The visitor returned several more times, Liz reported to her parents. He seemed to arrive like a smelly narcotic, but with decreasing effect—less fear, less lure. Either on her own or with a little reminder, Liz could make her own choice about having this guy around, and she usually sent him packing.

In short order, she began to feel less afraid and seemed more rested on many mornings. On her own, one day she thought to ask the visitor what he wanted. She said that he did not really have an answer. Her mom wondered if they might send him best wishes for his own growth, when Liz sent him on his way. She moved from feeling great fear to feeling considerably more in control and even having some pity and compassion toward him. Within a few weeks Liz learned to take control and set firm boundaries—"Go away now"—and even began to offer something to him—"Go toward the light."

If we are open to the purpose these acts have come forth to create, everyone involved takes lessons away. In Liz's case, her parents better understood the depth of their child and the influence of other dimensions, while Liz learned about her personal power and discernment. Perhaps even the visitor took away some understanding of love and limits.

A year after first telling her family about her visitor, Liz was speaking up more at school, was rarely moody or had tantrums, had increased self-confidence, and seemed more powerful, playful, and loving. "She was remarkably lighter and more joyful," her parents reported. While she was still seeing a great deal of the multidimensional world, there had been no sign of this particular visitor.

Obviously this is a tricky area. Some folks will think this story is just silly, others might believe it deeply but fear it so much that they become panicked or paralyzed, and others are just not sure what to make of it. But if children experience the world in this way, the only honorable path is to try to understand and face it with them. We can take a lesson from these parents about how we might approach such difficulties. These parents

- prayed for protection, guidance, and healing, and invited Liz to do the same;
- sent Liz healing and loving energy;
- listened, believed, and tried to understand their child;
- saw this as a possible learning opportunity;
- coached the child very gently to take charge and intend what she wanted as if she were working with a bully on the playground;
- treated this being with both compassion and clear limits.

Boundaries

Being human means we are both separate and interconnected. Balancing these dimensions means regulating boundaries. Without an ability to shut off as well as open up and to let go as well as take in, we may be so buffeted by the winds of the world that we have trouble navigating our own path. While the opportunity at this point in our evolution may be to become more aware of interconnection, we must equally regulate our separateness and individuality. Regulation of boundaries does not require rigid fortified armor, but instead a living permeable membrane directed by our intention and guided by our awareness. This is essential for children who are empathic, seeing multidimensionally, or highly sensitive, or those who just do not feel

like they fit. Following are a few principles for developing boundaries for children and for adults.

What's Mine and What's Theirs

Helping children understand that it is possible to pick up others' "vibes" can be tremendously clarifying and affirming. A child can
then think to ask, "What's mine and what's theirs?" This opens the
door to check out feelings or impressions with others— "Mom, are
you angry?" With time, practice, and dialogue, children can begin to
notice the patterns—"When I feel this way it means . . ."—and refine
their ability to discern and understand what they pick up directly.

One way we can help children develop discernment is through
our own congruence as adults. They may pick up an intuitive energy
packet from us and "read" that we are upset about something; maybe
we have brought home an emotional hangover from work. But if we
deny those feelings in response to their curious looks, their spontaneous offering of a back rub, their moving away from us, or maybe
just asking how we are today, we give them mixed signals. Their
response becomes, perhaps, "I feel that something's wrong with
Mommy, but she says there isn't. What's a girl to think?" The white
or polite lie, the incongruence between what we say and how things
are really going, fosters confusion instead of confirmation. Our being appropriately honest and congruent helps children to refine and
trust their perceptions.

Nonattachment

Can we have feelings, thoughts, and other sensations without
getting overly attached to our reactions? The process of mindfulness, of witnessing the contents of our consciousness, can lighten
and liberate. It is often not the feeling that is the problem, but our
reaction and clinging to it, as we talked about in chapter 7. The idea
is to invite children to notice and describe what they are experienc-

ing without initially having to do anything with it. We can encourage them to just take a deep breath, make a little space inside, get an arm's length from it, and describe the feelings (or whatever) as if they were talking about a friend, and just watch them. Being still and witnessing in this way can quickly change the intensity or quality of the feelings or thoughts, perhaps allowing them to be released, soften, or open to insight.

Resonance Chamber

Our bodies serve as a kind of resonance chamber in which all sorts of feelings and thoughts can vibrate within us. Helping children to ground themselves in their bodies (as we spoke of above) can increase their capacity for feelings. If they are "present" in their bodies, there is more space to feel what comes their way. They can learn to tolerate more feeling and become less easily blown over or apart by their feelings.

Since as humans we do experience so much—joy, fear, blocks, pain, a sense of flow—through our bodies, we can invite children to pay close attention to the messages from their bodies in the form of feelings and sensations. We might ask a child to notice where in his or her body a particular issue or feeling seems to be. We can then ask questions that elicit details: "What color is it? What shape does it have? How dense is it? What is the surface like? Does it have a sound? Does it move? What comes to mind as you notice this? Does this have a message for you?" Sometimes during this kind of looking, the sensation starts to change and dissipate.

When we bring this kind of precision to our seeing, we realize that the sensation occupies only a part of us, not our whole being as it may have felt, and therefore it may be easier to work with or release. If it is still hanging around, we might invite the child to take a deep breath anytime he or she feels this, letting him or her know that each breath helps to keep this process fluid rather than rigid. We might ask, "What does this need? What would help this to be released or healed? [Maybe a certain color, comfort, acceptance, expression, and so forth.] In your mind can you give it what you feel it needs and hear what it has to say?" As we tune into this resonance chamber that we call our body, we can learn to gain sensitivity and precision in understanding how the world around us vibrates within us.

The Martyr

Sometimes we think we are supposed to take on others' pain and carry it for them. This belief can be like an old family heirloom that is passed down from generation to generation. However, having compassion does not require that we take on other people's burdens as our own. Doing so can actually interfere with their growth and contribute to their drama, rather than supporting them in doing their own work. Some adults do want others, even children, to become enmeshed with their own problems. But children need to carry only their own lives.

What Do I Do with It?

If we do not take on the burden of another or shut it out, what do we do with it? It is often hard to know what to do with compassionate feelings or how to express them. Sometimes we feel a spontaneous impulse to act—a hug or kind word is offered, and something is said or done that connects us. But most of the time, we just have these feelings and thoughts toward another person or maybe even the planet. For example, a child walks along a street and feels the hopelessness or hostility of a hungry person. What should he or she do?

We can remind children that their reaction is their choice. First, we can invite them just to witness it—to make a little space to feel it without getting attached to it, as mentioned above. Next, we might invite them to send the person a packet of our best intentions, love, and hope. A moment of thoughtful prayer and of loving thoughts sent with a kind glance is spiritual power. Next time, perhaps they offer something else—a sandwich or money—or maybe they are so moved that their life's calling is to start a homeless shelter in years to come. If children have this gift of intention to offer in the face of suffering, they are more likely to remain open toward suffering because they have something to offer everyone.

Letting Go

Breathing in and breathing out, this is the natural rhythm of life. If all we did was to take in—whether food, air, water, or the world's woes—we would find our reservoirs full and bursting. We can help children apply this organic principle of letting go of what they have ingested empathically or multidimensionally. Something as simple as inviting children in school to take three deep breaths and shake their hands and arms between classes or on the way to lunch may help them to release the day's accumulations.

Linda felt like her daughter was picking up the energies of others during her elementary school day. Her daughter regularly came home from school agitated, even though there had not been a significant event or worries that had led to this reaction. To clear this response, Linda developed a three-minute after-school exercise in which she and her daughter would sit down facing each other and place their hands, palm to palm, over each other's. They would take some deep breaths and then imagine that together they were releasing the energies of the day harmlessly into the air and then rebalancing themselves. Her daughter said she could feel the energies in her hands and feel them leaving her body. This simple homemade cleansing ritual was all that was required for her to make the transition from school to home.

Overstimulation

When children are exposed to horrific, overly violent, or sexualized material, there is a kind of invasion of their boundaries. This is obvious with issues of abuse or traumatic accidents, but it also occurs through media exposure. John said, "I saw a horror film when I was eight years old about creatures that sucked your brains out, and it created nightmares for years afterward."

Images are so riveting to the psyche, especially today's over-the-top, high-tech, digitally-mastered, surround-sound presentations, that they penetrate and get seared into the subconscious. Sexuality and violence are part of life, but shocking, invasive, and disturbing material can overstimulate a young mind without a child having the ability to process or integrate it. When this occurs it may leak out in dreams like John had, manifest as extraordinary fear or disturbing mental images, or perhaps show up as an addiction to more of this stimulation as a kind of repetition compulsion. Before a child is ready to handle it, exposure fuels the basic aggressive and sexual drives of the lower self without offering any way to work through it. Rich, complex, or real-world themes are not the problem; it is sensationalized and shocking images that can violate boundaries. Regulating the media diet (without becoming overly provincial or puritanical) is a basic task in caring for young, growing minds.

Assertiveness

We set and practice boundaries in the world by asserting ourselves—being honest, learning to say no, and asking for what we need in constructive ways. As soon as we can assert ourselves, we establish boundaries of our privacy, power, and protection. I estimate that at least 85 percent of the adult and adolescent clients that I have seen in psychotherapy have not known how to assert themselves effectively; they would swing from aggressive outbursts to passive, begrudging compliance. They would feel invaded, taken advantage of, misunderstood, or powerless. They were unskilled at asking for what they needed or stating calmly and clearly what they did not. None of them learned this skill in childhood and have suffered all of their lives because of it.

Helping children say no to peer pressure or to their siblings in a constructive way, or even to an "invisible" visitor, can be tremendously empowering. Something as straightforward as having children practice asking for what they want or need—ordering food at a restaurant, being honest and speaking the truth, writing a letter expressing their hurt to someone who has betrayed them—are down-to-earth ways to develop assertion. Helping them to make "I" statements, such as "I feel_____ when you do _____," gives a simple and effective strategy for asserting without the attack and corresponding defensiveness of a blaming "you" statement, such as "You are such a jerk; why did you do that?" Role-playing assertiveness helps to turn these ideas into practice.

Cutting a Cord

Sometimes we are not just tuning into the frequencies around us, but it feels more like there is some kind of cord between ourselves and someone or something else. This is sometimes felt in the solar plexus (and other locations as well) as a tug or pain. These links can exist for all sorts of reasons: perhaps someone is especially close to us or unusually needy, or perhaps they are hostile or jealous toward us. While this is an intimate connection, it is not an optimal one. This way of connecting can become a kind of subtle bondage, can feels more like obligation than love, and can turn manipulative. Breaking or changing this connection gives us the freedom to connect in a healthy way, rather than being blindly bound to another.

Cutting cords may take assertiveness or overcoming some sense of martyred obligation; it may take recognizing "what's yours and what's mine." Mostly it will take intention to make that cut and liberate the relationship. Julie, five, and her mother had a loving but some-times difficult relationship. They seemed to antagonize each other, and her mom would become extremely frustrated and unhappy with her own reactions to Julie. It seemed that they had a strange connec-tion with each other that did not enable the most loving relationship. So Julie's mom decided to try an experiment one night. Before going to bed, the mother set the intention in her mind that she would like to cut any unhealthy cords that she and Julie had that got in the way of their love. After a few minutes of concentrating on this crystal-clear intention, she drifted off to sleep.

At about 2 A.M. Julie awoke crying. She seemed half-asleep, but after several requests from her father, who had gone in to check on her, she told what she had seen in a dream: "I'm in the water and Mom is in the back of a boat. She has an old rope that she is pulling away from me. I'm reaching for it, but I can't get it. There's a ring [life buoy] that I'm holding on to."

Julie's mom reported a significant change in their relationship that occurred almost immediately. She said, "It's hard to describe, but I'm just not as triggered by her as I was. It's so much easier to love her. We are so much lighter with each other. I really see a major change in her and in our relationship."

A Safe Boundary

Sometimes or in some situations, we may need to take a break from floating in the empathic and psychic seas. If we feel invaded or constantly bombarded, we will spend all our energy trying to keep the world out. Children (and adults) can create a space by imagining a bubble around them that can change from clear to opaque and porous to solid, depending on how much or how little they want to allow in and how much they want to project out. Since so much is felt in the body, many folks can also imagine and sense their physical skin boundary as a kind of protection. Even a heavy shirt or a hand, say, over the solar plexus can serve as a reminder to claim the bound-ary of one's own skin.

If we feel like we have got our own private space, we are much more likely to want to make contact with others on our own terms. Jason, an "impossibly unruly" child, was given some chalk by his frus-trated teacher. They were out on the playground, and just for fun she asked him to draw a boundary around himself that would make him feel comfortable and safe. Over the next fifteen minutes, Jason drew a line around the entire playground, around buildings and trees, and around other children and teachers. He finally came back to his teacher and, with a rather satisfied expression, said, "There!"

His teacher suddenly began to get a sense of how vulnerable and sensitive this child must be, and also how violated he must feel when so much was within his perimeter. She then proceeded to work with him on establishing boundaries in other ways than driving oth-ers out of his space with hostility or simply reacting as if he was out of control. He soon revealed that he had been abused, and his need for exaggerated personal space symbolically reflected this intrusion. Ending the abusive living situation, learning basic assertion skills, constructing safe spaces in his artwork and his imagery, and working through the violation in therapy helped this boy gain new control of his boundaries.

Several months later, Jason was on the playground again and asked his teacher if he could borrow some chalk. She gave him a piece and wondered what he was going to do. He drew a line that went about three feet around him. "There!" he said, with a smile on his face. The message here is that we may be willing to risk allowing people in if we know we have the power to keep them out. Paradoxi-cally, privacy can breed intimacy.

Children are evolution's front edge, and so they may push us with all sorts of new challenges. As parents, teachers, and spiritual friends, perhaps the most fundamental thing we can do for our children's spirituality-related difficulties is to deal with our own spiritual and psychological longings and lacks, and work on our own ways of knowing the Infinite. When we do so we may not come up with tidy answers to the issues that arise, but we have more presence, which allows us to open to the help necessary for the very individualized concerns that children face.

The world (including the world of children) discloses itself to us only to the extent that we open to it. We open by facing our shadows—fears and foibles, baggage and biases—as well as our light. If we do not, we may be left with a widening spiritual generation gap, unable to stay in touch with the inner lives of our children and growing further from our own. And amidst all this talk about how we might help children, we need to remember that sometimes children are the ones who lead us.

Chapter 9

And *a* Child Shall Lead Us

Children can be our spiritual teachers. They lead us to love, sacrifice, responsibility, and all sorts of things of which we hardly knew we were capable. As adults, we often think of our relationships with children as involving *our* helping *them* to develop, but they help us grow as well. Development is mutual.

There is something quite remarkable about the presence of a child that serves to activate our spiritual nature—our capacity for wonder, compassion, communion, and hope. I am still amazed to watch what happens to busy and serious adults when a child unexpectedly crosses their path. Our attention shifts when a child enters our busy workplace. Our heart reaches out when we see a child in pain or danger. We soften, even melt, as a child stares innocently at us or looks for a lap or a hug. We stoop down, become silly, want to draw in close, and suddenly lighten as if gravity no longer has the same pull when we are in their presence. These are signs that something deeply special and deeply spiritual is happening.

My wife asked her father one evening as we were sitting around the dinner table if he had ever had peak moments—ecstasy—in his life. He immediately started to tear up and quietly answered, "When you were born." Few things can transform us so quickly as a child.

Children's presence gives us hints that to enter the spiritual kingdom, we must be like them—"become as little children"—pure of heart, open to mystery, and spontaneously alive. Black Elk of the

Oglala Sioux said it this way: "Grown men may learn from very little children, for the hearts of little children are pure, and, therefore, the Great Spirit may show to them many things which older people miss."[1] Spirit is like a current deep within us and between us, and, ultimately, it *is* us. We sense that current more clearly in children. Maybe the secret is that they just do not struggle against it as much as we adults seem to. Whatever the reason, the child's presence, if we pay attention, leads us into the depths of spirit.

Lessons

Children may teach us all sorts of things, from sacrifice to patience. Their way of knowing and being in the world may offer some of the most fundamental instruction for our spiritual lives. Four of these themes follow.

See the Adventure

We tell children to be serious, that life is hard work, while they remind us that life is an adventure to be lived. Albert Einstein, who retained a remarkable childlike wonder and imagination as an adult, knew this truth: "Anyone who is really serious knows that life is only a big adventure."[2] Children teach us to play with life. They help us see that the spiritual is not a list to get through, but a story to be lived.

It was a very windy morning with sheets of heavy rain falling. As I left our house, I noticed a large pine tree squarely across my retired neighbor's driveway. I stopped and knocked on their door to see if they needed help getting it out of the driveway. As soon as the door opened, it was easy to feel the anxiety and fear, and see the marks of frightened tears that had been shed. What had happened? I wondered. The story unfolded that as this couple's grown son was driving into the driveway to drop off their three-year-old grandson for the day, a sixty-foot-tall pine tree fell just a few feet in front of them—a scary event, to be sure. The adults were in a tizzy. They were fearful and also angry because the owner of the lot next door had not taken down this dead tree. The grandfather even said that he was worried that his son would be afraid to bring his grandson next time.

In the midst of all this, a little face was peering up at me. He startled me when I first saw him because he was such a contrast to the adults. It looked like he was glowing, almost ecstatic. When the adults turned their attention back to each other, I quietly asked him if this was exciting. He quickly nodded with wide eyes—his whole body was trying to control the excitement. But in the next instant, he furtively looked around to check and see if it was OK to be excited or whether he was supposed to be scared. Sure, there is plenty to be scared of, but this child's response reminds us of the exhilaration of life. In that instant, a three-year-old helped me to feel the adventure even in the midst of all this fear, anger, and worry.

Children show us that when we take an adventurous attitude, the bumps and unexpected delights of our days are just grace to behold. Even the great curse of "nothing to do" is transformed by the mind of adventure: a stick becomes a sword; a leaf turns into a boat in a great sea; a dollop of paint becomes a tree; a castle, a whole galaxy. When we view something, even a crashing tree, through a child's eyes, life becomes fresh and awesome. In just a few moments of being on children's level or in their shoes, we can often feel the delight of seeing with "beginner's mind" and begin to feel ourselves in the tug of this incredible, mysterious current.

One of the most fundamental requirements for adventure is that we throw ourselves into it. The re-enchantment of the world comes when we immerse ourselves in the situations that life brings us. Children's ability to be totally absorbed and lost in time reminds us that the measure of our life is not merely how much we have gotten done, how fast we have done it, and how much it cost, but the *quality* of the encounter. Moments of quality change the nature of time and bring us to the "eternal now."³ Our consciousness is opened beyond the narrow march of our time-bound world and into one that is filled with the spaciousness of the present. As philosopher Alfred North Whitehead reminds us, "The present contains all that there is. It is holy ground. . . . The communion of saints is a great and inspiring assemblage, but it has only one possible hall of meeting, and that is, the present."⁴ The child's mind of adventure leads us to holy ground in the here and now.

Live Everything

As adults, we are to learn control of our feelings. Crying in public is a sign of weakness to most; singing and shouting out of delight is met with suspicion: Drugs? A mental disorder? But overly rigid control is not only a constriction of our expression of feeling, but it constricts the feeling itself. The message common in the adult world seems to be that we are supposed to live within a narrowly controlled bandwidth of feeling—not too low and not too high. (In our culture, attempts to break out of these confines in order to feel more vitality and intensity lead to all sorts of behavior, from extreme sports to drug use.)

Children, on the other hand, tend to let it all hang out. They feel and usually show what they feel—they teach us about being congruent. The long-awaited ice cream falls off the cone and into the dirt, and a screech of grief follows. A magician performs a trick, and a child gasps in joyful wonder.

Now I am not suggesting that as adults we should cry when our ice cream falls, or dance on the table at the board meeting, or that we should be lead around merely by emotions. In fact, some adults need more distance and perspective from their emotions, not less. (We spoke of this as mastering oneself in chapter 8). But many of us have restricted our range of affect and our spontaneity by overly filtering and prejudging the contents of our consciousness, rather than allowing the feelings and thoughts we have. If we deny those feelings, we tend to miss the vitality of our life. The spiritual does not fragment or discriminate; instead, it unites. If we predetermine a feeling or thought as good or bad rather than just allowing it, we create dark places within us that lodge and hide these shameful shadows.

By contrast, watch what happens sometime when a young child is allowed to just have his or her feelings. The feelings usually run their course and the child comes full circle. The feeling of pleasure or pain is just felt and then is gone. Unlike what happens when we judge or try to restrict our consciousness, it does not get stuck anywhere in the body or the mind, and the child is free to move on to the next vital moment without baggage.

The lesson for adults is to allow ourselves to feel what we feel, whatever it is. This is about being honest with ourselves. When we give the experience space to exist within us, we can witness it, enjoy its intensity, and then let it run its natural course without getting attached to it. We are controlled neither by the feeling nor by trying to keep certain feelings at bay. By having the experience without restricting it, our lives are opened to spontaneity rather than contracted by a controlling belief or judgment. Even, and maybe especially, the feelings that accompany tears have a special honored place. They are bearers of overwhelming grief, of deep contrition, and of unspeakable love. They are not the mark of weakness, but of power. Tears, like laughter, clean, clarify, and purify. The point of life is not to restrict it, but to live it, to feel it—just like a child.

Be in Our Bodies
Most developmental theorists, beginning with Piaget, have assumed that the pinnacle of development is an ability to think abstractly

and reflectively, which enables us to make models, maps, and theories about the world—mediating the world with the mental. But as we develop, we do not naturally lose our earlier capacities of more body-based knowing, such as smelling a rose or having a gut feeling about something. Healthy development involves integrating the capacities that emerge earlier with those, like abstract thinking, that emerge later.

However, as our cultural capacity for abstract thinking has increased, we have not always done so well at integrating the wisdom of our bodies. The result is alienation from our bodies, our senses, even our natural connection with the body of Earth. Instead of listening to our body, we may pop a pill or push ourselves to exhaustion, breakdown, and injury. Our disconnection from our bodies and the body of the planet makes it more likely that we will do violence to both and lose sight of their value. But the presence of a child can be a beacon in this sea of alienation. Children know through their body. A feeling is not just a mental flash, but a full-bodied experience. A taste from that ice cream cone is sensed right down to the toes. A day at the beach is an immersion in the texture and warmth of the sand, the rhythm of the surf, the heat and light of the sun.

Children help us to notice the simple pleasures of a taste, texture, or sound. I watched a young child play with mud for nearly an hour the other day. Nothing else, just mud through fingers and toes (and nearly everywhere else). The simple pleasure of a cup of tea, warm sun on our face, or the feeling of wet grass on bare feet brings our body back as a source of knowing. When children go to the museum, they want to touch the paintings. A young boy I know wants to touch the faces of people he meets.

Children remind us of the importance of touch in our lives: a big hug, a wrestling match on the living room floor, a stroke of the hair, or a "beep" on the nose between index finger and thumb. Research of all sorts has demonstrated that touch is basic sustenance.

An example will make the point: When infants were given brief daily massages, they showed increased weight gain, longer periods of quiet sleep, more stable temperature, less crying, and several other advantages over those who did not have the same contact.[5] When it is done without harm or hostility, touch is deeply healing, as anyone who has gotten a hug from a child lately can confirm.

"I could just eat you up!" a grandparent tells his or her grandchild. This weird-sounding expression is not a cannibal coming out of the closet. It is an indication that the body has awakened; the adult is feeling something intensely with his or her body. The nature of spirit in our lives is a visceral feeling, even a communion—the body and blood—to be eaten and drunk, in the language of Christian symbolism. This is why we do not say, "I'd like to think more about you." We say, "I could eat you!"

Our bodies are not only a source of sensory data, but also a link to intuitive knowing—the conduit through which spiritual insights often arise. While knowing is most often associated with the head, both the ancients and contemporary neuroscience support the idea of a bodywide mind. For example, researcher Candance Pert discovered that neurotransmitters and their receptor sites, once thought to exist only in the brain, are present throughout the body. She says, "I can no longer make a strong distinction between the brain and the body."[6] The reason, she suggests, that we speak of gut feelings is because the mechanisms for feeling in the gut are already in place. Likewise, research on energy cardiology and cellular memory in heart transplant patients suggests that knowing and memory are contained in an energy-information system associated not only with the brain, but also with the physical heart.[7] Our "heartfelt sense" does not just sound nice, it has biological reality. Once they come into their own body more, adults may find that it is a source of all sorts of messages about health, about what they like and what they do not, and about the world around them.

Sometimes simply doing what a child might do is a reminder to come into the body. One day I gave my university students Play-Doh during their general psychology quiz. For their last question, they were to make something with it that represented an aspect of themselves. I was impressed with the earnestness and pleasure with which they worked out this problem with their hands. After class several even asked if they could take the Play-Doh home with them. In the midst of intellectual tasks, they found a moment of richness that comes through the body. Such a simple activity brings us, child-like, into the sensuality of texture, smell, and movement. This is not regression; it is a movement toward integration. Spirit integrates and unites.

Being Vulnerable

For a moment, think of how vulnerable a newborn or a child going off to school for the first time is. By contrast, adults often think that the task of adulthood is to ward off feelings of vulnerability, and they try to gain security through such things as money, professional status, and a safe neighborhood. While adults provide the basic safety necessary for a child's survival, children demonstrate the grace of vulnerability that is essential for growth. We grow not merely from the places we control, but in those spaces where we are vulnerable and open to possibility.

We make ourselves vulnerable when we are honest about our feelings, when we speak truthfully, when we trust deeply, and when we ask genuine questions instead of feeling like we have to have all the answers—things children do all the time. And children are naturally thrown into all sorts of situations for which they are unprepared. The first time they play ball, try to ride a bike, or go off to school are all moments of vulnerability.

One young Southern schoolgirl described a moment of vulnerability during school desegregation in 1962 to researcher Robert

Coles: "I was all alone, and those [segregationists] were screaming, and suddenly I saw God smiling, and I smiled. A woman was standing there [near the school door], and she shouted at me, 'Hey, you little nigger, what are you smiling at? I looked right at her face, and I said, 'At God.' Then she looked up at the sky, and then she looked at me, and she didn't call me any more names."[8]

When we step back, living with such remarkable vulnerability is really an act of profound courage. If our children can face the playground bully, a new teacher, or just life in general with such little protection, maybe we can do more than try to control and protect. Maybe we can practice the spiritual art of vulnerability ourselves. Don Juan Mateus, a Yaqui shaman and spiritual guide for author and anthropologist Carlos Castenada, instructed his student that the spiritual path involves consuming your security in each step.[9] This does not necessarily mean that we try death-defying feats all the time or give away all our possessions to live in the wilderness or on a street corner. It means that we risk looking like a fool for love, speak honestly in the face of injustice, try new things, and trust our inner knowing even when the odds are against us. It means we risk having children. The presence of children reminds us of the spiritual lesson of vulnerability, a practice involving trust, and that profound balance of will and surrender.

Messengers of Love and Wisdom

Beyond reminding us of the mind of adventure, living directly, body wisdom, and the grace of vulnerability, children often lead us toward the most enduring spiritual principles, love and wisdom. One mom described the very common but mysterious impact of her young daughter. "She doesn't have to do anything. I don't know what it is, but just by her presence she teaches me to love." Another parent said, "I remember watching my child have this little epiphany about something. Her eyes brightened and I could see her understanding. I realized it was all so perfect; in this moment with her, my own epiphany was that love is all that matters—it is so perfect. When I turned that love inward, I thought about all the little changes that she has brought me through the ways I think, how I treat people. She just teaches me that in the midst of whatever we're involved in, it's love that matters."

Sometimes it is children's wisdom that triggers our own growth. Previously, we met Marshall Ball, a young and exceptional poet who cannot speak or walk but whose words are inspiring. For many adults, Marshall's messages carry a resonance that is, like wisdom itself, difficult to describe. He explains the power of words:

Words greatly present lessons,
oscillating finely bound,
opening great rich kind room
inside wonderful hearts.[10]

I asked Charlie, Marshall's father, what effect living with a wise child has had on his own spiritual life. He said, "We had been very active in our church for many years and left it because we felt it was too narrow-minded. In many ways, Marshall opened us up to that. While we still adhere to many of the tenets like the Golden Rule, we've found our faith very close to home now. He woke us up to the fact that your spirituality is in the here and now—it's not something you go get. If you go somewhere to get something, you are missing it. Our spirituality now seems simple: the Golden Rule and Marshall's one-liners echo in my head. I must say fifty times a week to myself Marshall's line [written at six years old] 'To judge someone is to judge God.'

"I suppose that if we really listened to Marshall, we would quit

our work and go be messengers like he is. But it takes a lot of courage, and we are too chicken right now. When I have looked at his
bookshelf and then I looked at mine, I saw how interesting his was,
how black and white mine was by comparison. He's got cool friends.
When I see my mail and then I see his, I am struck by the contrast.
He gets a basket of mail, and you sit and read and just cry because of
the stories that people tell about how Marshall's words have impacted
their lives. In many ways I feel like I am a humble cast member—
taking care of financial security and things like that. I now find myself
wanting to be a stay-at-home dad. I want to be his assistant, his 'guy.'"

Many parents have told me how their child has created a link
between themselves and the invisible world. One story is surprisingly typical. "When Julian was eighteen months old," said his mom,
"we were at my grandparents' house. We arrived that evening and all
three of us went to bed. I nursed Julian, and as we were falling asleep,
he started to cry and became very fussy. I nursed him for a long time,
but couldn't leave him for a moment without him screaming hysteri-
cally. Two hours of trying to calm him went by, asking him if his
teeth hurt, was he hungry, checking his diaper, was he mad? We
couldn't figure out what was going on; we had never heard him scream
like this before.

"Then he got up and pointed, saying, 'PaPu.' That's the name
that he called his grandfather and we couldn't figure out why he was
calling his name. I asked Julian if he was scared. He nodded yes and
continued to cry. My husband asked if there was someone in the
room, and Julian said, 'Yes.' Carl asked, 'Where?' Julian pointed to
the same corner of the room that he had earlier. While Julian was
sitting on me, he was staring at something for a while in another
direction, and I turned to see what he was staring at. It was a picture
of my mother as a child. She had died several years before. I felt
chills up my spine like I had never had in my life, and asked him
while pointing to the picture if that was who was in the room. 'Yeah!'

he said. I spontaneously said, 'We need to pray now.' I told Julian to say 'good-bye' and tell the person to go. He then finally calmed down and fell asleep.

"The next night the scene renewed," Julian's mother continued. "We had taken the picture out of the room. Julian started screaming again and pointed to another part of the room near the mirror. 'There! There!' Julian said. 'Say good-bye, say, bye,' I said. He did and we prayed. He calmed down and fell asleep. In the following days, my husband and I had separate and similar occurrences with Julian. He would be pointing to areas in the room and pointing to the picture and saying, 'Bye.' He calmed down, now that he seemed to have more control. All this was strange enough, but the funny thing was that in some very deep way, this really helped in my own healing and in my saying good-bye to my mother. I felt like Julian was sort of the bridge between us; he helped to give me the chance to really say good-bye."

While Julian seemed to be an unknowing link, another mom expressed feelings that I have heard from many parents: "It's strange, but I feel like a part of my daughter knows exactly what she's doing. She provokes me in ways that force me to deal with my own stuff. Sometimes I think she does stuff just to drive me crazy, but when I look at it a little differently, I wonder if she's doing it so I can learn my own lessons."

Chris was reading some information to help understand her very demanding son when he suddenly jumped into her lap and said, "You're the best mom!" "Then," related Chris, "he hopped down and began playing with his Legos. I tried to tell him about what I was reading, but he just wanted to talk to me about his Legos. Then I asked him if he could give me a few minutes of quiet so that I could read. Well, he couldn't be quiet. So I proceeded to tell him that I was reading in order to understand him better and to help him connect with other children like him. I thought this might help him respect my request for quiet.

"This is when it happened," she went on. "I don't know how to describe it, but his energy became bigger than his body could contain; it engulfed me, and his eyes seemed to pull me into him. Then this little five-year-old spoke with an authority that seemed like that of a grown man. He said, 'I connect with the others without words; they are in my mind when they need to be.' Then he became his five-year-old self again.

"The most important thing that I took away from this experience is that I move very slowly compared to him. I felt completely exhausted after he said that to me. He understands all of this, of course! He's just waiting for me to catch up. I don't know if my mind can move that fast. I feel like Mother Theresa must have felt when she said, 'I know God doesn't give me anything that I can't handle, I just wish he didn't trust me so much!' I have come across few adults in my life that I am blown away by, and my five-year-old blows me away daily!"

Children are evolution's arrow. And when we join with them, they can help lead us to the front edge of the wave of creation. In fact, the mission of this book and the ChildSpirit Institute has been led by these children about whom you have been hearing.

On the ride to school one morning, I asked Haley, who was nine at the time, whether it would be all right if I told other people about her angel. She quickly said, "I don't want to talk about it." She paused and then said, "But I think you should." I asked, "Why should I talk about it?" She said, "I don't know." I then rephrased the question. "Well, what does your angel think about this?" She fell silent for a moment and then said, "My angel said it's important to tell other people about this so that they can find each other and find their own angel."

The Wellspring Within

Something else happens in our relationship with children. The child beside us helps us to find the child within us. Carl Jung understood that "in every adult there lurks a child—an eternal child, something that is always becoming, is never completed, and calls for unceasing care, attention, and education. That is the part of the human personality that wants to develop and become whole."[11]

Our own childhood and the way that we were cared for can be stirred up in the presence of children. Whatever is unfinished, unhealed, or fragmented within us surfaces in our relationships with children. Development is often like a spiral in that we revisit similar themes in our life, but at new levels of the spiral. The grief, for example, of our seven-year-old self may be reactivated throughout our life each time we sense a loss. The challenge is to heal and learn as we go, to "get" another piece of the learning at each new opportunity. Spending time with children may remind us of our own childhood, our own first date, our struggles and pleasures within our family of origin, or the joy and disappointments of school and friends.

We may even be unconsciously drawn to children of a particular age because we experienced something especially important in our own life at that time. We can simply ask ourselves, What was our life like when we were their age? What is there for me to remember or heal? As one second-grade schoolteacher said, "Once I reclaimed the second grader inside me, I no longer felt like I had to teach these kids. I recovered a part of me—the real me—that I had shut down so long ago. Once I did, I felt like I was both free and myself at the same time. But you know what? I kept teaching second grade, but now I do it with much more pleasure. I let that little girl within me tell me what will help these kids that I teach, and I make sure that I bring her to class with me. I see what the gifts are that I want to offer, and I love it. I don't know if I'll always do it, but for now it's completely my choice. This is where I want to be. Before it felt like I had to be here."

When we are faced with caring for a child, we will often act in a way that was modeled by our own caretakers. Many of us swore that, however good our caregivers were, we would not make the same mistakes they did. Yet sometimes, despite our best intentions, we find ourselves sounding an awful lot like that parent or teacher. Sometimes it takes only a poor night's sleep or a demanding child to push us into the place, the tone, the words that we swore we would never use: "Why do I have to do that, Mom?" "Because I said so, that's why!"

The opportunity as we parent or teach a child is to reparent ourselves at the same time. Remember, we grow right along with our children; our development is mutual. If we are harsh or withholding of our love to the child, we are usually also, deep on the inside, harsh and withholding to ourselves. Children mirror and amplify us so we can see ourselves more clearly. As we feel provoked or frustrated, our opportunity is not only to parent the child, but also to reparent ourselves—to unwind the knots, salve the wounds, and forgive the trespassers that have taken root within us.

Dana entered therapy when she realized she was so depressed that she could hardly get off the sofa to take care of her young daughter when she arrived home on the school bus. Through the haze of depression, she knew that she was not there for her daughter, and deep down, this was gut-wrenching for her.

One day, her therapist asked Dana to take some deep breaths, close her eyes, and deeply relax. She then said, "Put your intellect in suspended animation and just let your imagination take over. See yourself as a child standing on a bridge. Now allow that emotional child to come over that bridge." Dana did as the therapist suggested, and in a few moments she was able to see the little girl approaching from over that bridge. She was surprised at how vivid and real the girl seemed to her. "Does she have anything to tell you?" the therapist asked. Dana was shocked by what she heard next. The little girl looked her in the eye and said, "Just let me be me."

Dana said, "In that instant I realized that I hadn't been me since I didn't know when. Growing up in my own household was like, 'This is how we are and we want you to be this way, so anything outside of these lines is not permitted.' It was like you couldn't really be accepted; nothing was unconditional. The message from my family was, 'If you don't think and do like we do, then there is something wrong with you and you will be rejected.' So I stuffed that little kid away and developed a false self for the world; everything else disappeared, got pushed underground, except for those fleeting moments when some glimmer of knowing would break through."

Dana had had moments of ecstasy and wonder during childhood. As a young child of three or four, these moments were awesome and ecstatic. But because her family did not accept these experiences, her response to ecstasy began to change. She said, "Instead of beautiful blissful experiences, these now had a negative quality. There was a sense of burden, even though I might see incredible beauty or connection. The experiences were still awesome, but my reaction was so negative. When they popped up, it was like, 'Oh no! I can't have these things.' It was not OK to have these experiences in my family, and because I tried to shut them out so tightly, when they popped up it was a bad thing. I was afraid someone would find out; I was afraid they wouldn't love me because I was different than they wanted me to be." Instead of knowing herself, Dana's energy was spent on pushing herself away and building a false self in order to be accepted.

However, meeting that little girl on the bridge of her imagination turned Dana's life around. Her vitality came back, her depression lifted, and she came to trust herself in new ways. She learned firsthand that the more children shut down, the more they suffer. As she opened back up, so did her intuition and ecstasy. She began to have more of those powerful moments of connection, bliss, and revelation that she had experienced as a child. But now she worked to honor and learn from these, rather than judge and fear them. Dana turned her life around by understanding and being true to herself rather than adhering to an image her family had of her. She entered a graduate program quite different from the one she had dropped out of years before. She found a new energy for living and her intuitive awareness opened up. Now in her role as a therapist, she helps others to reclaim their own inner child.

Since that meeting on the bridge, Dana has been sure to parent her own child differently from how she was parented. She said, "Within limits, we give her [her daughter] a long leash. I had one of those moments the other day when you feel like all this work has paid off. You don't always see the fruits of the work until later. My daughter said, 'I can tell you about anything, Mom, because you understand me.'

"Unlike what happened to me growing up, we really work on letting her have her feelings, within limits. We allow her to have her anger, let her be who she is in the moment. One thing I noticed that my own parents did and still do is to tell us how we feel—'Oh, that's not scary'—instead of acknowledging that we were scared. I want my child to have the emotional freedom to feel what she is feeling first, and then we might help her to work it through. But what happened to me was that I wasn't allowed the freedom even to have my own feelings, so I became an expert at shutting myself down, and that was the root of my own depression."

Like Dana, Claire reported what so many adults do: "My own childhood experiences have to be revisited because of her [her daughter]. Long ago, I abandoned that part of my life and that way of being; my ego took over. But since my daughter has been here, I find myself retrieving my own childhood. I'm more alive, more playful, and I think I'm just easier to be around."

As we reclaim that child within us, we not only find grief and pain, but also a source of wonder and wisdom, meaning and mystery, and deep interconnection— all those things we've been talking about as spiritual. We can draw nourishment from the inner child like drawing clear, pure sustenance from a wellspring.

In times of intellectual doubt, Christina said, she finds a source of comfort and guidance that she discovered and never lost sight of as a young child. She has always asked the big questions about life and meaning: Why are we here? Is God real? Why is this happening? She explained, "I needed proof, my own direct experience of these answers. Instead of having to trust someone else, I just had to know for myself. And at five—and there have been other moments in my life, too—I felt the answer. I found the place where those answers are. I saw the perfection of the world. It was amazing and it was comforting; when I get back into that place, it always brings a sense that everything is OK. Even in times of intellectual doubt, I always really know. If someone asks, 'What do you know in your heart?' it's that experience. There have been other moments in my life where I felt the perfection of the world, but really that moment at five was the absolute foundation. Even now, I'm going through a period of intellectual doubt, and it's neat that I'm talking to you because of course I know the place where I feel the answer. It's that knowing inside that I had when I was five."

Just like the child beside us, the child within us serves as both a wellspring for our spiritual life and a mystery to unravel and clarify.

Conclusion

My own children have opened my heart to the spiritual life of childhood: a visit with Haley's angel, a view of the invisible through Maia's eyes, and, even more importantly, the everyday wonders of learning patience, feeling love that is overwhelming, learning to play more, appreciating something tiny, and asking more questions than offering answers. Perhaps the children in your life have catalyzed your spiritual growth as my children have for me. And when I can remember to pay attention, my time with them each day is a spiritual practice. I am reminded to ask myself, Is my heart uncontracted? Am I honest and trustworthy? Am I willing to learn? Am I living up to my sacred contract with them? Do I appreciate their uniqueness? Can I find what is most important even in the hurry of a busy day?

I cannot express the depth of my amazement, love, and gratitude for the grace children give without trying. The secret spiritual world of children reminds us to listen for inner wisdom, find wonder in the day, see through the eye of the heart, live the big questions, and peer into the invisible. When we open to the spiritual world through the presence of a child in our neighborhood, our classroom, our household, or even in our own hearts, we honor their spirit and simultaneously renew our own.

Afterword

Lifting *a* Veil

Are children growing up these days different from those in the past? Do they represent an evolutionary leap? Are they, as some more recent labels claim, Star Kids, Millennial Children, Indigo Children, Crystal Children, Psychic Children, and so on?

The term *Indigo* has been the most popular label for a new kind of child, so let us look at it for a moment. Nancy Ann Tappe may have been the first to use this term. She claimed that beginning around 1980, she clairvoyantly saw this color around particular children. Essentially, the Indigo label is used as a kind of new personality classification for children who are technically savvy, are often labeled as attention disordered and nonconforming, and have a sense of entitlement, or "deserving to be here." Tappe also suggested that the children who have been the perpetrators in recent school shootings like Columbine have been frustrated Indigo children.[1]

The positive impact of these ideas is that parents have come to recognize that a child who exhibits these characteristics is not alone. It has provided an opportunity to reconsider our assumptions and our habits of who children are and how we can work with them most successfully. This has been a service, and if you are interested, you can find plenty of resources under "Indigo Children" on the Web.

However, there are two difficulties. The first occurs when "naming" turns to "labeling." Naming is often empowering. It gives us a way to talk about and work with something. When we can name the source of a vague ache in our body or a fear in our minds for example, we can work with it more effectively. When children who think they are dumb discover that they have a different learning or attention style from other people, they gain power to bridge the learning gap. On the other hand, labeling is often disempowering and distancing. In this case, a child labeled "Indigo" means that the child starts to become an Indigo in our minds, rather than Jane or Bob or Katy. The individual tends to get homogenized and identified with a group. Trouble, whether in a psychiatric diagnosis or a metaphysical one, arises when we give too much attention to the label and not enough to the individual child. We have to work one mind at a time if we are to see who children are.

Categorization, whether as an Indigo or ADD or whatever, is a double-edged sword. While the description may help us to understand and ask better questions about the child in front of us, it can also get in the way of our understanding the uniqueness of each child; categorization can interfere with direct contact. Our children are not "Indigos," they are spiritual beings, like you and I, who happen to be our children. Unlike a car or a quark that does not care what we call it, children interact and are affected by such labels. As philosopher of science Ian Hacking notes, changes in names lead to changes in treatment and, ultimately, to changes in children themselves.[2]

I have had children (and parents) come up to me and say, "I'm an Indigo. Are your kids?" Some well-meaning parent's label becomes a category of haves and have-nots, worthy and not-so-worthy, perhaps. What if my response is, "No"? Do non-Indigos become irrelevant in this child's world? Evolutionary dinosaurs? What this label, this category, does is prejudge—otherwise known as "prejudice"—which is anathema to a spiritual path. It gives the ego plenty of material to feel special about and build on, but it does little to serve real spiritual growth.

Perhaps most importantly, the vast majority of the children I have been with who are highly intuitive or demonstrate spiritual capacities *do not* meet the characteristics of a so-called Indigo. Some do, others seem to have some characteristics, but most of our children do not fit this profile. My intellectually astute and highly intuitive sixteen-year-old friend said it this way: "Much of what I hear and read about Indigo children makes it seem as though the only people who are able to be spiritual in some way are young oversensitive hyperactives! Now I'm certainly not saying there aren't people like that, and I'm not saying they don't deserve just as much respect as others. However, I've always felt that spirituality and the perception of nonphysical realms is an innate capacity in all human beings, not just an unusual few."

But this Indigo label has been surprisingly popular. Why? First, it does describe some characteristics of fascinating children. Secondly, and most importantly, it has gained wider appeal because it speaks to the cultural longing for dealing with the spiritual life of children in general. We sense the spirit in our children (and ourselves) and feel the gap between prevailing views of children's spirituality and the child in front of us. The popularity speaks to parents' needs for support, information, and insight to make sense of their children in a more well-rounded, spiritually sensitive way.

Every era has had those whose very presence pushes at the accepted order and at evolution's edge; think of Jesus or Buddha, for example. Paul after his revelation on the road to Damascus told of the coming of the new age, one guided by profound love. In the nineteenth century, Helena Blavatsky, who launched the Theosophical movement, also hailed the dawning of a new age. She believed humanity was on the horizon of new potential and might see the harbingers of evolution in individuals, including children, with expanded human capacities (such as telepathy or great compassion).[3] Throughout history, child prodigies of all sorts have nudged at societies' understanding of human potential and were often seen as portents of change.[4]

Is there physical evidence of changes among today's children? Researcher and author Joseph Chilton Pearce has suggested that evolution may currently be giving us some children with very large prefrontal cortexes, the largest and most recently evolved brain structures. These children are recognizable by a large protruding forehead (indicating a large prefrontal cortex), extending to or even beyond the tip of their noses (along a vertical axis). The prefrontal cortex is associated with higher intellectual functions, such as analytic and creative thinking, and higher virtues, such as empathy and compassion.

Perhaps one of the most important factors to consider is evidence that a mother "who is emotionally mature, stable, loved, and feels secure gives birth to a child with advanced forebrain and . . . an infant protected and nurtured has a larger prefrontal growth after birth."[5] The stunning implication is that our evolution is bioculturally dependant. That is, the growth of higher-order functions is tied to our social environment, to our cultural norms, and to our state of mind. As Pearce says, "That neural growth will shift from a defensive, combative stance to one that is reflective and intellectual—or vice versa, according to the mother's emotional state—offers us the chance to make a profound shift in our history and to take our evolution in hand."[6]

Are there any viable statistics indicating significant changes in the child population? There has been a steady increase in IQ scores since the 1950s. Someone with average IQ measured in the 1950s would be considered as bordering on low IQ today. Interestingly, the increase is seen most in visual-spatial intelligence.[7] The meaning of IQ scores is a slippery issue in nearly any circumstance, and to what this increase is attributable is far from clear. Is it the result of improved nutrition, increased visual stimulation in this technology-rich environment, demands of current problems, or a more fundamental change in human capacity? It is hard to say definitively. Concomitantly, there are also stunning increases in the diagnosis of difficulties such as attention disorder and autism. For example, diagnoses of autism in the United States increased over 500 percent between 1992 and 2001.[8] But it is difficult to tease out how much is attributable to an actual increase in autism or a change in diagnostic awareness.

So are the children coming in these days different, no matter what we call them? Do they represent an evolutionary leap? What is different is not necessarily or exclusively the children. As we in our contemporary culture have become freer to talk about and to pursue our own direct connection with Spirit, we are naturally more able to recognize it in others and in ourselves. There have always been wise souls, healers, children with different learning styles, prodigies, and highly intuitive beings in the world. Many adults with whom I have spoken also had rich and powerful spiritual lives as children. And I have presented evidence that children have had spiritual experiences for at least hundreds of years, no doubt much longer. So this is not new. But are there more or different "special" children coming in now? Maybe. But when we step back, the most important consideration is that it is not just the children who are different. It is the adults, too, and it is the world around us.

It is no news that these are remarkably intense, dynamic times, and it does not look like this is going to change anytime soon. Nearly everything appears to be in dynamic flux, as evidenced by global politics, unthinkable violence, and challenges to traditional values. And the intensity has been arriving in other forms as well, such as the remarkable availability of information, the expansion of credit (my daughter received her first credit card application at age eleven!), the unparalleled creation of wealth, and the widening gap between the haves and the have-nots.

These times are not merely intense, but perhaps they are even apocalyptic in proportion. A surprising number of traditions point to these days as the "end times." In a talk some years ago, psychologist James Hillman hinted at these mythic times by reinterpreting the image of the four horsemen of the Apocalypse as described in the Book of Revelation in the Bible.

The horsemen arrive on different-colored mounts and each serves as a portent of the end times. The first rider approaches on a red horse. This has traditionally been interpreted to mean war. A more subtle form of war may be seen as hypercompetition, the chronic striving for power over another that takes away peace (from corporate America to the structure of classrooms) and has been a predominant motif for modern American culture. The next horseman rides on a white horse and represents the bright light of a pseudo-spirituality that offers prepackaged, tidy, glossy, absolutist, and fundamentalist answers. The horseman on the black horse arrives holding a set of balances. This is the horseman of money and materialism, which measure the worth of everything and everyone by its current market value. The last rider approaches on a pale mount, which we will interpret to mean apathy. This is the turning away from injustice, suffering, hypocrisy, and the atrocities committed in the name of greed or ideology. Apathy turns hearts to stone, does not rock the boat, and goes along to get along.

As we look at today's newspaper headlines, it may not seem so wild to ask, Are the horsemen upon us? Is the apocalypse at hand? Perhaps. But what does "apocalypse" mean beyond the connotations of vast devastation and destruction? The word *apocalypse*, from ancient Greek, actually means revealing, revelation, or lifting a veil.

What is happening is that we are becoming able to see more, understand more—the veil is lifting. We have the power to become more conscious of our choices and their consequences across the street and across the globe. As we wake up, we can recognize even more poignantly the power of the heart when we feel a loving touch from someone or learn of selfless sacrifice. We live in a time when we are becoming conscious of our own evolution and therefore are increasingly responsible for it. We have the power to join with the wave of creation and actually move evolution along.

As the veil lifts, questions emerge: What's waking up in me? What is truly important? How do I want to live this moment, this day, and this life? How am I treating others? How can I understand and serve this child, this world, this spirit? Do my intentions and my actions spread love and wisdom, peace and generosity, or selfishness? What does the way I live my life teach this child? What does this child offer to teach me? Every moment is an invitation to reconsider priorities, but these times grab our attention by the throat. Our greatest opportunity these days is not the chance to make our lives safer, but to align with that deep current through which our lives flow. Children are different in some way, but so are we, and so is this world. As we open to and nourish the spiritual world of children, we contribute to and join with the wave of evolution and of Spirit itself.

Notes

Introduction

1. Peter L. Nelson, "A Survey of Mystical, Visionary, and Remote Perception Experiences," in *Exploring the Paranormal: Perspectives on Belief and Experience*, ed. G. K. Zollschan, J. F. Schumaker, and G. F. Walsh (Dorset, U.K.: Prism, 1989), 184–214.

2. Edward Robinson, *The Original Vision: A Study of the Religious Experience of Childhood* (1977; reprint, New York: Seabury Press, 1983).

3. Tobin Hart and Peter L. Nelson, "Children's Spiritual Experience." Manuscript in preparation at time of printing.

4. William Penn, as cited in Aldous Huxley, *The Perennial Philosophy* (New York: Harper & Row, 1945), 14.

5. James M. Robinson, ed., *The Nag Hammadi Library in English* (New York: Harper & Row, 1977), 126.

6. Paul Tillich, *Dynamics of Faith* (New York: Harper & Row, 1957).

7. Henry Corbin, *The Man of Light in Iranian Sufism*, trans. N. Pearson (New Lebanon, NY: Omega Publications, 1994).

8. John G. Neihardt, *Black Elk Speaks: Being the Life Story of a Holy Man of the Oglala Sioux* (1932; reprint, Lincoln: University of Nebraska Press, 1988), 21.

9. Fiona Bowie and Oliver Davies, ed., *Hildegard of Bingen*, trans. R. Carver (New York: Crossroads Publishing Company, 1990), 20.

10. Raymundus de Vineis, *The Life of St. Catherine of Siena*, trans. G. Lamb (New York: P. J. Kennedy & Sons, 1960).

11. Swami Nikhilananda, trans., *The Gospel of Sri Ramakrishna*, abridged ed. (New York: Ramakrishna-Vivekananda Center, 1970), 3–4.

12. Alexander Gilchrist, *Life of William Blake* (Totowa, NJ: Rowman & Littlefield, 1973), 7.

13. Arthur Osborne, *Ramana Maharshi and the Path of Self-Knowledge* (New York: S. Weiser, 1970).

Notes

14. Erik H. Erikson, *Gandhi's Truth: On the Origins of Militant Nonviolence* (New York: W. W. Norton & Company Inc, 1969).

15. Edith Cobb, *The Ecology of the Imagination of Childhood* (New York: Columbia University Press, 1977), 90.

Chapter 1

1. Robin Waterfield, "Socrates' Defense: Introduction," in *Xenophon: Conversations of Socrates* (New York: Penguin, 1990), 35.

2. Jon Klimo, *Channeling: Investigations on Receiving Information from Paranormal Sources* (Los Angeles: Jeremy P. Tarcher, 1987).

3. Hirsch Loeb Gordon, *The Maggid of Caro* (New York: Shoulson Press, 1949).

4. Mitchell B. Liester, "Inner Voices: Distinguishing Transcendent and Pathological Characteristics," *The Journal of Transpersonal Psychology* 28, no. 1 (1996): 1.

5. Jelaluddin Rumi, *The Essential Rumi*, trans. Colman Barks, with J. Moyne, A. J. Arberry, and R. Nicholson (San Francisco: HarperSanFrancisco, 1995), 178.

6. Sri Aurobindo, *The Essential Aurobindo*, ed. R. A. McDermott (1973; reprint, Hudson, NY: Lindisfarne Press, 1987).

7. Meister Eckhart, *Meister Eckhart: Selected Treatises and Sermons*, trans. J. M. Clark and J. V. Skinner (London: Faber & Faber, 1958).

8. Ralph Waldo Emerson, "The Oversoul," in *The Collected Works*, vol. 2, ed. J. Slater and A. R. Ferguson (1841; reprint, Cambridge: The Belknap Press of Harvard University Press, 1979), 157–175.

9. Roberto Assagioli, *The Act of Will* (New York: Penguin Books, 1973).

10. William James, *Principles of Psychology* (1890; reprint, New York: Dover, 1950).

11. Carl Gustav Jung, "The Archetypes and the Collective Unconscious," in *Collected Works of C. G. Jung*, 2d ed., vol. 9, part 1, ed. M. Fordham and R. F. C. Hull (Princeton, NJ: Princeton University Press, 1981).

12. John Steinbeck, *Grapes of Wrath* (1939; reprint, New York: Penguin Books, 1976).

13. Erwin Schrodinger, *What Is Life? With Mind and Matter* (London: Cambridge University Press, 1969), 145.

14. James M. Robinson, ed., *The Nag Hammadi Library in English* (New York: Harper & Row, 1977).

15. Charles Tart, *Waking Up: Overcoming the Obstacles to Human Potential* (Boston: Shambhala, 1987).

16. Nathaniel Needle, "The Six Paramitas: Outline for a Buddhist Education," *Encounter: Education for Meaning and Social Justice* 12, no. 1 (1999): 9–21.

17. Merton M. Sealts, *Emerson on the Scholar* (Columbia, MO: University of Missouri Press, 1992).

18. John G. Neihardt, *Black Elk Speaks: Being the Life Story of a Holy Man of the Oglala Sioux* (1932; reprint, Lincoln: University of Nebraska Press, 1988).

19. Ted Andrews, *Animal Speak: The Spiritual and Magical Powers of Creatures Great and Small* (St. Paul, MN: Llewellyn Publications, 1993).

20. G. N. M. Tyrrell, *The Personality of Man* (London: Penguin Books, 1946), 31.

21. Sabina Flanagan, *Hildegard of Bingen: A Visionary Life* (London: Routledge, 1989), 196.

22. Alexander Gilchrist, *Life of William Blake* (Totowa, NJ: Rowman & Littlefield, 1973), 7.

23. Alex Ayers, ed., *The Wisdom of Martin Luther King, Jr.* (New York: Meridian, 1993), 95.

24. Vita Sackville-West, *Saint Joan of Arc* (New York: Doubleday, 1964), 51.

25. Ken Wilber, *Eye to Eye* (Garden City, NY: Anchor, 1989).

26. Ken Wilber, *Sex, Ecology, and Spirituality: The Spirit of Evolution* (Boston: Shambhala, 1995), 334–335.

27. Fredrich Nietzsche, *Werke 1–5*, vol. 1, ed. Karl Schlechta (1969; reprint, Frankfurt am Main. Ulstein, 1972), 88.

28. Liester, "Inner Voices," 17.

29. Marshall Stewart Ball, *Kiss of God* (Deerfield Beach, FL: Health Communications, Inc, 1999), 3.

30. Ibid., 133.

31. Ibid., 31.

32. Ibid., 201.

Chapter 2

1. Walt Whitman, as cited in Richard Maurice Bucke, *Cosmic Consciousness: A Study in the Evolution of the Human Mind* (1901; reprint, New York: Dutton, 1969), 228.

2. Richard Maurice Bucke, *Cosmic Consciousness: A Study in the Evolution of the Human Mind* (1901; reprint, New York: Dutton, 1969).

3. Ibid., 73.

4. William James, *The Varieties of Religious Experience* (New York: The Modern Library, 1936).

5. John G. Neihardt, *Black Elk Speaks: Being the Life Story of a Holy Man of the Oglala Sioux* (1932; reprint, Lincoln: University of Nebraska Press, 1988), 40–41.

Notes

6. Paul Tillich, *The Eternal Now* (New York: Charles Scribner's Sons, 1956).

7. Peter L. Nelson, "The Technology of the Praeternatural: An Empirically Based Model of Transpersonal Experiences," *The Journal of Transpersonal Psychology* 22, no. 1 (1990): 35–50.

8. Jean Pierhal, *Albert Schweitzer: The Story of His Life* (New York: Philosophical Library Inc, 1957).

9. Plato, *Ion*, trans. W. R. M. Lamb (Cambridge: Harvard University Press, 1962).

10. Evelyn Underhill, *Mysticism* (1911; reprint, New York: E. P. Dutton, 1961).

11. Joseph Campbell, *The Power of Myth*, reissue ed., ed. B. S. Flowers, with B. Moyers (Garden City, NY: Anchor, 1991).

12. Neihardt, *Black Elk Speaks*, 41.

13. Edward Robinson, *The Original Vision: A Study of the Religious Experience of Childhood* (1977; reprint, New York: Seabury Press, 1983), 133.

14. P. M. H. Atwater, *Children of the New Millennium: Children's Near-Death Experiences and the Evolution of Humankind* (New York: Three Rivers Press, 1999).

15. Lex Hixon, *Coming Home: The Experience of Enlightenment in Sacred Traditions* (Burdett, NY: Larson Publications, 1978).

    Swami Nikhilananda, trans., *The Gospel of Sri Ramakrishna* (New York: Ramakrishna-Vivekananda Center, 1958).

16. Marghanita Laski, *Ecstasy in Secular and Religious Experience* (Los Angeles: Jeremy P. Tarcher, 1961).

17. Matt. 13:33, *The Holy Bible: Containing the Old and New Testaments* (New York: T. Nelson, 1953).

18. William Blake, "Auguries of Innocence," in *The Portable Blake*, ed. A. Kazin (1804; reprint, New York: Penguin Books, 1976), 150.

19. Abraham Heschel, *God in Search of Man* (1955; reprint, New York: Octagon, 1972), 74, 75.

20. Matt. 18:2, *The Holy Bible: Containing the Old and New Testaments* (New York: T. Nelson, 1953).

21. Lao Tzu, *Tao Te Ching*, trans. S. Mitchell (New York: Harper Perennial, 2000).

22. Mary Catherine Richards, *Centering in Pottery, Poetry, and the Person* (1962; reprint, Hanover, NH: Wesleyan University Press, 1989), 8.

Chapter 3

1. Martin Buber, *I and Thou*, trans. R. G. Smith (1923; reprint, New York: Charles Scribner & Sons, 1970), 89.

Notes

2. Martin Buber, *I and Thou*, trans. R. G. Smith (1923; reprint, New York: Charles Scribner & Sons, 1958), 11.

3. Huang Po, *The Zen Teachings of Huang Po: On the Transmission of Mind*, trans. J. Blofield (New York: Grove Weidenfeld, 1958).

4. Houston Smith, "Educating the Intellect: On Opening the Eye of the Heart," in *Can Virtue be Taught?* ed. B. Darling-Smith (Notre Dame, IN: University of Notre Dame Press, 1993), 17–31.

5. Hyemeyohsts Storm, *Seven Arrows* (New York: Ballantine Books, 1972).

6. P. Abrams (producer), and M. Leder (director), *Pay it Forward* (film, 2000). Available from Warner Bros. Studios, 4000 Warner Blvd., Burbank, CA 91522.

7. Albert Einstein, "The World as I See It," in *Ideas and Opinions*, ed. C. Seelig (New York: Bonanza Books, 1954), 8–11.

8. Benjamin Shield and Richard Carlson, eds., *For the Love of God: New Writings by Spiritual and Psychological Leaders* (San Rafael, CA: New World Library, 1990), 151.

9. Antoine de Saint-Exupéry, *The Little Prince*, trans. K. Woods (1943; reprint, San Diego, CA: Harcourt Brace Jovanovich, 1971), 87.

10. Doc Lew Childre and Howard Martin, *The Heartmath Solution: The Institute of Heartmath's Revolutionary Program for Engaging the Power of the Heart's Intelligence* (SanFrancisco: HarperSanFrancisco, 2000).

11. Evelyn Fox Keller, *A Feeling for the Organism: The Life and Work of Barbara McClintock* (New York: Freeman, 1983), 198.

12. J. Krishnamurti, *Krishnamurti on Education*, ed. Krishnamurti Foundation Trust Limited (New York: Harper & Row, 1974), 176.

13. David Kherdian and Nancy Hogrogian, *The Animal* (New York: Random House, 1984).

14. Thich Nhat Hanh, *The Heart of Understanding: Commentaries on the Prajnaparamita Heart Sutra* (Berkeley, CA: Parallax Press, 1995).

15. Walt Whitman, *Leaves of Grass* (1855; reprint, New York: Bantam Classics, 1983).

16. Tobin Hart, "Deep Empathy," in *Transpersonal Knowing: Exploring the Horizon of Consciousness*, ed. Tobin Hart, Peter L. Nelson, and Kaisa Puhakka (Albany: State University of New York Press, 2000), 253–270.

17. Dean I. Radin, *The Conscious Universe* (San Francisco: HarperSanFrancisco, 1997).

18. Lex Hixon, *Coming Home* (Burdett, NY: Larson Publications, 1978), 26.

19. Jacques Lusseyran, *And There Was Light*, trans. E. Cameron (New York: Parabola Books, 1963), 28.

20. Larry Dossey, *Reinventing Medicine* (San Francisco: HarperSanFrancisco, 1999).

Notes

21. P. M. H. Atwater, *Children of the New Millennium: Children's Near-Death Experiences and the Evolution of Humankind* (New York: Three Rivers Press, 1999).

22. Saint Augustine, *Confessions*, trans. R. S. Pine-Coffin (New York: Penguin Books, 1961), 39.

23. D. Wigg, "George Harrison Interview, March 1969" on *The Beatles Tapes* (London: Polydor, 1976). LP.

Chapter 4

1. Jean Piaget, *The Essential Piaget*, ed. H. Gruber and J. Voneche (New York: Basic Books, 1977).

2. Gareth B. Matthews, *Philosophy and the Young Child* (Cambridge: Harvard University Press, 1980), 85.

3. Paul Tillich, *Dynamics of Faith* (New York: Harper & Row, 1957).

4. David Bohm, "Insight, Knowledge, Science, and Human Values," in *Toward the Recovery of Wholeness*, ed. D. Sloan (New York: Teachers College Press, 1981), 8–30.

5. Ranier Maria Rilke, *Letters to a Young Poet*, trans. M. D. Herter Norton (New York: Norton, 1993), 35.

6. Patricia K. Arlin, "Wisdom: The Art of Problem Finding," in *Wisdom: Its Nature, Origins, and Development*, ed. R. J. Sternberg (New York: Penguin Books, 1990), 230–243.

7. Ranier Maria Rilke, *Rodin and Other Prose Pieces* (London: Quartet Books, 1986), 4.

8. Buddhaghosa, *Visuddhimagga*, 3d. ed. (San Francisco: W. H. Freeman, 1975).

9. Zia Inayat Khan, "Illuminative Presence," in *Transpersonal Knowing: Exploring the Horizon of Consciousness*, ed. Tobin Hart, Peter L. Nelson, and Kaisa Puhakka (Albany: State University of New York Press, 2000), 147–159.

10. Shihab al-Din Suhrawardi, *Majmu'a-yi Musannafat-i Shaykh-i Ishraq*, vol. 1, ed. H. Corbin and S. H. Nasr (Tehran: Pazuhishgah-i 'Ulum-i Insani va Mutalafat-i Farhangi, 1993), 71–72.

11. Ramana Maharshi, *Who Am I?* (Tiruvannamalai, S. India: Sri Ramanasramam, 1982).

12. Gary Zukov and D. Finkelstein, *The Dancing Wu Li Masters: An Overview of the New Physics* (New York: Bantam Books, 1980), 193.

13. Tobin Hart, *From Information to Transformation: Education for the Evolution of Consciousness* (New York: Peter Lang Publishing, 2001).

14. Thomas Merton, *What Is Contemplation?* (1948; reprint, Springfield, IL: Templegate, 1978), 183.

15. Peter Fenner, *The Ontology of the Middle Way* (Dordrecht, Holland: Kluwer Publishing Company, 1991).

16. Donald Rothberg, "Spiritual Inquiry," in *Transpersonal Knowing: Exploring the Horizon of Consciousness*, ed. Tobin Hart, Peter L. Nelson, and Kaisa Puhakka (Albany: State University of New York Press, 2000), 172.

17. Idries Shah, *The Exploits of the Incomparable Mulla Nasrudin* (London: The Octagon Press, 1966), 9.

18. Umberto Eco, *The Name of the Rose*, trans. W. Weaver (London: Picador, 1984), 492.

19. Rachel Livsey and Parker Palmer, *The Courage to Teach: A Guide for Reflection and Renewal* (San Francisco: Jossey-Bass, 1999), 43–48.

20. Pablo Neruda, *The Book of Questions*, trans. W. O'Daly (1974; reprint, Port Townsend, WA: Copper Canyon Press, 1991), 24.

21. Carl Gustav Jung, *Memories, Dreams, Reflections* (New York: Vintage Books, 1965), 20.

22. Gareth B. Matthews, *Philosophy and the Young Child* (Cambridge: Harvard University Press, 1980).

23. Rosalie Maggio, *Quotations on Education* (Paramus, NJ: Prentice Hall, 1997), 150.

24. Arthur Schopenhauer, from the author's personal collection of quotations, no reference information available.

25. R. B. Blakney, ed. and trans., *Meister Eckhart: A Modern Translation* (New York: Harper Torch Books, 1957), 288.

Chapter 5

1. *Hamlet* 1.5.

2. Edith Cobb, *The Ecology of the Imagination of Childhood*. (New York: Columbia University Press, 1977), 90.

3. Gershom G. Scholem, ed., *Zohar: The Book of Splendor* (1949; reprint, New York: Schocken Books, 1995), 79.

4. Kaku Michio, *Hyperspace* (New York: Oxford University Press, 1994).

5. Stephen Larsen, James F. Lawrence, and William R. Woofenden, *Emanuel Swedenborg*, ed. Robin Larsen (New York: Swedenborg Foundation, 1988).

6. Richard Gerber, *Vibrational Medicine* (Santa Fe, NM: Bear & Company, 1988).

7. Richard J. Finneran, ed., *The Collected Poems of W. B. Yeats* (New York: Collier Books, 1983), 180–190.

8. Maurice Merleau-Ponty, *The Phenomenology of Perception*, trans. C. Smith (1945; reprint, New York: Humanities Press, 1962), 229.

Notes

9. Evelyn Underhill, *Mysticism* (1911; reprint, New York: E. P. Dutton, 1961), 7.

10. R. E. M. Harding, *An Anatomy of Inspiration* (London: Frank Cass and Co. Ltd, 1967).

11. William Blake, "The Marriage of Heaven and Hell," in *Blake: Complete Writings*, ed. G. Keynes (1790–93; reprint, London: Oxford University Press, 1966), 154.

12. Pete A. Sanders, *You Are Psychic!: The Free Soul Method* (New York: Fireside Books, 1999).

13. *The Qur'an*, trans. E. H. Palmer (Delhi: Motilal Banarsidass, 1965), 24:35.

14. Jacques Lusseyran, *And There was Light*, trans. E. Cameron (New York: Parabola Books, 1963), 12–13.

15. Ibid., 16–21.

16. Ibid., 16, 17, 18.

17. T. S. Eliot, *Four Quartets* (New York: Harcourt, Brace, and World, 1971), 16.

18. Fiona Bowie and Oliver Davies, ed., *Hildegard of Bingen*, trans. R. Carver (New York: Crossroads Publishing Company, 1990), 20.

19. Ian Stevenson, *Twenty Cases Suggestive of Reincarnation* (Charlottesville: University Press of Virginia, 1974).

    Ian Stevenson, *Children Who Remember Previous Lives* (Charlottesville: University Press of Virginia, 1987).

20. Scholem, *Zohar*.

21. Matt. 17:10–13, *The Holy Bible: Containing the Old and New Testaments* (New York: T. Nelson, 1953).

22. Kahlil Gibran, *The Prophet* (1923; reprint, New York: Alfred A. Knopf, 1980), 94–95.

Chapter 6

1. Kahlil Gibran, *The Prophet* (1923; reprint, New York: Alfred A. Knopf, 1980), 17.

2. Forrest Carter, *The Education of Little Tree* (Albuquerque, NM: University of New Mexico Press, 1976), 38.

3. Thich Nhat Hanh, *The Miracle of Mindfulness* (Boston: Beacon Press, 1975).

4. Ira Progoff, *The Symbolic and the Real: A New Psychological Approach to the Fuller Experience of Personal Existence* (New York: Julian, 1963), 165–166.

5. Julia Cameron, *The Artist's Way: A Spiritual Path to Higher Creativity* (Los Angeles, CA: Jeremy P. Tarcher/Perigee, 1992), 53.

6. Carl R. Rogers, *A Way of Being* (Boston: Houghton Mifflin, 1980), 129.

7. John 16:23–25, *The Holy Bible: Containing the Old and New Testaments* (New York: T. Nelson, 1953).

8. Johann Wolfgang von Goethe, *Wisdom and Experience*, ed. and trans., H. J. Weigand (1829; reprint, New York: Pantheon Books, 1949), 184.

9. Friedrich Froebel, *The Education of Man*, trans. W. N. Hailmann (New York: D. Appleton, 1887), 55.

10. James Hillman, *The Soul's Code: In Search of Character and Calling* (New York: Warner Books, 1996).

11. David Henry Feldman, *Nature's Gambit* (New York: Basic Books, 1986), 118.

12. Oriah Mountain Dreamer, *The Invitation* (San Francisco: HarperSanFrancisco, 1999), 1.

Chapter 7

1. V. K. Gokak, *Bhagavan Sri Sathya Sai Baba* (New Delhi: Abhinav Publications, 1975), 116.
   Alfred North Whitehead, *The Aims of Education and Other Essays* (1929; reprint, New York: The Free Press, 1967), 57.

2. Thomas Merton, *Love and Living* (New York: Farrar, Straus & Giroux, 1979), 3.

3. Ramana Maharshi, *Who Am I?* (Tiruvannamalai, S. India: Sri Ramanasramam, 1982).

4. *Hamlet* 1.3.

5. Martin Buber, *Tales of Hasidism: The Early Masters* (New York: Schocken Books, 1975), 251.

6. Edward Robinson, *The Original Vision; A Study of Religious Experience of Childhood* (New York: The Seabury Press, 1988), 101.

7. Carl Gustav Jung, *Collected Works of C. G. Jung*, vol. 11, ed. H. Read, M. Fordham, G. Adler, and W. McGuire, trans. R. F. C. Hull (Princeton, NJ: Princeton University Press, 1953–78), 131.

8. Jelaluddin Rumi, *The Essential Rumi*, trans. Colman Barks, with J. Moyne, A. J. Arberry, and R. Nicholson (San Francisco: HarperSanFrancisco, 1995), 109.

9. Marshall Stewart Ball, *Kiss of God* (Deerfield Beach, FL: Health Communications, Inc, 1999), xix.

10. Eleanor Roosevelt, *You Learn by Living* (New York: Harper and Bros., 1960), 18.

11. James Hillman, *The Soul's Code: In Search of Character and Calling* (New York: Warner Books, 1996), 21, 22.

12. Whitehead, *Aims of Education*, 51.

13. Joseph Campbell, *The Power of Myth*, ed. B. S. Flowers, with B. Moyers (Garden City, NY: Anchor, 1991).

Notes

14. Jiddu Krishnamurti, *Krishnamurti on Education*, ed. Krishnamurti Foundation Trust Limited (New York: Harper & Row, 1974), 76.

15. Barbara Cooney, *Miss Rumphius* (New York: Viking Press, 1982).

16. *As You Like It* 2. 7.

17. Ranier Maria Rilke, *Letters to a Young Poet*, trans. M. D. Herter Norton (New York: Norton, 1993), 35.

18. Gal. 6:6–9, *The Holy Bible: Containing the Old and New Testaments* (New York: T. Nelson, 1953).

19. M. Nagler, "Nonviolence and Peacekeeping Today," *ReVision: A Journal of Consciousness and Transformation* 20, no. 2 (1997): 12–17.

20. John G. Neihardt, *Black Elk Speaks: Being the Life Story of a Holy Man of the Oglala Sioux* (1932; reprint, Lincoln: University of Nebraska Press, 1988).

21. Alfred North Whitehead, *Process and Reality: An Essay in Cosmology* (1929; reprint, New York: The Free Press, 1978), 21.

22. Ken Wilber, *Sex, Ecology, and Spirituality: The Spirit of Evolution* (Boston: Shambhala, 1995), 334–5.

23. Elaine Pagels, *The Gnostic Gospels* (New York: Vintage Books, 1979), 126.

24. Ralph Waldo Emerson, "The American Scholar," in *Ralph Waldo Emerson: Essays and Journals*, ed. L. Mumford (1837; reprint, Garden City, NY: Doubleday, 1968), 46.

25. Marsha Sinetar, *Spiritual Intelligence: What We Can Learn from the Early Awakening Child* (Maryknoll, NY: Orbis Books, 2000), 87.

   E. Paul Torrance, *Guiding Creative Talent* (Englewood Cliffs, NJ: Prentice-Hall, 1962).

26. Vaclav Havel, *The Art of the Impossible*, trans. P. Wilson (New York: Alfred A. Knopf, 1997), 17–18.

27. Gerald G. May, *Will and Spirit: A Contemplative Psychology* (San Francisco: HarperSanFrancisco, 1982), 208.

28. T. S. Eliot, *Four Quartets* (New York: Harcourt, Brace, and World, 1971), 15.

29. Daniel Goleman and Robert A. Thurman, ed., *Mindscience* (Boston: Wisdom, 1991).

30. Merton M. Sealts, *Emerson on the Scholar* (Columbia, MO: University of Missouri Press, 1992), 257.

31. Thich Nhat Hanh, *The Miracle of Mindfulness* (Boston: Beacon Press, 1975).

32. Meister Eckhart, *Meister Eckhart: Selected Treatises and Sermons*, trans. J. M. Clark and J. V. Skinner (London: Faber & Faber, 1958).

33. Eugene T. Gendlin, *Focusing*, 2d. ed. (New York: Bantam Books, 1988).

34. Tobin Hart, "Opening the Contemplative Mind in the Classroom" (submitted for publication 2003).

35. Rabindranath Tagore, *Rabindranath Tagore: Pioneer in Education* (London: John Murray, 1961), 57.

36. Pierre Teilhard de Chardin, *Toward the Future*, trans. R. Hague (1973; reprint, New York: Harcourt Brace Jovanovich, 1975), 86–87.

Chapter 8

1. Jacques Lusseyran, *And There Was Light*, trans. E. Cameron (New York: Parabola Books. 1963), 66, 67.

2. William James, *The Varieties of Religious Experience* (New York: The Modern Library, 1936).

3. Annette Hollander, *How to Help Your Child Have a Spiritual Life: A Parent's Guide to Inner Development* (New York: A & W Publishers, Inc., 1980), 27.

4. Carl Gustav Jung, *Modern Man in Search of a Soul* (San Diego: Harvest / Harcourt Brace Jovanovich, 1933).

5. F. S. C. Northrop, *The Meeting of East and West: An Inquiry Concerning World Understanding* (New York: Macmillian, 1946).

   Jean Paul Richter, *The Doctrine of Education for English Readers*, trans. B. Wood (London: Swan Sonnenschein, 1887).

   James J. Dillon, "The Spiritual Child: Appreciating Children's Transformative Effects on Adults," *Encounter: Education for Meaning and Social Justice* 13, no. 4 (2000): 4–18.

6. Gordon Allport, *The Individual and His Religion* (New York: Macmillian, 1955), 101.

7. Mitchell B. Liester, "Inner Voices: Distinguishing Transcendent and Pathological Characteristics," *The Journal of Transpersonal Psychology* 28, no. 1 (1996).

8. American Psychological Association, *Diagnostic and Statistical Manual of Mental Disorders*, 4th ed. (Washington, DC: American Psychological Association, 2000).

9. John Welwood, "Principles of Inner Work: Psychological and Spiritual," *The Journal of Transpersonal Psychology* 16, no. 1 (1984): 63–73.

10. Robert A. Johnson, *Balancing Heaven and Earth: A Memoir of Visions, Dreams, and Realizations* (San Francisco: HarperSanFrancisco, 1998), 2.

11. P. M. H. Atwater, *Children of the New Millennium: Children's Near-Death Experiences and the Evolution of Humankind* (New York: Three Rivers Press, 1999).

12. John G. Neihardt, *Black Elk Speaks: Being the Life Story of a Holy Man of the Oglala Sioux* (1932; reprint, Lincoln: University of Nebraska Press, 1988), 43.

13. M. A. J. McKenna, "Attention Deficit Disorder Rate Nears 7%," in *Atlanta Journal Constitution*, 22 May 2002, A1.

14. Samuel H. Young, *Psychic Children* (Garden City, NY: Doubleday and Company, 1977), 29–30.

15. Herman Hesse, *Siddhartha*, trans. H. Rosner (New York: Bantam, 1971).

    Paulo Coelho, *The Alchemist: A Fable About Following Your Dream*, trans. A. R. Clark (New York: HarperPerennial, 1993).

    J. R. R. Tolkien, *The Lord of the Rings* (London: Allen & Unwin, 1954).

16. John 16:23–25, *The Holy Bible: Containing the Old and New Testaments*, (New York: T. Nelson, 1953).

17. Ian Stevenson, *Twenty Cases Suggestive of Reincarnation* (Charlottesville: University Press of Virginia, 1974).

    Ian Stevenson, *Children Who Remember Previous Lives* (Charlottesville: University Press of Virginia, 1987).

18. Carol Bowman, *Children's Past Lives: How Past Life Memories Affect Your Child* (New York: Bantam Books, 1997).

19. Ibid.

20. Barbro Karlen, *And the Wolves Howled: Fragments of Two Lifetimes* (London: Clairview Books, 1997).

Chapter 9

1. Joseph Epes Brown, ed., *The Sacred Pipe: Black Elk's Account of the Seven Rites of the Oglala Sioux* (Norman, OK: University of Oklahoma Press, 1953), 74–75.

2. Peter A. Bucky, *The Private Albert Einstein* (Kansas City, MO: Andrews & McMeel, 1992), 118.

3. Paul Tillich, *The Eternal Now* (New York: Charles Scribner's Sons, 1956).

4. Alfred North Whitehead, *The Aims of Education and Other Essays* (1929; reprint, New York: The Free Press, 1967), 3.

5. Ruth Rice, "Neurophysiological Development in Premature Infants Following Stimulation," *Developmental Psychology* 13, no. 1 (1977): 69–76.

6. Candice B. Pert, "The Wisdom of the Receptor: Neuropeptides, the Emotions, and Bodymind," *Advances* 3, (1986): 8–16.

7. Paul Pearsall, *The Heart's Code: Tapping the Wisdom and Power of our Heart Energy* (New York: Broadway Books, 1999).

Gary Schwartz and Linda G. Russek, "Energy Cardiology: A Dynamical Energy Systems Approach for Integrating Conventional and Alternative Medicine," *Advances* 12 (1996): 4–14.

8. Robert Coles, *The Spiritual Life of Children* (Boston: Houghton Mifflin, 1990), 19–20.

9. Carlos Casteneda, *Journey to Ixtlan: The Lessons of Don Juan* (New York: Pocket Books, 1972).

10. Marshall Stewart Ball, *Kiss of God* (Deerfield Beach, FL: Health Communications, Inc, 1999), xix.

11. Carl Gustav Jung, *Collected Works of C. G. Jung*, vol. 17, ed. H. Read, M. Fordham, G. Adler, and W. McGuire, trans. R. F. C. Hull (Princeton, NJ: Princeton University Press, 1953–78), 286.

Afterword

1. Nancy Anne Tappe, *Understanding Your Life Through Color* (Carlsbad, CA: Starling Publishers, 1982).

   Lee Carroll and Jan Tober, *The Indigo Children: The New Children Have Arrived* (Carlsbad, CA: Hay House, 1999).

2. Ian Hacking, *Rewriting the Soul* (Princeton, NJ: Princeton University Press, 1995).

   Ian Hacking, *The Social Construction of What?* (Cambridge, MA: Harvard University Press, 1999).

3. Helena Petrovna Blavatsky, *The Secret Doctrine* (Pasadena, CA: Theosophical University Press, 1999).

4. David Henry Feldman, *Nature's Gambit* (New York: Basic Books, 1986).

5. Joseph Chilton Pearce, *The Biology of Transcendence: A Blueprint for the Human Spirit* (Rochester, VT: Park Street Press, 2002), 251.

6. Ibid., 116.

7. Phyllida Brown, "Brain Gain," *New Scientist* 173, no. 2334 (2 March 2002): 24–27.

8. See www.mercola.com/2002/apr/17/autism_epidemic.htm.

About ChildSpirit Institute

ChildSpirit Institute is a nonprofit 501[c]3 organization dedicated to understanding and nurturing the spirituality of children and adults. The institute serves as a research and educational hub for the growing field of children's spirituality.

ChildSpirit helps to nourish our innate spirituality through innovative research, education, publishing, consulting, and programming. ChildSpirit partners with organizations around the globe to promote spirituality in young people and adults; is creating a global resource network of experts in the field of children's spirituality; consults with a wide range of organizations and individuals; conducts research to help us better understand the inner world of childhood; and offers trainings and talks for educators, therapists, researchers, parents, and children.

The Institute is not affiliated with any particular religious group but honors the spiritual heart of all wisdom traditions. Its work bridges academic disciplines and religious differences to recognize the deep and diverse current of spiritual life. ChildSpirit does not award grants but instead provides expertise, resources, and partnerships to support the development of innovative programs and projects.

To learn more or offer support, or to share a story about your own spiritual life as a child or that of a child close to you, please contact us at the appropriate address below. If you are sharing a story, please include your name and any contact information, and be sure to let us know if we have your permission to share this story with others in print or on our website. Also indicate if you would like to remain anonymous if the story is made public.

For more information:
ChildSpirit Institute
35 Camp Court
Carrollton, GA 30117
www.childspirit.net

To share a story:
Stories
ChildSpirit Institute
35 Camp Court
Carrollton, GA 30117
Childspirit@aol.com
(include the word "stories" in the subject line)

About the Author

Tobin Hart, Ph.D., is a university professor, psychologist, speaker, husband, and father of two girls. He is cofounder and chairman of the board of directors of ChildSpirit Institute, a nonprofit organization that is a research and educational hub with a mission of understanding and nurturing the spirituality of children and adults. He serves as an associate professor of psychology at the State University of West Georgia where his teaching and research examines consciousness, spirituality, psychotherapy, and transformative education. Over the past twenty years, he has provided psychotherapy to individuals and families, done consulting for organizations, and served as an academic dean, director of counseling, and director of a school for gifted students. His four books and numerous scholarly articles explore human consciousness and potential through an interdisciplinary and spiritual approach.

Inner Ocean Publishing

Expanding horizons
with books that
challenge the mind,
inspire the spirit,
and nourish the soul.

We invite you to visit us at:
www.innerocean.com

Inner Ocean Publishing, Inc.
PO Box 1239, Makawao
Maui, HI 96768, USA
Email: info@innerocean.com